THE FRENCH CODE OF CIVIL PROCEDURE IN ENGLISH

2005

Translated by
Christian Dodd

OCEANA PUBLICATIONS

ISSN 1548-0917

ISBN 0-379-21852-6

Manufactured in the United States of America on acid-free paper.

THE FRENCH CODE OF CIVIL PROCEDURE IN ENGLISH
2005

Translated by Christian Dodd

SUMMARY TABLE OF CONTENTS

THE FRENCH CODE OF CIVIL PROCEDURE IN ENGLISH 2005

Translated by Christian Dodd

TABLE OF CONTENTS

GLOSSARY AND INDEX

ABOUT THE EDITOR

CHRISTIAN DODD - Born, London, 21.10.56

Mr. Dodd graduated with an Honours Degree in law from Brunel University, London, in 1979, was called to the Bar of England Wales at Gray's Inn in 1985, and was admitted as Solicitor in 1994.

Between 1986 and 2002, Mr. Dodd first worked as an in-house Legal Counsel for Smith-Klein Beecham, and thereafter spent four years in the City of London as a Claims Executive and jurist for shipowners' legal liability mutual insurers, the UK P&I Association (managed by Thomas Miller & Co.). He then practiced with the London law firm, Constant & Constant, for whom he helped to establish a Paris office in 1991, where he worked for three years mainly handling shipping litigation. Returning to England, he was a partner for six years with the Ipswich firm, Birketts, handling all aspects of shipping and transport law.

In September 2002, Mr. Dodd and his family moved back to France, where he currently practices with the French law firm, d'Ornano & Associés, Marseille, as a solicitor handling shipping and transport matters, in both English and French law, as well as international trade disputes and cross-border litigation.

Mr. Dodd is registered at the Bar of Marseille as an avocat under the E.U. Freedom of Establishment Directive. He is a member of the Law Society of England and Wales and is a Member of the Committee of the U.A.E. (European Lawyers' Union). He is also a regular speaker at international legal conferences and a contributor to legal journals and the international marine and insurance press.

He speaks fluent French and Danish and is competent in Italian.

Mr. Dodd lives with his family outside of Marseille in the famous wine producing region of Bandol, in the delightful hills behind the Mediterranean Sea.

THE FRENCH CODE OF CIVIL PROCEDURE IN ENGLISH

2005

Translated by Christian Dodd

(Note: Footnotes are Editor's Notes, not part of the official text.)

BOOK ONE
PROVISIONS COMMON TO ALL COURTS

TITLE I
PRELIMINARY PROVISIONS

Chapter I
Guiding Principles for Trial

Section I
Proceedings

Article 1

Only the parties may institute proceedings unless the law provides otherwise. They shall have the right to terminate the proceedings prior to a judgment or by virtue of the law.

Article 2

The parties must conduct the proceedings according to the duties incumbent upon them. They must carry out the procedural steps in the manner and within the time limit prescribed.

Article 3

The judge shall supervise the proper progress of the proceedings; he/she shall have the power to impose time limits and to issue directives as necessary.

Section II
The Subject Matter of a Dispute

Article 4

The subject matter of a dispute shall be determined according to the respective claims of the parties.

Such claims shall be set out in the originating application and in the defense. Notwithstanding the above, the subject matter of a dispute may be amended by interlocutory claims where they demonstrate a sufficient link with the original claim.

Article 5

A judge must rule upon all the points at issue and only upon them.

Section III
The Facts

Article 6

In support of their claims, the parties are obliged to allege the relevant facts to support them.

Article 7

A judge may not found his/her decision on facts which are not in issue.

A judge may also take into consideration facts which the parties have not specifically pleaded in support of their contentions.

Article 8

A judge may invite the parties to provide such factual explanations as he/she shall deem necessary for the resolution of the dispute.

Section IV
Evidence

Article 9

It shall be incumbent on each party to prove the facts necessary to establish its claim in accordance with the law.

Article 10

A judge may of his/her own initiative give issue directives as may be legally permitted.

Article 11

The parties are bound to comply with the implementation of any directives, although it is for the judge to draw any conclusions from the abstention or refusal of a party to do so.

Where a party withholds an item of evidence, the judge may, on the application of the other party, order him/her to produce the same, if necessary under the sanction of a fine. He/she may, on the application by one of the parties, request or order, if necessary subject to the same sanction, the production of all documents in the possession of third parties, provided that there are no legal reasons preventing their production.

Section V
The Law

Article 12

A judge shall determine a dispute in accordance with the rules of law applicable thereto.

He/she shall establish the dispute in relation to the facts and documents at issue without limiting him/herself to the meaning which might be suggested by the parties.

Notwithstanding the above, he/she may not change such meaning or legal bases when the parties, by virtue of an express agreement and in the exercise of the rights to which they may be entitled, have limited him/her to the legal definitions and points of law to which they seek to restrict the argument.

Once a dispute has arisen, the parties may, where it relates to the same matters and in the same circumstances, vest the judge with the powers of an arbitrator, subject to a right of appeal where the parties have not expressly waived such right.

Article 13

A judge may invite the parties to make such submissions on points of law as he/she shall deem necessary for the resolution of the dispute.

Section VI
Participation of the Parties[1]

Article 14

No party may be adjudged without having been heard or called to appear.

Article 15

The parties must, within the prescribed time, disclose to each other the facts giving rise to their claim, the items of evidence they shall provide and the points of law upon which they shall rely, so that each of them shall be in a position to prepare his/her case in reply.

Article 16

A judge shall, at any event, enforce, and shall him/herself comply, with the *inter partes* principle.

---

1 The French term "contradiction" refers to a principle of French jurisprudence that is wider that the Anglo-Saxon *audi alteram parte*. It also requires that evidence be gathered jointly by the parties. In fact, evidence that is gathered in the absence of the other party, which is a common practice in the Anglo-Saxon world, will probably be rejected by French courts.

A judge may not in his/her decision take into consideration issues, explanations and documents relied upon or produced by the parties, unless the latter have been considered by the parties with an opportunity to raise arguments in an adversarial manner.

A judge shall not base his/her decision on points of law which he/she has raised of his/her own initiative, without having first invited the parties to comment thereon.

Article 17

Where the law shall allow or where the circumstances shall require that a directive be issued *ex parte*, the other party shall have an appropriate right of recourse if he/she is aggrieved by that directive.

Section VII
The Defense

Article 18

A party may defend him/herself except in circumstances where legal representation is mandatory.

Article 19

A party shall choose freely his/her representative either to represent him/her or to assist him/her as the law permits or orders.

Article 20

A judge may hear the parties themselves at any time.

Section VIII
Mediation

Article 21

The judge has the duty to mediate between the parties.

Section IX
Oral Arguments

Article 22

Oral pleadings must be held in public, unless the law allows or directs that they be held in chambers.

Article 23

A judge is not bound to use an interpreter if he/she knows the language used by the parties.

Article 23-1

If one of the other parties is deaf, the judge shall appoint, by an order that is not subject to appeal, an interpreter competent in sign language or in spoken language or any person who is qualified in a language or method of communicating with the deaf to assist him/her. The judge may also have recourse to any technology that enables communication with such a party.

However, the preceding paragraph shall not apply where the party who is deaf, appears assisted by a person of his choice who is able to communicate with him/her.

Section X
Duty of Courtesy

Article 24

Parties are bound to act at all times with due respect to the law.

A judge may, depending on the seriousness of the breach, order on his/her own initiative, injunctive relief, strike out written pleadings, declare them to be defamatory or order the issuance and publication of his/her judgments.

Chapter II
Rules Applicable to Non-Contentious Matters

Article 25

In non-contentious matters the judge shall rule where, in the absence of a dispute, he/she is asked to consider a claim which, by virtue of its subject matter or the status of the claimant, the law requires should be submitted for his/her consideration.

Article 26

A judge may base his/her decision on all the facts relating to the case submitted before him/her, including those which have not been alleged.

Article 27

A judge shall proceed with all necessary investigations, even on his/her own motion.

He/she shall have the power to hear informally persons who may provide guidance to him/her as well as those whose interests may be affected by his/her decision.

Article 28

A judge may rule upon a matter without hearing oral arguments.

Article 29

A third party may be granted leave by the judge to consult the case file and to have copies given to him/her if he/she can demonstrate that he/she has a legitimate interest in the case.

TITLE II
THE ACTION

Article 30

An action, as regards the maker of a claim, is entitled to be heard on its merits so that the judge may decide on its admissibility.

The opponent is entitled to contest the merits of a claim.

Article 31

An action shall be open to all persons with a legitimate interest in the success or the dismissal of a claim except where the law only confers *locus standi* on those persons specifically allowed to bring or contest a claim or to defend a specific interest.

Article 32

A claim made by or against a person with no right of action, shall be inadmissible.

Article 32-1

A litigant who pursues a legal action in a dilatory or vexatious manner may be fined between of 15€ to 1,500€, without prejudice to any damages which may be claimed against him/her.

TITLE III
JURISDICTION

Chapter I
Specific Jurisdiction

Article 33

The jurisdiction of a chamber in relation to the subject-matter shall be determined by the rules relating to judicial organization and to its specific provisions.

Article 34

The jurisdiction in relation to the amount of a claim or in relation to the value-limit above for which there is no right of appeal, shall be determined by the rules applicable to each court and by the following provisions.

Article 35

Where several claims based on different facts and which are not connected with one another are made by a claimant against the same defendant and joined in the same proceedings, the appropriate court and its claim value-limit shall be determined according to the nature and the value of each claim considered separately.

Where consolidated claims are based on the same facts or are connected with each other, the appropriate court and its claim value-limit shall be determined according to the aggregate value of the claims.

Article 36

Where claims are brought in a single action pursuant to a common cause of action by several claimants or against several defendants, the appropriate court and its claim value-limit for all of the claims shall be determined according to the claim with the highest value.

Article 37

Where the jurisdiction of a court depends on the amount of the claim, the court shall hear all counterclaims and set-offs which are lower than its claim amount limit even if, when combined with the amount of the claimant's claim, they exceed the said claim amount limit.

Article 38

Where the incidental claim exceeds the claim value-limit of a court, a judge of the same court, where a party alleges that it has no jurisdiction, may either rule solely upon the original claim or may order the parties to litigate the whole matter before the court that has jurisdiction so that the incidental claim may be heard. However, where a counterclaim for damages is related exclusively to the original claim, the judge shall be competent to hear the matter irrespective of the value of the claim.

Article 39

Subject to the provisions of Article 35, the judgment cannot be appealed if none of the incidental claims exceed the claim value-limit of the court of last resort.

If one claim exceeds such limit, the judge shall rule as a court of first instance on all of the claims. He/she shall, however, rule as a court of last resort if the only claim that exceeds the jurisdictional claim limit is a counterclaim for damages based exclusively on the original claim.

Article 40

A judgment which has ruled upon an unspecified claim is, unless otherwise provided, subject to an appeal.

Article 41

Once a dispute has arisen, the parties may nevertheless agree to submit their dispute to a court which otherwise would have lacked jurisdiction by reason of the amount of the claim.

Furthermore, they may, under the same conditions and in accordance with their unfettered rights, agree expressly that their dispute should be decided without any right of appeal, even where the amount of the claim exceeds the claim amount limit of the first court.

Chapter II
Territorial Jurisdiction

Article 42

The court that is territorially competent shall be, subject to any contrary provisions, the one where the defendant lives.

Where there are several defendants, the claimant shall, at his/her choice, apply to the court where one of the defendants lives.

Where the defendant has no known domicile or known residence, the claimant may apply to the court where he/she lives or if he/she lives abroad, to the court of his/her choice.

Article 43

Where the defendant lives shall mean:

- in relation to a natural person, the place where he/she has his/her domicile or, in default thereof, his/her residence,
- in relation to a corporate entity, the place where it is established.

Article 44

In actions relating to real property, only the court where the property is situated shall have jurisdiction.

Article 45

Matters involving succession must be brought before the court in whose[2] judicial district the succession was opened up to the distribution, including:

– claims between heirs;

– claims brought by creditors of the deceased;

– claims regarding the implementation of dispositions taking effect upon death.

Article 46

At his/her choice, the claimant may, instead of the court where the defendant resides, bring his/her claim to a different court:

– in contractual matters, before the court within whose jurisdiction the subject matter of the contract was performed or where the performance of the agreed services had been contemplated;

– in tortious matters, before the court within the whose jurisdiction the wrongful act was done or the where the loss or damage incurred;

– in mixed matters, before the court within whose jurisdiction the property is situated;

– in matters of family maintenance or contribution to the expenses of marriage, before the court within whose jurisdiction the creditor resides.

Article 47

Where a judge or a judicial officer is a party to an action which relates to the court in which the latter sits, the claimant may apply to a court sitting in a neighboring judicial district.

The defendant and any parties to an appeal may likewise ask to refer the matter to a court selected under the same conditions; the matter shall be dealt with as provided under Article 97.

Article 48

Any clause which, directly or indirectly, offends against territorial jurisdiction of the court shall be deemed invalid and void except where it has been agreed in a contract entered into between businessmen and that the same has been clearly provided in the undertaking given by the party against whom it is being enforced.

---

2 Linguistic purists may object to the use of "whose" in connection with things, but it is much less clumsy than the more grammatically correct "of which" formulation.

Chapter III
Common Provisions

Article 49

A court with jurisdiction over a claim, shall hear all the grounds raised in defense, even where it may require an interpretation of a contract, except where such grounds raise issues which might come under the exclusive jurisdiction of another court.

Article 50

Interlocutory matters shall be heard by the court before which the proceedings to which they relate are conducted.

Article 51

The regional court[3] shall hear all interlocutory claims which do not fall within the exclusive jurisdiction of any other court.

Other courts shall only hear interlocutory claims which fall within their jurisdiction.

Article 52

Claims in relation to costs, fees and disbursements relating to an action that have been incurred before a court by law officers and public officers[4] are brought before that court.

Claims in relation to costs, fees and disbursements in connection with an action that have not been incurred before a court are brought, according to the amount of

3 I have translated the French term "tribunal de grande instance" as "regional court" as there are at least one of these courts in every department of France. The regional courts constitute, together with the specialized courts (e.g. Commercial Courts, administrative courts, industrial relations tribunals) the second rung of the French judicial hierarchy for civil matters. They are situated above the local courts and below the courts of appeal and the French Court of Cassation (*see* notes 6 and 8). They hear all civil cases that do not go to the specialized courts and have exclusive jurisdiction over actions relating to real property, enforcement of judgments and intellectual property rights. The judges of regional courts are appointed and are called "magistrats" in French. The president of a regional court may issue orders (ordonannces) or summary orders (référés—*see* note 9) but generally a regional court hears the case in full. Appeals lie as of right from a regional court to a court of appeal on points of law and fact (*see* note 6).

4 The French has two terms—"officier public", which means a member of certain professions, such as a notary, who is entitled to make officially recorded documents, and "officier ministériel", which means a member of certain professions, again like a notary, who are officially appointed. I have translated both terms as "public officer".

the costs, before the district court[5] or regional court in the judicial district where the public officer or law officer carries out his/her duties.

TITLE IV
THE CLAIM BEFORE A COURT

Chapter I
The Initial Claim

Section I
Claims in Contentious Matters

Article 53

The initial claim is the one whereby a litigant shall take the initiative in legal proceedings by submitting his/her allegations to a judge.

It shall begin the proceedings.

Article 54

Except for cases where proceedings are instituted by an application or a declaration to the court registry office and those instituted by a voluntary appearance of the parties before a judge, the originating application shall be made by summons or by the filing of a joint application at the court registry office.

Article 55

The summons is the document of the court bailiff in which a claimant shall require his/her opponent to appear before the judge.

Article 56

At the risk of being declared invalid and void, the summons must, subject to particulars prescribed for legal process served by a court bailiff, contain:

1. The name of the court before which the claim is brought;

2. The subject-matter of the claim with a presentation of the issues of facts and of law;

5 The French term is "tribunal d'instance". I have translated this term as "district court". These courts are found in each locality all over France and are on the lowest rung of the French judicial hierarchy for civil matters and deal with less serious cases in place of the regional or Commercial Courts. There is an appeal as of right from this court to a court of appeal on matters of fact and law (*see* note 6).

3. The statement that, should the defendant fail to appear, he/she shall run the risk that a judgment be entered against him/her based solely on the evidence produced by his/her opponent;

4. Where appropriate, statements relating to the identity of real property as required by the land registry in relation to their advertisement.

Further, it shall contain details of the exhibits in support of the claim. Such exhibits shall be listed in a separate sheet attached to the summons.

It shall constitute the required pleadings.

Article 57

The joint application shall be the legal process in common whereby the parties shall submit to a judge their respective claims, the points on which they disagree as well as their respective grounds in support.

Furthermore, it shall contain, at the risk of being otherwise inadmissible:

1. a) in relation to natural persons: the family name, first names, occupation, domicile, nationality, date and place of birth of each of the plaintiffs;

b) in relation to corporate entities: their type, name, the address of their registered office and the body which shall legally represent them;

2. the name of the court before which the claim is brought;

3. where appropriate, any statement relating to the identity of real property as required by the land registry in relation to their advertisement.

It must also contain details of the exhibits in support of the claim.

It must be dated and signed by the parties.

It is considered to be a written submission.

Article 58

Under the provisions of Article 12, the parties may, in a joint application, if they have not yet done so since starting the proceedings, confer upon the judge the function of arbitrator, or limit his/her jurisdiction to such legal definitions and points of law to which they are seeking to limit the dispute.

Article 59

At the risk of having his/her defense declared inadmissible, the defendant must declare:

a) in relation to a natural person: his/her family name, first name, address, nationality, date and place of birth;

b) in relation to a corporate entity: its type, name, registered office and the organ which shall represent it legally.

Section II
Claim in Non-Contentious Matters

Article 60

In non-contentious matters, the claim shall be brought by an *ex parte* application.

Article 61

The judge shall be empowered to hear the claim by the filing of the request at the court registry.

Article 62

Furthermore, a claim may be brought before a regional court, and the court empowered by an oral declaration recorded by the court registry office.

Chapter II
Incidental Claims

Article 63

Incidental claims are: counterclaims, additional claims and interlocutory claims.

Article 64

A counterclaim is one whereby the original defendant claims something, beyond simply rejecting the claim made by his/her opponent.

Article 65

An additional claim is one whereby a party amends his/her previous claim.

Article 66

An interpleader is a claim whose effect is to join a third party to an action which involved the original parties.

Where the claim comes from a third party, the interpleader shall be voluntary: an intervention shall be a ordered where a party has summonsed a third person.

Article 67

The incidental claim must contain the claims and grounds of the party bringing it and must identify the supporting documents.

Article 68

Incidental claims are brought against parties to proceedings in the same way in which defenses are filed.

They must be made against defaulting parties or third parties in the manner prescribed for instituting proceedings. In relation to appeals, they must be brought by a summons.

Article 69

The document by which an additional claim is made is deemed part of the pleadings; notice of it is given to the other parties.

Article 70

Counterclaims or additional claims are only admissible where they are connected sufficiently with the original allegations.

However, a claim for set-off shall be admissible despite the absence of such a connection, although the judge may order a disjoinder if the said claim is likely to cause an excessive delay to the judgment on the whole claim.

TITLE V
GROUNDS OF DEFENSE

Chapter I
Defense

Article 71

Any allegation which, after an examination of the law on the merits, tends to reject the claims of the opponent as being without justification, shall constitute a defense.

Article 72

Substantive defenses may be advanced at any stage of the proceedings.

Chapter II
Procedural Pleas

Article 73

A procedural plea is an allegation that either declares that the proceedings are irregular or have lapsed or which stays proceedings.

Article 74

At the risk of otherwise being inadmissible, objections must be raised simultaneously and prior to any defense on the merits of the case or application to strike out. This is the case even if the rules invoked to support the objection might be those of public policy.

A request for inspection of the documents does not constitute a ground for declaring an objection to be inadmissible.

The provisions of the first paragraph shall not prevent the application of Articles 103, 111, 112 and 118.

Section I
Pleas of Lack of Jurisdiction

Sub-Section 1
Lack of Jurisdiction Raised by the Parties

Article 75

If the court which is dealing with the matter is alleged to lack jurisdiction, the party making such an allegation must, at the risk of it otherwise being held to be inadmissible, provide reasons therefore and state, in all cases, before which court the matter should be brought.

Article 76

A judge may, in the same judgment, but by separate provisions declare him/herself to be competent and may rule upon the merits, as long as he/she puts the parties on notice to plead on the merits.

Article 77

Where the judge does not rule upon the merits of the dispute, but where the determination of a point of jurisdiction is subordinate to the merits, the judge must, in the provisions of his/her judgment, rule upon the merits and upon jurisdiction separately.

Sub-Section 2
Appeal

Article 78

Where the judge declares him/herself to be competent and where he/she rules upon the merits of a case in the same judgment, the latter may only be challenged by appeal, either on all of its findings if they are subject to an appeal, or on the grounds of jurisdiction if the decision on the merits has been issued in the first and last resort.

Article 79

Where a court overturns the judgment on the issue of jurisdiction, it must, nevertheless, rule upon the merits of the case if the decision is subject to an appeal in its entirety and if the court has appellate jurisdiction in relation to the lower court which would have been competent in this matter.

Otherwise, in overturning a judgment on the issue of jurisdiction, a court must refer the matter to a court that has appellate jurisdiction over that lower court which would have been competent in this matter as a court of first instance. That decision shall be binding on the parties and the court to which the matter is referred.

Sub-Section 3
Objections

Article 80

Where the judge rules on an issue of jurisdiction without determining the merits of the case, his/her decision may only be challenged by a plea objecting to jurisdiction, even though the judge may have decided the question on the merits which determines the jurisdiction.

Likewise, the decision may, subject to the special rules on expert opinions, only be challenged by way of a plea objecting to jurisdiction where the judge rules on the issue of jurisdiction and orders procedural or interlocutory measures.

Article 81

Where the judge holds him/herself competent, the proceedings shall be stayed until the expiration of the time-limit for lodging the appellate plea objecting to jurisdiction and, where the same is lodged, until the court of appeal[6] has delivered its decision.

---

6 I have translated the French term "cour d'appel" as court of appeal, but one must not confuse the French court of appeal with its Anglo-Saxon counterpart. There are a number of courts of appeal in France although there is not necessarily one for each department. The French courts of appeal comprise the third rung of the French judicial hierarchy for civil matters above the local, district and Commercial Courts and below the French Court of Cassation. Appeals to these courts may be made as of right on matters of law and fact, and the court of appeal proceeds by way of a trial *de novo*. Appeals to the French Court of Cassation may be made from a court of appeal on a matter of law.

Article 82

The plea objecting to jurisdiction must, at the risk of it otherwise being inadmissible, set out the grounds therefore, and must be sent to the court registry which issued the decision within fifteen days from its date of issuance.

Where the plea objecting to jurisdiction gives rise to any court costs, the filing of the same may only be accepted if the appellant has paid the court an amount covering the costs.

An acknowledgment shall be issued upon its filing.

Article 83

The clerk of the court which has issued the decision on jurisdiction must without delay send a copy of the plea to the opposing party by registered mail with acknowledgement of receipt and must similarly inform his/her representative where he/she has instructed one.

At the same time, he/she must remit to the chief registrar of the court the case file together with the plea and a copy of the judgment.

Article 84

The first president will fix the hearing date, which must take place as soon as possible.

The court registrar shall inform the parties by registered mail with acknowledgement of receipt.

Article 85

The parties may, in support of their claims, submit any written arguments which they consider appropriate. Such submissions, bearing the stamp of the judge, shall be placed on the record.

Article 86

The court must refer the matter to the one which it deems to be competent. Such a decision is binding on the parties and on the referral judge.

Article 87

The court registrar must notify the parties of the decision on the plea objecting to jurisdiction immediately by registered mail with acknowledgment of receipt.

Such judgment may not be open to an objection. The time limit for an application to the Court of Cassation shall run from the date of its notification.

Article 88

Any costs relating to the plea objecting to jurisdiction shall be borne by the losing party on the issue of jurisdiction. Where the latter filed the plea objecting to jurisdiction, he/she may further be ordered to pay a fine of 15€ to 1,500€ without prejudice to any claim for damages which may be brought against him/her.

Article 89

If a court has appellate jurisdiction in relation to the lower court that it considers in charge of a case, it may, after having itself given, where appropriate, procedural directions, make a decision on the substance of the case if it deems it to be in the interest of justice that the case be definitively concluded.

Article 90

Where it decides to hear the merits of the case, the court must invite the parties, in that case, by registered mail with acknowledgment of receipt, to instruct an attorney[7] within the time that it decides, where such instruction is required by the rules applicable to appeals of the lower court which gave judgment on the issue of jurisdiction.

Where none of the parties has instructed an appeal advocate, the court may of its own motion strike out the matter by a reasoned decision which shall not be subject to appeal. A copy of such decision shall be brought to the notice of each of the parties by regular mail sent to their address or residence.

Article 91

Where the court considers that the decision which is brought before it by way of a plea of lack of jurisdiction should have been brought by way of an appeal, it nevertheless retains the right to hear the matter.

The matter is then prepared and decided according to the rules that apply to appeals against decisions made by the court where the judgment originates that is being challenged on the basis of lack of jurisdiction.

If, according to these rules, the parties are obliged to instruct an appeal advocate, the appeal shall automatically be declared inadmissible if the party who filed the plea of lack of jurisdiction has not instructed an appeal advocate within one month of the notice given to the parties by the registrar.

---

7 The French "avoué" does not exist in the Anglo-Saxon legal system. It is a person who prepares appeals. I have translated the term as "appeal advocate" to distinguish this person from the "avocat" or "attorney".

Sub-Section 4
Lack of Jurisdiction Raised by the Court of Its Own Motion

Article 92

Lack of jurisdiction may be declared automatically in the event that a rule of special jurisdiction is breached which involves a matter of public policy or where the defendant fails to appear. This is possible only in these two cases.

Before a court of appeal and the Court of Cassation[8], this lack of jurisdiction may only be claimed automatically if the matter concerns the jurisdiction of a criminal or administrative court or is outside the knowledge of the French courts.

Article 93

In non-contentious matters, the judge may of his/her own initiative claim his/her lack of territorial jurisdiction. He/she may only do so, in contentious matters, in disputes relating to the civil status of persons in cases where the law has conferred exclusive jurisdiction to another court or where a defendant does not appear.

Article 94

A plea objecting to jurisdiction shall be the only recourse available where a court ruling upon a matter as a court of first instance automatically declares that it lacks jurisdiction.

Sub-Section 5
Common Provisions

Article 95

Where the judge, in considering his/her jurisdiction, resolves the substantive question which determines his/her jurisdiction, the judge's decision shall be final in relation to this question.

Article 96

Where a judge considers that a matter comes within the jurisdiction of a criminal, administrative, arbitral or foreign court, he/she merely instructs the parties to take proceedings to the proper court.

---

8 The French term "Cour de cassation" refers to the highest court in the French judicial hierarchy for civil and criminal matters. I have not translated the term as "Supreme Court", because the Council of State fulfils the role of court of final instance for the administrative court system. The Court of Cassation hears appeals on points of law from the lower courts. It may only confirm or set aside a judgment of a lower court; unlike the supreme courts of Anglo-Saxon countries, it may not substitute its own judgment for that of the lower court.

In all other cases, a judge who declares that he/she lacks jurisdiction designates the court that he/she deems to have jurisdiction. This designation is binding on the parties and the judge to whom the matter is referred.

Article 97

Where a matter is referred to the court that has been designated, the case file is immediately transferred to it by the court registry, with a copy of the decision to refer. However, the transfer is only done in the absence of any plea challenging jurisdiction within the time limit where such a recourse is available against the decision to refer.

Upon receipt of the file, the parties shall be invited by registered mail with acknowledgment of receipt from the clerk of the designated court to begin the proceedings and, where necessary, to instruct an attorney or an appeal advocate.

Where, before such a court, the parties are required to be represented, the matter shall be struck off the list automatically if none of the parties has instructed an attorney or an appeal attorney, as appropriate, within one month of the notice to do so being given to them.

Where the referral is to the court which originally heard the matter, the proceedings shall be prosecuted in the judge's chambers.

Article 98

The filing of an appeal shall be the only recourse available against summary procedure orders and against a decree of the conciliating judge in matters of divorce or judicial separation.

Article 99

As an exception to the rules of the present Section, the court may only be informed by an appeal, where the lack of jurisdiction has been relied upon or claimed automatically on the grounds that the matter should have been heard by an administrative court.

Section II
Pleas of Lis Alibi Pendens and Against Duplication of Actions

Article 100

Where the same cause of action is pending between two courts of the same level, which are equally competent to handle the matter, the last court informed shall decline jurisdiction in favor of the first one informed if one of the parties so requests. In the absence of such a request, the court may do so of its own motion.

Article 101

If there is a link between matters which are before two different courts, which in the interests of justice requires that they should be determined together, one of the courts may be asked to decline jurisdiction and to refer the whole matter to the other.

Article 102

Where the courts informed are not of the same level, pleas of *lis alibi pendens* or those against duplication of action may only be raised before the lower one.

Article 103

A plea against duplication of action may be raised at any time during the proceedings, but that it may be dismissed when raised at a late stage with an intention to delay matters.

Article 104

Appeals against decisions made in relation to *lis alibi pendens* or duplication of actions by courts of first instance shall be requested and determined in the same manner as those relating to an objection against jurisdiction.

Where there are several appeals, it shall be for the court of appeal first informed to decide, where it upholds the plea, to refer the matter to another court which in the circumstances appears to be the most competent to decide.

Article 105

The decision made on the pleas of exclusion on the above-mentioned grounds, whether made by the court, informed or pursuant to an appeal, shall be binding on both the court to which it is referred and on the court which was ordered to decline jurisdiction.

Article 106

Where both courts have to decline jurisdiction, the last decision which was given shall be deemed to be invalid and void.

Article 107

Where on a question of duplication of action, difficulties arise between different benches of the same court, they shall be resolved informally by the president of the court. His/her decision shall be deemed to be an act of judicial administration.

Section III
Dilatory Pleas

Article 108

The judge must stay the proceedings if the party requesting the same is entitled either to a certain period of time in order to carry out an inventory or to effect a deliberation, or has a vested right to a discussion or a benefit of separation of liability, or is entitled to such other periods of adjournment as afforded by law.

Article 109

The judge may grant a defendant an adjournment to issue third party indemnity proceedings.

The substantive proceedings shall resume upon the expiration of the time-limit granted for the third party to enter an appearance, unless the indemnity claim shall be ruled upon separately if the third party has not been summoned within the time period set by the judge.

Article 110

Moreover, the judge may also stay proceedings where one of the parties relies upon a decision, challenged by a third party, on objection, or on an appeal to the Court of Cassation.

Article 111

The party who benefits from an adjournment to prepare an inventory and to effect a deliberation may only raise such other pleas of exclusion after the expiration of the adjournment period.

Section IV
Pleas of Invalidity

Sub-Section 1
Invalidity of Instruments Owing to Formal Irregularity

Article 112

The invalidity of written pleadings may be raised as and when they are served; but their invalidity shall be waived where the person seeking to declare an invalidity, has, subsequent to the service of the pleadings at issue, raised a substantive defense or a plea seeking a declaration of inadmissibility without pleading the invalidity.

Article 113

Any grounds alleging the invalidity of written pleadings which have already been served must be pleaded at the same time, at the risk of the inadmissibility of those grounds, which have not been so pleaded.

Article 114

No written pleadings may be declared invalid by reason of a defect in their form unless the invalidity is expressly provided for in law, except where it is a case of a failure to comply with an important formality or one of public policy.

The invalidity may only be declared by the opponent who seeks to rely upon it, in order to prove the damages which the irregularity has caused him/her, even if it concerns an important formality or a rule of public policy.

Article 115

The invalidity is waived by the subsequent regularization of the document, if no time-limitation has expired and if such regularization does not allow any other loss to be suffered.

Article 116

The sanction for failure to observe a procedural formality prior to the oral hearing shall be subject to the rules provided in this sub-section.

Sub-Section 2
Invalidity of Documents by Reason of an Essential Defect

Article 117

The following shall constitute a substantive irregularity affecting the validity of a document:

- any lack of capacity to appear in the proceedings;
- any lack of authority of a party or a person who appears in the proceedings as the representative of either a corporate entity or of a person under a legal incapacity;
- any lack of capacity or authority of a person who legally represents a party before a court of law.

Article 118

Pleas of invalidity based on failure to comply with the substantive rules relating to written pleadings, may be raised at any stage of the proceedings, but the judge may award damages against a party who, with an intention to delay matters, has failed to raised such pleas at an earlier stage.

Article 119

Pleas of invalidity based on failure to comply with substantive rules relating to written pleadings shall be admissible without the party raising them having to prove any prejudice to him/her even where the invalidity does not arise under any express provisions.

Article 120

Pleas of invalidity based on failure to comply with substantive rules relating to written pleadings, must be raised by the judge where they relate to matters of public policy.

The judge may raise a plea of invalidity at his/her discretion where there is a lack of capacity to appear in the proceedings.

Article 121

In cases where the invalidity can be rectified, it shall not be declared invalid if the defect has been rectified before being ruled upon by the judge.

Chapter III
Summary Declaration of Inadmissibility

Article 122

A ground for a summary declaration of inadmissibility shall be one which, without any examination on the merits of the case, demonstrates that the opponent's claim is inadmissible on the grounds that it does not show any cause of action, a *locus standi* or an interest, or that it is time-barred, or is *res judicata.*

Article 123

A plea seeking a summary declaration of inadmissibility may be brought at any stage of the proceedings, except that the judge may order damages against those who, with an intention to delay, have failed to raise them earlier.

Article 124

A plea seeking a summary declaration of inadmissibility is admissible without the party raising it having to prove any prejudice to him/her, even if the inadmissibility does not derive from any express provisions.

Article 125

A summary declaration of inadmissibility must be made by the court where it relates to matters of public policy, and in particular where it concerns the failure to comply with a time-limit within which rights of recourse should be exercised or the failure to exercise such rights of recourse.

The judge has the right to strike out an action on the grounds of lack of standing to sue, lack of authority or *res judicata*.

Article 126

In the case where the situation which would justify a summary declaration of inadmissibility is capable of being rectified, such inadmissibility shall be waived where the grounds no longer exist before being ruled upon by the judge.

The same shall apply if, before the operation of any time limitation for suit, a person having standing to sue shall be joined to the proceedings as a party.

TITLE VI
SETTLEMENT

Article 127

Parties may negotiate a settlement between themselves or a settlement may be engineered by the judge at any time during the proceedings.

Article 128

Any attempt at settlement may be made at such time and place as the judge shall deem proper, except where special provisions apply.

Article 129

The parties may always request the judge to record their settlement.

Article 130

The terms of the settlement agreement, if only in part, must be recorded in a statement signed by the judge and by the parties.

Article 131

Extracts of the statement recording the agreement may be issued and they shall be enforceable.

TITLE VI[Bis]
MEDIATION

Article 131-1

A judge presiding over a dispute may, with the agreement of the parties, appoint a third person to hear them and their points of view to enable them to resolve the issues between them.

The same power may be exercised by the judge in summary proceedings.

Article 131-2

A mediation may deal with whole or a part of a dispute.

In any event, it shall remove the matter from the jurisdiction of the judge who may at any time take whatever steps deemed necessary to him/her.

Article 131-3

The initial time period for mediation shall not exceed three months. It may be renewed once, for the same duration, at the request of the mediator.

Article 131-4

The mediation may be assigned to a person or to an association.

Where the appointed mediator is an association, its legal representative shall submit for the approval of the judge the name or names of the person or persons who shall conduct the mediation on its behalf.

Article 131-5

The person conducting the mediation must satisfy the following conditions:

1. He/she shall not have been the subject of a criminal conviction, of an incapacity or a forfeiture as set out in the No. 2 Criminal Record Bulletin;

2. He/she shall not have been the responsible for any acts which might be dishonorable or contrary to probity and good virtue and which gave rise to disciplinary or administrative penalties of dismissal, the removal, revocation, withdrawal of consent or authority to act;

3. He/she shall hold, by virtue his/her previous or present occupation, the required qualifications to deal with the nature of the dispute;

4. He/she shall demonstrate that he/she has, where relevant, the training or experience appropriate for the practice of mediation;

5. He/she shall demonstrate sufficient proof of the independence necessary to conduct a mediation.

Article 131-6

The decision which orders a mediation must disclose the agreement of the parties, appointment of the mediator, the initial duration of his/her assignment and indicate the date at which the matter shall be called for a hearing before the judge.

It shall fix the amount of the mediator's fees at a level which is as close as possible to the estimated cost and shall indicate the party or parties who shall make the payment within the stated time-limit; where several parties are named, the decision must specify the contribution of each party towards the payment on account.

In the absence of a payment on account, the court's decision to allow mediation shall have no effect and the legal proceedings shall continue to be prosecuted.

Article 131-7

Regarding the issue of the decision appointing the mediator, the court registry shall send a copy of the decision by regular mail to the parties and the mediator.

The mediator shall immediately notify the judge of his/her acceptance of the assignment.

As soon as the mediator is informed by the court registry of the payment on account, he/she must convene the parties to attend the mediation.

Article 131-8

The mediator shall not have any powers to give directions. However, he/she may, with the agreement of the parties and as required by the mediation, hear third parties consenting to the take part in the mediation.

The mediator may not be instructed, in the course of the same proceedings, to implement directions.

Article 131-9

The person who conducts a mediation shall inform the judge of any difficulties which he/she may have encountered in the execution of his/her assignment.

Article 131-10

The judge may, at any time, terminate the mediation on application by a party or at the initiative of the mediator to the same.

The judge may, on his/her own motion, terminate it where the proper progress of the mediation appears to have been compromised.

In any event, the matter must be dealt with at a hearing to which the parties shall be summoned to attend by registered mail with acknowledgment of receipt letter from the court registry.

At such hearing, the judge, should he/she terminate the assignment of the mediator, may restore the legal proceedings. The mediator shall be informed of his/her decision.

Article 131-11

On the termination of his/her assignment, the mediator must inform the judge in writing whether the parties have or have not resolved the issues between them.

On the appointed day, the matter is brought before the judge.

Article 131-12

At the request of the parties the judge shall by way of ratification, approve the agreement which they shall submit to him/her.

Such approval shall concern non-contentious matters.

Article 131-13

On the termination of his/her assignment, the judge must fix the fees of the mediator.

The burden of the costs of the mediation shall be apportioned in accordance with the provisions of Article 22 of Act No. 95-125 of 8 February 1995 relating to the organization of courts and civil, criminal and administrative procedure.

The judge shall grant the mediator leave to have the amount paid on account of his/her fees to the court registry, to be released to him/her up to the sum which is due to him/her.

Where necessary, he/she shall order the payment of any additional sums and shall indicate the party or parties who shall have to pay them, or order the return of the excess amount paid on account.

An enforceable title to payment shall be given to the mediator on his/her request.

Article 131-14

The findings of the mediator and the statements which he/she has recorded may not be produced, or relied upon in the course of the subsequent legal proceedings, without the agreement of the parties, or, in any case, be referred to in any other proceedings.

Article 131-15

A decision which orders, renews or terminates the mediation is not subject to any appeal.

TITLE VII
THE TAKING OF EVIDENCE

SUB-TITLE I
DOCUMENTS

Chapter I
Discovery of Documents Between Parties

Article 132

The party who is relying upon a document is bound to disclose it to the other party to the proceedings.

The discovery of documents must be spontaneous.

In the course of an appeal, a further discovery of documents already on record in relation to the hearing at first instance shall not be required. Any party may nevertheless require that such further discovery of documents be made.

Article 133

Where discovery of documents has not taken place, the judge may, without any formality, be requested informally to order such discovery.

Article 134

The judge shall fix the time limit for discovery, subject to a fine in default thereof, if appropriate, and where necessary, the method of discovery.

Article 135

The judge may exclude from the hearing those documents which have not been communicated in time.

Article 136

The party who does not return any original documents communicated may be compelled to do so, possibly by means of a fine.

Article 137

The amount of the fine may be fixed by the judge who ordered it.

Chapter II
Obtaining Documents Held by a Third Person

Article 138

Where, in the course of the proceedings, a party wishes to rely on an original document of record or private contract to which he/she was not a party or a document held by a third party, he/she may request the judge hearing the matter to order that a certified copy of the same should be produced or that the original document itself should be produced.

Article 139

The request shall be made informally.

Should he/she deem the request to be valid, the judge shall order the production of the original deed or document, or a copy or extract thereof as the case may be, under such conditions and upon such undertakings as he/she shall determine, and where appropriate, subject to a fine.

Article 140

The decision of the judge shall be enforceable, and where it appears necessary, be rendered with a written decision.

Article 141

In cases of difficulty, or where a lawful impediment is raised, the judge who ordered the production may, upon an informal application made to him/her, revoke or amend his/her decision. The third party may appeal against the new decision within fifteen days from the date when it is made.

Chapter III
Production of Documents Held by a Party to the Proceedings

Article 142

Requests for the production of items of evidence held by the parties shall be made, and complied with, in accordance with Articles 138 and 139.

SUB-TITLE II
DIRECTIONS

Chapter I
General Provisions

Section I
Decisions Providing for Directions

Article 143

The facts leading to the outcome of the dispute, may, at the request of the parties or in the judge's discretion, lead to any legally permissible directions from the judge.

Article 144

Directions may be given at any time in the course the proceedings, where the judge does not have sufficient evidence to be able to determine the matter.

Article 145

If, before any proceedings have been commenced, there is a legitimate reason to preserve, or to establish the method of proving, the facts upon which the outcome of the of the dispute shall turn, legally permissible directions may be given at the request of any party, pursuant to an application or by way of a summary application.

Article 146

Directions may only be given in relation to facts which the party who alleges the same is unable to prove sufficiently.

In no case may directions be given for the sake of remedying any deficiency in the presentation of evidence of a particular party.

Article 147

The judge shall limit his/her choice of directions to that which shall be sufficient for the resolution of the dispute, by endeavoring to select the simplest and least onerous directions.

Article 148

The judge may give several different directions. He/she may at any time, even while they are being implemented, decide to give any directions which are necessary, in addition to those which have already been given.

Article 149

The judge may at any time extend or restrict the scope of his/her directions.

Article 150

Any decision which gives or amends directions may not be set aside; it may not be overturned by way of an appeal or an appeal to the Court of Cassation, independently of the judgment on the merits of the case, except where this is allowed by the law.

The same shall apply to any decisions rejecting a request for a direction or for the variation of those already given.

Article 151

When it may not be appealed against independently of the judgment on the merits of the case, such a decision may be simply noted on the court file or in the transcript of the hearing.

Article 152

A decision which, in the course of proceedings, makes or varies any directions shall not be notified. The same shall apply to decisions rejecting a request for directions or providing for a variation of those already given. The clerk of the court shall send a copy of the decision by regular mail to the defaulting or absent parties at the time when the decision is made.

Article 153

A decision ordering directions may not bring the matter out of the judge's jurisdiction.

Article 154

Directions shall be implemented at the initiative of the judge or of one of the parties according to the rules applicable to each matter and in consideration of an extract of a certified copy of a judgment, where applicable.

Section II
Implementing Directions

Article 155

Directions must be implemented under the supervision of the judge who made them if he/she does not proceed with the implementation him/herself.

If directions have been made by a panel of judges, their implementation shall be supervised by the judge to whom the request for directions was made, and in default thereof, by the president of the panel of judges if the matter has not been entrusted to any panel member.

The judge specified in the sentence above and the panel-judge may also have recourse to a judge appointed in the manner provided for in Article 155-1.

Article 155-1

The president of the court may, in the interests of the proper administration of justice, appoint a judge especially to deal with the supervision the implementation of directions, as conferred to a technician in the application of Article 232.

Article 156

The judge may travel outside of the jurisdiction of his/her court in order to implement a direction or to supervise its implementation.

Article 157

Where the physical distance between the parties or persons who must assist with the directions, or the distance of the place, shall render traveling to and from it too difficult or too onerous for the judge, he/she may request another court having the same or lesser jurisdiction to implement all or part of the directions ordered.

Such a decision shall be communicated with all useful documents by the registry of the issuing court to the appointed court. On receipt thereof, the specific directions shall be implemented at the initiative of the appointed court or by the judge whom the president of the latter has designated for that purpose.

The parties or persons who shall assist in the implementation of the directions shall be directly summoned or informed by the appointed court. The parties shall not be required to instruct an attorney or appeal advocate before such a court.

As soon as the directions have been implemented, the registry of the court which dealt with them, must send to the original/issuing court an official document of implementation, together with any documents or filed objects.

Article 158

Where several directions have been given, they shall be implemented simultaneously wherever possible.

Article 159

Any directions given may be immediately implemented.

Article 160

Parties and third parties who must assist in the implementation of the directions shall be summoned, as the case may be, by the clerk of the judge dealing with them or by a designated legal officer. The summons must be made by registered mail with acknowledgment of receipt. The parties may similarly be summoned by the delivery of a simple memorandum to their legal representative.

Parties and third persons may also be summoned verbally if they are present at the time when the date for the implementation of the directions is set by the court.

The legal representatives of the parties must be advised by regular mail if they have not been advised verbally or by a memorandum.

Defaulting parties must be advised by regular mail.

Article 161

The parties may be assisted in the implementation of directions.

They may be excused from personal attendance if the implementation of such directions does not require the hearing of their testimony.

Article 162

The person who represents or assists a party before a court which has given directions may follow its implementation wherever it may take place, make any written submissions or present any request relating to its implementation in the absence of the parties.

Article 163

The State Prosecution Service may always attend the implementation of any directions even if it may not be a principal party to the action.

Article 164

Directions to be implemented before the court shall take place in open court or in chambers according to the rules applicable to oral arguments on substantive issues.

Article 165

The judge may, in order to implement or be present at the implementation of a direction, travel outside the court's jurisdiction without being assisted by the clerk of the court.

Article 166

The judge appointed to implement a direction or to supervise its implementation may give such other directions as might help with its implementation of the directions already given.

Article 167

Any difficulties encountered in the course of the implementation of directions must be resolved, at the request of the parties, at the initiative of the designated officer, or of the court's own motion, either by the judge dealing with it or by the judge appointed to supervise its implementation.

Article 168

The judge must give an immediate ruling where a difficulty arises during the course of the implementation of a direction with which he/she is dealing, or at which he/she is present.

In other cases, a judge who is informally appointed, shall set the date on which the parties and, where appropriate, the agreed expert, shall be summoned by the clerk of the court.

Article 169

Where a third party is involved in the proceedings, the clerk of the court shall inform the judge regarding the mutually acceptable expert as soon as possible.

The third party shall be given the opportunity to make submissions in relation to the directions which have already been implemented.

Article 170

Decisions relating to the implementation of directions may not be challenged by way of an objection; they may only be challenged by way of an appeal to the Court of Cassation at the same time as the judgment on the merits.

Challenges shall take the form of a simple note recorded on the court file or in the transcript of the hearing, or where necessary, in an order or a judgment.

Article 171

Decisions made by a delegated judge or by the supervising judge shall not be deemed to be final as regards any consideration of the case on the merits.

Article 172

As soon as a direction has been implemented, the substantive proceedings shall continue at the initiative of the judge.

The latter may, within the limits of his/her jurisdiction, hear immediately the observations of the parties or closing speeches and rule *ex tempore* on their claims.

Article 173

The statements, opinions or reports made at the time or following the implementation of a direction shall be sent or given in their original form or a copy thereof to each of the parties by the clerk of the court which issued them, or by the officer who drafted them, as the case may be. A note to this effect shall be made on the original document.

Article 174

The judge may make an audio, visual or audiovisual recording of all or part of the directions which he/she is implementing.

The recording shall be kept at the court registry. Each party may, at his/her own expense, ask to be provided with a duplicate, copy or a transcript thereof.

Section III
Invalidities

Article 175

The invalidity of any decision or documents relating to directions shall be subject to the provisions governing the invalidity of written pleadings.

Article 176

Such invalidity shall only affect those directions which are irregular.

Article 177

The directions may be remedied or re-implemented, even immediately, where the defect which affects them is capable of being removed.

Article 178

An omission or an inaccuracy in a note intended to demonstrate the compliance with a direction shall not render it invalid, if it is shown by whatever means, that the legal requirements have, in fact, been satisfied.

Article 178-1

Where a procedural measure ordered from outside France pursuant to (EC) Council Regulation 1206/01 of May 28, 2001 on cooperation between the courts of the Member States in the taking of evidence in civil or commercial matters gives rise to costs of translating the forms which must be sent to the requested court, the judge shall order a payment on account of these costs, the amount of which is fixed in accordance with the tariff set out in Article R. 122 of the Code of Criminal Procedure. The judge shall decide which party or parties shall make the payment to the court registry within a time limit that he/she shall determine in accordance with the procedures set out in Articles 270 and 271 of this Code.

Article 178-2

Where a procedural measure ordered from outside France pursuant to the Regulation mentioned in Article 178-1 may give rise to interpreting costs when implemented by the requested court, the judge shall fix the amount of the payment on account of such costs in accordance with the procedures set out in Articles 269, 270 and 271 of this Code.

Upon receipt of the request for reimbursement of the amount of the interpreting costs by the requesting court, the court registry shall proceed with the payment up to the amount of the provision on account.

Chapter II
Personal Verifications by the Judge

Article 179

The judge may in any matter, for his own information, take a personal interest in the facts in issue, where the parties are present or have been summoned.

He/she shall proceed to make such findings, evaluations, appraisals or reconstructions as he/she shall deem necessary and, should the need arise, visit the location in question.

Article 180

Where he/she does not proceed in such manner immediately, the judge shall set the place, date and time for the verification process; where appropriate, he/she may appoint a member of the adjudicating panel for such purpose.

Article 181

The judge may, during the process of verification, at the hearing or in any other venue, call upon the assistance of a technical expert, or hear the parties or such other person whose testimony will be helpful in establishing the truth.

Article 182

An official document shall be prepared recording the findings, evaluations, appraisals, reconstructions or declarations.

Notwithstanding the above, the drafting of an official document may be replaced by a note in the judgment where the case is being heard in the last resort.

Article 183

A judge who is implementing another direction may, even though he/she is not a member of the adjudicating panel, proceed with any personal verifications which might be appropriate to the implementation of that direction.

Chapter III
Personal Appearance of the Parties

Article 184

A judge may order one or all of the parties to appear in person.

Article 185

The personal appearance may only be ordered by the panel of judges or by a member of such panel entrusted with the management of the case.

Article 186

Where the personal appearance is ordered by a panel of judges, the latter may decide that the appearance shall be before one of its members.

Where it is ordered by the judge entrusted with the management of the case, he/she may proceed with the same him/herself or decide that the appearance shall be before the panel of judges.

Article 187

When making such an order, the judge must determine the place, date and time for the personal appearance, unless this is dealt with on the spot.

Article 188

Personal appearances may take place in chambers.

Article 189

The parties shall be examined in each other's presence except where the circumstances require them to be examined separately. They must be cross-examined where one of the parties so requests.

If the appearance of only one party has been ordered, such party shall be examined in the presence of the other party, unless the circumstances require him/her to be examined immediately or not in other party's presence, subject to the absent party's right to be immediately informed of the statements made by the party being heard.

The absence of a party shall not prevent the testimony of the other being heard.

Article 190

The parties may be examined in the presence of a technical expert and be confronted by witnesses.

Article 191

The parties must personally answer the questions put to them without referring to any notes.

Article 192

Personal appearances shall take place in the presence of the legal representatives of all the parties.

Article 193

The judge shall, where he/she deems it necessary, ask the questions which the parties may submit to him/her after the examination.

Article 194

A formal record shall be made of the statements of the parties, their absence or their refusal to answer.

The drafting of the record may, notwithstanding the above, be replaced by a written note in the judgment if the case is being heard in the last resort.

Article 195

The parties being examined shall sign the formal record after first having verified or certified that it conforms to their statements, in which case the same is stated on the record. Where relevant, it shall be stated that the parties have refused to sign or to certify the same.

The record shall, furthermore be dated and signed by the judge and, if need be, by the clerk of the court.

Article 196

Where one of the parties is unable to be present at court, the judge who ordered his/her appearance, or the judge appointed by the panel of judges on which he/she sits, may travel to meet that party, after having called the opposing party to accompany him/her.

Article 197

The judge may order the appearance of persons with a mental incapacity subject to the rules relating to the capacity of persons and to the administration of evidence, as well as their legal representatives or those assisting them.

He/she may order the appearance of corporate entities including public bodies or public corporations in the person of their authorized representatives.

He/she may, moreover, order the appearance of any member or agent of a corporate entity to be examined on facts personal to him/her, as well as those which he/she might have known by virtue of his/her position.

Article 198

The judge may draw whatever legal conclusions he/she likes from the statements of the parties, and from the absence or refusal by one of them to answer, which fact is deemed to have the same evidential weight as written evidence.

Chapter IV
Statements of Third Parties

Article 199

If oral evidence is admissible, the judge shall admit statements from third parties in order to clarify the facts in issue of which they have personal knowledge. Such statements shall be given in writing or given by means of an inquiry, depending on whether they are written or oral.

Section I
Statements in Writing

Article 200

Statements in writing must be produced by the parties or at the request of the judge.

The judge shall forward to the parties those statements which are transmitted directly to him/her.

Article 201

Written statements must be made by persons who fulfill the requirements for persons to be heard as a witness.

Article 202

A formal written statement must contain an account of the facts which the maker has witnessed or which he/she has personally noted.

It must indicate the family name, date and place of birth, address and occupation of the maker as well as, where necessary, his/her relationship, by blood or by marriage, to the parties, his/her employment by, or working relationship or common interest with them.

Furthermore, it must indicate that it has been drafted for production before a court of law and that the maker is aware that any false statement made by him/her shall be punishable by criminal sanctions.

The statement shall be written, dated and signed by its author. The latter must attach to it the original or a photocopy thereof of any official document proving his/her identity and containing his/her signature.

Article 203

The judge may, as part of his/her investigation, always hear the maker of a written statement.

Section II
The Investigation

Sub-Section 1
General Provisions

Article 204

Where an investigation is ordered, conflicting evidence may be adduced by way of witnesses without a new order being required.

Article 205

Any person may be heard as a witness except those who might be deemed to be unfit to give witness evidence by reason of a legal incapacity.

Persons who cannot stand as a witness may, notwithstanding the above, be heard under the same conditions but without taking the oath. However, children of a marriage may never be heard as witnesses in support of allegations made to the court by spouses relating to a petition for divorce or judicial separation.

Article 206

Any person summoned to testify shall be bound to do so. Persons who can demonstrate a legitimate reason may be excused from giving their testimony. Parents or relatives directly related to one of the parties, or a partner or previous partners to a marriage, may object to testifying.

Article 207

Defaulting witnesses may be called at their expense where their testimony is deemed necessary.

Defaulting witnesses and persons who, without any legitimate excuse, have refused to testify or to take the oath may be ordered to pay a fine of between 15€ to 1,500€.

A person who can demonstrate that he/she was unable to attend on the appointed day may be relieved of the fine and the costs of the summons.

Article 208

The judge shall hear the testimony of the witnesses separately and in the order which he/she shall decide.

The witnesses shall be heard in the presence of the parties or where the latter have been called to be present.

By way of exception, if the circumstances shall so require, the judge may ask a party to withdraw during the testimony of a witness, subject to the right of the former to have the statements of witnesses heard in his/her absence to be produced to him/her immediately thereafter.

The judge may, where there is a risk that its evidential value might be weakened, proceed without delay to hear the testimony of a witness after having, wherever possible, called the parties to attend court.

Article 209

An investigation shall take place in the presence of the legal representatives of the parties or when it has been proven that they have been called.

Article 210

The witnesses shall state their family name, first names, date and place of birth, address, occupation, and, where relevant, their relationship by blood or by marriage to the parties, any employment by them by, or working relationship or common interest with them.

Article 211

Persons who are heard as witnesses must swear an oath to tell the truth. The judge must remind them that perjury is punishable by a fine or imprisonment.

Persons who are heard without taking the oath must be informed of their obligation to tell the truth.

Article 212

Witnesses may not read from notes.

Article 213

The judge may hear or examine the witnesses on all facts in relation to legally admissible evidence, even if these facts are not stated in the decision ordering the investigation.

Article 214

The parties shall neither interrupt, nor question, nor attempt to influence the witness who is giving evidence, nor address them directly at the risk off being excluded from attending the examination.

After an examination of a witness, the judge must, where he/she deems it proper, put to the witness any questions submitted to him/her by the parties.

Article 215

The judge may recall the witnesses and may confront them with each other or with the parties; where relevant, he/she may proceed with a hearing in the presence of a technical expert.

Article 216

Except where they have been permitted or directed to leave the court after having given their testimony, witnesses shall remain at the disposal of the judge until the close of the inquiry or the hearing. They may, up to that time, add to or amend their testimony.

Article 217

If a witness proves that it is impossible for him/her to travel on the appointed day, the judge may give him/her a time-limit or travel him/herself to meet the witness in order to take his/her evidence.

Article 218

The judge who proceeds with an inquiry may, of his/her own initiative or at the request of the parties, call or hear any person whose testimony he/she deems to be necessary for a establishing the truth.

Article 219

The testimony shall be recorded in a statement.

However, where the testimony is given in the course of the hearing, a note shall simply be made in the judgment, of the family name of the persons heard and the weight attached to their testimony if the matter has to be ruled on as of last resort.

Article 220

The record must note the presence or absence of the parties, the family name, first names date and place of birth, address and occupation of the parties being heard as well as, where appropriate, the oath taken by them and of their statements relating to their relationship to the parties, any subordination to, or working relationship or joint interests with them.

Each person heard must sign the record regarding his/her testimony, after having first verified or certified that it conforms to it, in which case a note to that effect shall be made in the record. Where appropriate, a note must be made of his/her refusal to sign or to certify.

The judge may note in the record, his/her findings in relation to the behavior of a witness during the hearing of his/her testimony.

The comments of the parties must be noted down in the record, or must be annexed to it where they are in writing.

Any documents presented at the inquiry must also be annexed to it.

The record must be dated and signed by the judge and, where appropriate, by the clerk of the court.

Article 221

The judge shall grant leave to the witness, at his/her request, to claim such expenses to which he/she is entitled.

Sub-Section 2
Ordinary Inquiry

§ 1 Determination of facts to be proved

Article 222

The party requesting an inquiry must state the facts for which he/she requires proof.

It shall be for the judge who orders the inquiry to determine the pertinent facts to be proved.

§ 2 Naming of witnesses

Article 223

The party who requests an inquiry must state the family name, first names and address of the persons they intend to produce as witnesses.

The same obligation shall apply to the opponents who intend to produce witnesses in relation to those facts they intend to prove.

The decision ordering an inquiry shall indicate the family name, first names and address of the persons to be heard.

Article 224

If the parties are unable to specify at the outset the persons who will be heard, the judge may nevertheless grant them leave without any further formality, either to attend the inquiry with those persons whom they wish to be heard as witnesses, or to inform the court registry of the family name, first names and address of the persons they intend to produce as witnesses within a time limit to be specified by the preceding judge.

Where the inquiry has been ordered on his/her own motion, the judge shall direct the parties to proceed as set out in the above paragraph, if he/she is unable to specify in his/her order the family name of the witnesses to be heard.

§ 3 Determination of the method and the timetable for the inquiry

Article 225

A decision ordering an inquiry must specify whether it should be conducted before the panel of judges, a member of such panel, or, where necessary, before any other judge of the court.

Article 226

Where the inquiry is to be heard before the judge who ordered it, or before one of the members of the panel of judges, the decision must indicate the date, time and place where it is to be conducted.

Article 227

Where the judge appointed by the court is not a member of the panel of judges, the decision ordering the inquiry may be limited to indicating the time period within which it must be conducted.

Where the enquiry is to be by way of a commission on behalf of another court, the decision must specify the time period within which the inquiry must be conducted. Such period may be extended by the president of the commissioned court and he/she shall inform the judge thereof who originally ordered the inquiry.

The commissioned judge shall set the date, time and place for the inquiry.

§ 4 Subpoena of witnesses

Article 228

Witnesses shall be subpoenaed by the clerk of the court at least eight days before the date of the enquiry.

Article 229

The subpoenas shall indicate the family name and first names of the parties and shall recite the provisions of the first two paragraphs of Article 207.

Article 230

The parties shall be notified of the date of the inquiry verbally or by regular mail.

Sub-Section 3
The Immediate Inquiry

Article 231

The judge may, at the hearing or in chambers, as well as in any other place where a direction is being implemented, hear immediately those persons whose testimony he/she deems necessary in order to establish the truth.

Chapter V
Directions Carried Out by a Technical Expert

Section I
Common Provisions

Article 232

The judge may appoint any person of his/her choice to provide him/her with guidance in the form of observations, written advice or by way of a report on a question of fact which calls for such technical guidance.

Article 233

The expert, given certain powers by the judge by reason of his/her qualifications, must personally fulfill the duties given to him/her.

If the appointed expert is a corporate entity, its authorized representative shall submit, for the judge's approval, the family name of the person or persons within its organization who will insure the implementation of the direction on its behalf.

Article 234

Experts may be challenged on the same grounds as judges. In the case of a corporate entity, the challenge may be directed to the corporate entity as well as against a natural person or persons approved by the judge.

The party who intends to challenge an expert must do so before the judge who appointed him/her, or before the judge assigned to supervise the inquiry before it starts or from the time when grounds for such a challenge have arisen.

Where the expert considers that he/she might be challenged, he/she must declare this immediately to the judge who appointed him/her or to the judge assigned to supervise the inquiry.

Article 235

If a challenge is justified, or if an expert refuses an assignment, or if there exists a lawful impediment, the judge who appointed the latter or the judge assigned to supervise the enquiry, shall replace the expert.

The judge may also, at the request of the parties or of his/her own initiative, replace the expert who has failed in his/her duties after having asked him/her to provide explanations for the same.

Article 236

The judge who has appointed the expert or the judge assigned to supervise the enquiry may extend or reduce the task given to the expert.

Article 237

The appointed expert must carry out his/her duties conscientiously, objectively and impartially.

Article 238

The expert must provide his/her opinion on the issues which he/she has been asked to examine.

He/she may not consider other questions without written agreement by the parties.

He/she shall never express an opinion on a point of law.

Article 239

An expert must comply with any time limits imposed upon him/her.

Article 240

A judge may not commission an expert to reconcile the parties.

Article 241

The judge assigned to supervise the inquiry may attend the expert's inquiry.

He/she may ask him/her to provide explanations and impose time limits upon him/her.

Article 242

The expert may accept any oral or written information from any person as long as their family name, first names, address and occupation are specified as well as, where the necessary, his/her relationship to the parties, by blood or by marriage, by employment, working relationship or common interests with them.

Where the appointed expert or the parties request that these persons should be heard by the judge, the latter shall proceed to hear them if he/she considers this to be useful.

Article 243

The expert may request any documents from the parties or third persons and the judge may request the same in difficult cases.

Article 244

The expert must in his/her opinion disclose all the information which might provide clarification of the questions to be examined.

He/she shall be prohibited from disclosing other information which might have come to his/her knowledge in the course of conducting his/her duties.

He/she may only refer to information lawfully received by him/her.

Article 245

The judge may always invite the expert to complete, clarify or to explain his/her observations or conclusions either in writing or at the hearing.

The expert may at any time demand a hearing before the judge.

The judge may not, without having first received the observations of the appointed expert, extend the latter's assignment or give a further assignment to another expert.

Article 246

The judge shall not be bound by the observations or conclusions of the expert.

Article 247

When the publication of the expert's opinion might constitute an invasion of a party's privacy or any other legitimate interest, it may not be used for any other purpose than the legal proceedings, without the judge's permission or the consent of the party concerned.

Article 248

The expert may not receive any remuneration directly from a party in any form whatsoever even as a reimbursement of expenses unless ordered by the judge.

Section II
Reporting of Facts

Article 249

The judge may entrust the persons he/she has appointed to proceed with the finding of facts.

The examiner shall not give any opinion on the factual and legal consequences which may result from such findings.

Article 250

Fact-findings may be ordered at any time including at the conciliation stage or during the deliberation. In the latter case, the parties shall be advised of the same.

The findings of fact shall be recorded in writing unless the judge should decide on their oral presentation.

Article 251

The judge who orders a fact-finding exercise shall set the time limit within which a report must be presented or the date of the hearing at which they shall be presented orally. He/she shall indicate the party or parties who shall be obliged to provide an interim payment for remuneration of the examiner, which shall be determined by the judge.

Article 252

The examiner of the facts shall be notified of his/her assignment by the clerk of the court.

Article 253

The report shall be delivered to the court registry.

A record shall be drafted of the findings which are presented orally. The preparation of the record may, notwithstanding the above, be replaced by a note made in the judgment where the matter is being decided immediately without any appeal.

Documents in support of the findings of fact shall be added to the file on the matter.

Article 254

Where a fact-finding operation has been ordered during the private consultation, the judge, after such a direction has been carried out, shall order the re-opening of the hearing if one of the parties so requests or if the judge considers it necessary.

Article 255

The judge shall fix the payment to the examiner upon proof of the completion of his/her assignment. He/she may issue to him/her an enforceable document.

Section III
Consultation

Article 256

When a purely technical question does not require complex investigation, the judge may instruct the person he/she shall appoint to provide him/her with a simple opinion.

Article 257

A consultation may be required at any time including during the conciliation stage or during the private consultation of the judges. In the latter case, the parties shall be informed.

The consultation shall be presented orally unless the judge requires that it should only be submitted in writing.

Article 258

The judge who orders a consultation shall set the date of the hearing at which it shall be presented orally or the time limit within which it shall be submitted.

He/she shall indicate the party or parties who shall pay the consultant's fees, the amount of which shall be fixed by the judge.

Article 259

The consultant shall be notified of his/her assignment by the clerk of the court who will call him/her where necessary.

Article 260

If the consultation is given orally, it shall be recorded in an official report. The preparation of the record may, notwithstanding the above, be replaced by a memorandum made in the judgment if the matter is being decided immediately without any appeal.

If the consultation is written, it shall be delivered to the court registry.

The documents in support of the consultation shall be placed on the file of the matter.

Article 261

If the consultation has been ordered during the deliberations, the judge, after such a direction has been carried out, shall order the re-opening of the hearing if one of the parties so requests, or if the judge considers it necessary.

Article 262

Upon proof of the completion of the assignment, the judge shall set the payment due to the consultant. He/she may issue him/her an enforceable document.

Section IV
Expert Opinion

Article 263

A expert opinion shall only be ordered in cases where a finding of fact or an independent advice would not be sufficient to provide the judge with guidance.

Sub-Section 1
The Decision Ordering the Survey

Article 264

Only one person shall be appointed as an expert, unless the judge deems it necessary to appoint several persons.

Article 265

The decision which orders the survey must:

- set out the circumstances which make a survey necessary and, where applicable, which makes the appointment of several surveyors necessary;
- name the surveyor or surveyors;
- specify main headings for the surveyor's appointment;

– impose the time limit within which the surveyor shall have to provide his/her opinion.

Article 266

The same decision may also specify a date on which the surveyor and the parties shall have to appear before the judge who has made it or before the judge entrusted with the supervision of the survey operations so that the extent of the surveyor's duties and, where necessary, the timetable of the survey operation, may be determined.

Documents useful for the survey shall be given to the surveyor at this hearing.

Article 267

As soon as the decision appointing the surveyor is issued, the clerk of the court shall send him/her a copy thereof by regular mail.

The expert shall without delay notify his/her acceptance to the judge; he/she must commence the survey as soon as he/she has been informed that the parties have deposited the sum on account of his/her fees to which they are liable to contribute, or the amount of the first installment as may be due under the order for payment on account, unless the judge directs him/her to start his/her survey immediately.

Article 268

The files of the parties or the documents necessary for the survey shall provisionally be kept at the court registry, subject to the judge's authorization to the parties who submitted them to remove certain documents or to have copies made and sent to them. The surveyor may consult them even before accepting his/her assignment.

From the moment of his/her acceptance, the surveyor may remove the files or the documents, or have them sent to him/her by the clerk of the court, upon the latter making a note in the margin of the file, or issuing a receipt.

Article 269

The judge who orders the survey or the judge entrusted with its supervision must, at the time of the expert is appointed or as soon as he/she is able to do so, set the amount of the sum to be paid on account of the surveyor's fees, as close as possible to the estimated final payment. He/she shall indicate the party or parties who shall have to deposit the payment on account with the court registry within the time limit which he/she shall determine; where several parties are named, he/she shall indicate the proportions which each of the parties shall have to pay. He/she shall, where necessary, adjust the installments in which the payments must be made.

Article 270

The registrar shall invite the parties who are liable to contribute to the deposit, whilst reminding them of the provisions of Article 271, to deposit the payment on account with the court registry within the time limit and in the manner specified.

He/she shall inform the surveyor of the payment.

Article 271

In default of payment of the deposit within the specified time limit and manner, the appointment of the expert shall lapse unless the judge, at the request of one of the parties who can provide a legitimate excuse, shall grant a further time limit or shall waive the lapse. The legal proceedings shall continue, but subject to any consequences which may flow from the abstention or refusal to pay the deposit.

Article 272

The decision ordering the survey shall be subject to appeal where there are serious and legitimate grounds, by authorization of the first president of the court of appeal, independently of any judgment on the merits of the case.

The party who wishes to appeal must apply to the president who shall give a summary order.[9] The summons must be served within one month of the decision.

If he/she accepts the request, the first president shall set the day when the matter shall be heard by the court, which shall be empowered and shall give a ruling as in matters for fixed-date proceedings, or as provided for under Article 948, as the case may be.

If the decision ordering the survey has also ruled upon the issue of jurisdiction, the court may deal with the challenge over jurisdiction even though the parties may not have filed an appeal against jurisdiction.

---

9 A "référé" is an order given on an *inter partes* application. It is made by a district court (*see* note 5) or Commercial Court (*see* note 19) to deal with urgent matters. I have translated the term as "summary order" or "summary proceeding" depending on the context. In cases where there is a serious dispute as to the substance of the case, a summary order is given for conservatory measures that are deemed necessary by the president to prevent imminent loss or manifestly unlawful activity. In cases where there is no serious dispute on the substance of the case, a summary order may be given to award a sum of money to a creditor or even order performance of the obligation itself.

Summary orders do not bind the court that subsequently hears the case and gives judgment on the merits. They may be modified or rescinded by a subsequent summary order if new circumstances justify this action.

Sub-Section 2
Survey Operations

Article 273

The surveyor must inform the judge of the progress of his/her survey and the steps taken by him/her.

Article 274

Where the judge attends the survey operations, he/she may record in a report his/her observations, the explanations of the surveyor as well as the statements of the parties and of third persons; the report shall be signed by the judge.

Article 275

The parties must, without delay, give the expert all documents which he/she might deem necessary for the conduct of his/her duties.

If the parties have failed to do so, the surveyor must inform the judge thereof and the latter may order the production of documents, where appropriate, subject to fine, or, as the case may be, grant him/her leave to proceed with the matter and to submit his/her report as it stands. The court which is hearing the matter may draw any legal inferences which it chooses from the failure to produce the necessary documents to the surveyor.

Article 276

The surveyor must take into consideration the parties' observations or assertions, and, where they are made in writing, he/she shall attach them to his/her report if the parties so request.

He/she must indicate in his/her report the weight which he/she has given to them.

Article 277

If the State Prosecution Service[10] is present at the survey operations, its observations shall, at its request, be quoted in the surveyor's opinion as well as the weight which he/she has attached to them.

Article 278

The surveyor may take the initiative of obtaining the opinion of another technical expert, but only in a specialized field different from his/her own.

---

10 The French term "ministère publique" refers to the administrative department of the French government responsible for State Prosecutions. I have translated it as "State Prosecution Service".

Article 279

If the surveyor encounters difficulties which might obstruct the completion of his/her duties, or if an extension of his/her duties appears to be necessary, he/she must report this to the judge.

The latter, in his/her ruling, may extend the time limit within which the expert must provide his/her opinion.

Article 280

The surveyor who can demonstrate that he/she has made some progress may be granted leave to withdraw a part payment on the sum deposited in court.

If the surveyor can show that the sum on paid on account is going to be insufficient, the judge shall order the deposit of a further sum on account. In default of payment of a [further] deposit within the time limit and in the manner specified by the judge, and unless there is an extension of such a time limit, the surveyor shall file his/her opinion as it is.

Article 281

Where the parties have reached a settlement, the surveyor shall record that his/her duty has become pointless; he/she shall report accordingly to the judge.

The parties may request the judge to issue an enforceable certificate in relation to the document containing their agreement to settle.

Sub-Section 3
The Surveyor's Opinion

Article 282

Where the surveyor's opinion does not need to be explained in writing, the judge may grant him/her leave to present it orally at the hearing; a record shall be made thereof. The drafting of the record may, notwithstanding the above, be substituted by a written note in the judgment, where the matter is being heard in the final instance without an appeal.

Otherwise, the surveyor must file a report at the court registry. Only one report shall be prepared, even where there are several surveyors; where they cannot agree, each one shall provide his/her view.

Where the surveyor has obtained the opinion of another expert in a different field to his/her own, such an opinion shall be attached, where appropriate, to the surveyor's report, to the record of the hearing of the oral report, or to the court file.

Article 283

Where the judge does not find sufficiently clear explanations in the report to guide him/her, he/she may hear the expert, the parties being present or summonsed to be present.

Article 284

As soon as the report is filed, the judge shall determine the surveyor's fees, based on the steps taken, compliance with the time limit imposed and the quality of the work provided.

He/she shall grant the surveyor leave to be paid up to the amount of the sums deposited at the court registry. He/she shall order, where appropriate, either the payment of further sums due to the surveyor, indicating the party or parties who shall pay the same, or the return of the excess amount deposited by the parties.

If the judge anticipates setting the surveyor's fees at an amount which is less than the sum requested, he/she must first invite the expert to submit his/her comments in relation to the same.

The judge may issue an enforceable deed to the surveyor, at his/her request.

Article 284-1

If the surveyor so requests, a copy of the judgment which is made taking account of his/her opinion, may be sent to him/her or given to him/her by the registrar.

SUB-TITLE III
DISPUTES RELATING TO PRIVATE DOCUMENTS

Article 285

Verification of private documents comes within the jurisdiction of the judge dealing with the main issue when it is requested as an interlocutory matter.

It falls within the jurisdiction of the regional court where it is requested as a principal issue.

Article 286

An allegation of forgery in respect of an official document of record comes within the jurisdiction of the judge hearing the main issue where it is brought as an interlocutory matter before a regional court and a court of appeal.

In other cases, an allegation of forgery comes within the jurisdiction of the regional court.

Chapter I
Disputes Relating to Written Documents and Private Signature

Section I
Verification of Handwriting

Sub-Section 1
The Motion for Verification

Article 287

Where one of the parties denies the handwriting that is attributed to him/her, or declares that he/she does not recognize that which is attributed to its author, the judge shall verify the handwriting in dispute, unless he/she is able to make a ruling without doing so. Where the handwriting in dispute only relates to certain grounds of the claim, the judge may rule upon the other grounds.

If the denial or refusal of recognition involves an electronic document or signature, the judge shall verify if the conditions provided in Articles 1316-1 and 1316-4 of the Civil Code for the validity of an electronic document or signature are satisfied.

Article 288

The judge shall verify the handwriting based upon the material available and if necessary require the parties to provide documents or handwriting samples for comparison.

When considering the documents to be compared, the judge may retain any useful documents provided by one or other of the parties, whether or not they may have been written at the time of the litigious act.

Article 288-1

When an electronic signature can be considered to be reliable, the judge may determine whether the documents at his/her disposal justify the rebuttal of such a presumption.

Article 289

If he/she does not make an immediate ruling, the judge shall keep the handwriting to be verified and the exhibits for comparison, or may order that they be filed at the court registry.

Article 290

If it is necessary to compare the disputed handwriting with third-party documents, the judge may order, under his/her own motion and under threat of a fine, that those documents be filed at the court registry in original form or copies thereof.

He/she shall issue all the necessary directives, particularly those relating to the preservation, consultation, reproduction, return or restoration of the documents.

Article 291

If necessary, the judge may order the personal appearance of the parties and, where appropriate, in the presence of an advisor, or shall issue any other directives.

He/she may hear the alleged author of the disputed handwriting.

Article 292

If a handwriting expert is required, the latter may be given leave by the judge to remove the disputed handwriting and the exhibits to make a comparison, after so noting in the court record, or to have the record sent to him/her by the clerk of the court.

Article 293

Persons who witnessed the disputed document being written or signed, or those whose testimony appears to be useful for ascertaining the truth, may be heard as witnesses.

Article 294

The judge shall rule upon the difficulties in carrying out the verification of the handwriting, in particular determining the exhibits to be compared.

His/her decision shall take the form either of simple notes recorded in the court file, or in the records of the hearing, or, where necessary, in an order or a judgment.

Article 295

Where it is ruled that the document was written or signed by the person who denied it, the latter shall be ordered to pay a fine of between 15€ and 1500€ without prejudice to any damages which might be claimed.

Sub-Section 2
The Verification of Handwriting Requested as a Main Issue

Article 296

If the verification of handwriting is raised as a main point of claim, the judge shall consider the handwriting as being his/her own if the defendant who is summonsed to appear in person, fails to appear.

Article 297

Where the defendant recognizes the handwriting, the judge shall find for the claimant.

Article 298

Where the defendant denies or does not recognize the handwriting, the provisions under Articles 287 to 295 shall be followed.

The same shall apply where the defendant who has not been summonsed to appear in person, does not appear.

Section II
Falsification

Sub-Section 1
The Plea of Forgery

Article 299

Where a private document that is produced in the course of the proceedings is alleged to be forged, the document in dispute is examined as provided in Articles 287 to 295.

Sub-Section 2
Forgery Raised as a Main Allegation

Article 300

Where the allegation of forgery of a private document is raised as a main point of the claim, the summons must indicate the grounds for the allegation and shall require the defendant to declare whether or not he/she intends to rely upon the document which is alleged to be forged or falsified.

Article 301

Where the defendant declares that he/she does not wish to use the document which is alleged to be forged, the judge shall find for the claimant.

Article 302

Where the defendant does not appear or where he/she declares that he/she wishes to use the disputed handwritten document, the provisions under Articles 287 to 295 shall be followed.

Chapter II
Pleas of Forgery Against Official Documents

Article 303

A plea of forgery against an official document shall be sent to the State Prosecution Service.

Article 304

The judge may order that the person who drew up the disputed document be heard.

Article 305

The claimant whose plea of forgery fails shall be ordered to pay a fine of 15€ to 1,500€ without prejudice to any damages which may be claimed.

Section I
The Incidental Plea of a Forgery Against an Official Document

Sub-Section 1
The Incidental Plea Raised Before the Regional Court or the Court of Appeal

Article 306

The plea of forgery shall be entered by the filing at the court registry office of a notice by the party or his/her authorized agent.

The notice, in duplicate, must, at the risk of it otherwise being inadmissible, state precisely the grounds upon which the party is relying in order to prove the forgery.

One of the copies shall immediately be placed in the court file and the other, dated and stamped by the registrar, shall be returned to the party to enable him/her to serve the plea on the defendant.

The notice must be served by and upon the parties' attorneys or by serving the opposing party within one month from the filing of the notice.

Article 307

The judge shall rule upon the forgery unless he/she can decide without considering the exhibit which is alleged to be forged.

Where the allegedly forged document relates only to one of the grounds of the claim, the judge may rule upon the other grounds.

Article 308

The judge shall admit or reject the disputed document on the basis of the material at his/her disposal.

Where appropriate, the judge shall, as regards the forgery, order any procedural measures that are necessary, and the matter proceeds as for verification of handwriting.

Article 309

The judge shall decide on the basis of the grounds raised by the parties or him/herself.

Article 310

The decision declaring a forgery shall be noted in the margin of the forged document.

The decision shall specify whether the original of the authentic document of record will be returned to the place from which it was obtained or will be kept at the court registry office.

The implementation of such provisions shall not be enforced until the judgment has become final or until the losing party has accepted the judgment.

Article 311

If the plea of forgery is withdrawn or settled, the State Prosecution Service may demand all measures appropriate to the prosecution of a criminal action.

Article 312

Where criminal proceedings are brought against the authors of or accomplices to the forgery, the civil judgment shall be suspended until after the decision in the criminal proceedings has been given, unless the main issue can be judged without taking account of the allegedly forged document or unless there has been a withdrawal or settlement with respect to the forgery.

Sub-Section 2
The Incidental Plea Raised Before Other Courts

Article 313

Where the plea is raised before a court other than the regional court or the court of appeal, the judgment shall be stayed until a ruling on the issue of forgery has been given, unless the disputed exhibit has been withdrawn from the proceedings so that it is possible to rule upon the main issue without taking the same into consideration.

The plea of forgery shall proceed as provided in Articles 314 to 316. The notice of the plea of forgery must be lodged at the court registry office of the regional court within the month of the decision to stay the judgment, failing which the plea shall be disregarded and the disputed document shall be considered to have been accepted as being valid between the parties.

Section II
The Plea of Forgery as a Principal Allegation

Article 314

The principal claim of forgery shall be preceded by a plea of forgery entered as provided in Article 306.

A copy of the notice entering the plea shall be attached to the summons which shall contain a formal request to the defendant to declare whether or not he/she intends to rely upon the documents which are alleged to be forged or falsified.

The summons must be served within one month of the plea of forgery being entered under penalty of it otherwise being struck out.

Article 315

Where the defendant declares that he/she does not wish to use the document which is alleged to be false, the judge shall acknowledge this fact in the claimant's favor.

Article 316

Where the defendant fails to appear or declares that he/she wishes to rely upon the disputed document, matters shall proceed as provided in Articles 287 to 294 and 309 to 312.

SUB-TITLE IV
THE OATH BEFORE THE COURT

Article 317

The party who tenders evidence on oath must set out the facts in relation to which the oath shall be given.

The judge shall order evidence to be sworn where it is permissible and shall specify the facts on which the oath shall be given.

Article 318

Where the oath is required by the court in any event, the judge determines the facts in relation to which it shall be given.

Article 319

The judgment ordering the oath shall fix the date, time and place where it shall be taken. It shall state the question in relation to which the oath is to be taken and shall point out that perjury will subject a witness to criminal sanctions.

Where the oath is requested by a party, the judgment shall further specify that the party against whom the oath is called shall fail in his/her claim if he/she refuses to take the oath and fails to request one in return.

In all cases, the judgment shall be served upon the party from whom the oath is called as well as his/her representative, where appropriate.

Article 320

The judgment which orders or refuses to order a decisive oath may be appealed, independently of the decision on the substantive issue.

Article 321

The oath shall be taken by the party in person and at the hearing.

Where the party shows that he/she is unable to travel, the oath may be taken either before a judge commissioned for that purpose who shall travel to the residence of the party, assisted by the clerk, or before the court of that party's place of residence.

In any case, the oath shall be given in the presence of the other party.

Article 322

The person duly authorized as a legal representative may not request an oath without showing that he/she has a special power to do so.

TITLE VIII
MULTIPLE PARTIES

Article 323

Where the claim is made by or against several persons with a common interest, each of them shall exercise and discharge, the rights and obligations of the parties to the proceedings, insofar as they relate to those persons.

Article 324

The acts performed by or against the persons with a common interest shall neither benefit nor prejudice the others, subject to the provisions of Articles 474, 475, 529, 552, 553 and 615.

TITLE IX
INTERPLEADERS

Article 325

An interpleader shall not be allowed unless it is sufficiently connected to the claims of the parties.

Article 326

Where the interpleader might excessively delay the judgment on the whole matter, the judge shall first rule upon the main cause of action and thereafter consider the interpleader.

Article 327

The interpleader at first instance or on appeal is implemented either by voluntary joinder of parties or interpleading summons.

Before the Court of Cassation, only a voluntary joinder of parties is allowed where it is of secondary importance to the main cause of action.

Chapter I
The Voluntary Joinder of Parties

Article 328

The voluntary joinder of parties shall be of principal or secondary importance.

Article 329

The joinder shall be of principal importance if it helps to establish a claim for the benefit of the party who is requesting it.

It shall only be allowed where the party requesting it has a right of action in relation to that claim.

Article 330

The intervention shall be of secondary importance if it supports the claims of a party.

It shall be allowed where the party requesting it has, in order to protect his/her rights, an interest in joining that party, who may unilaterally withdraw his/her intervention in the proceedings.

Chapter II
Interpleading Summons

Section I
Provisions Common to All Third-Party Proceedings

Article 331

A third party may be joined for the purpose of having an order made against him/her by any party who has the right to bring a claim against the former.

He/she may likewise be joined by a party who has an interest in obtaining a judgment against him/her which is common to all concerned.

The third party must be summonsed with sufficient time for him/her to establish his/her defense.

Article 332

The judge may invite the parties to issue proceedings against all interested persons whose presence appears necessary for the resolution of the dispute.

In non-contentious matters, he/she may order proceedings to be issued against persons whose rights or duties may be affected by the decision.

Article 333

The third party against whom proceedings have been issued shall be bound to proceed before the court dealing with the original claim, without being able to challenge the territorial jurisdiction of the court even by relying upon a specific jurisdiction clause.

Section II
Special Provisions for Third Party Notices

Article 334

The indemnity claim may be simple or formal depending on whether the defendant seeking the contribution is him/herself being sued personally or only as the holder of an asset.

Article 335

The defendant seeking a simple indemnity shall remain the main party.

Article 336

The defendant in a formal indemnity claim may always request that he/she should be dismissed from the action, and that the third party/guarantor should be substituted as the main defendant.

However, the defendant seeking a contribution or indemnity, although being dismissed from the action may remain in the action in order to preserve his/her rights; the original claimant may also ask that he/she should remain in the action to preserve his/her rights.

Article 337

A judgment issued against the formal guarantor may, in any case, be enforced against the person who is being guaranteed on the sole condition that he/she has been served with it.

Article 338

Costs are only recoverable against the person who is being guaranteed in the case of the insolvency of the formal guarantor and on condition that the person who is being guaranteed should remain as a party to the proceedings, even as a minor defendant.

TITLE IX Bis
TESTIMONY OF A CHILD BEFORE A COURT OF JUSTICE

Article 338-1

Where a minor asks to be heard as provided by Article 388-1 of the Civil Code, the following provisions shall apply.

Article 338-2

The request shall be made informally to the judge by the person concerned. It may be made at any stage of the proceedings and even for the first time on appeal.

Article 338-3

The ruling on the request made by the minor cannot be appealed.

The decision whereby the testimony is ordered may, notwithstanding the above, be amended or set aside by another special reasoned decision if the judge is aware of a serious reason why the testimony of the minor should not be heard, under the previously stated conditions.

Article 338-4

The decision ordering the testimony may be recorded as a simple note in the court file or in the transcript of the hearing.

Article 338-5

A summons to appear to give testimony shall be sent to the minor by registered mail with acknowledgment of receipt, and also sent by regular mail.

The summons shall inform him/her of his/her right to testify alone, or in the presence of an attorney or another person of his/her choice.

On the same day, the court registry office shall inform the legal representatives of the parties by an ordinary notice and, in default thereof, the parties themselves shall be informed by registered mail with acknowledgment of receipt of the decision ordering the testimony. The notice shall contain the provisions of Article 338-3.

Article 338-6

Where the judge is requested to give evidence in the presence of the parties and the minor, the hearing of his/her testimony may take place immediately. If it is not dealt with immediately, the summons of the minor and the information contained in the second paragraph of Article 338-5 shall be given orally by the judge.

Article 338-7

Where the minor appears alone in order to give evidence, the judge must inform him/her of his/her right to give evidence in the presence of an attorney or a person of his/her choice. If the minor exercises such a right, the hearing of his/her testimony shall be adjourned to a later date.

The attorney instructed by the minor shall inform the judge of this.

Where the minor requests to give evidence in the presence of an attorney and where he/she does not choose one him/herself, the judge shall ask the Chairperson of the Bar to appoint an attorney for him/her.

Article 338-8

The decision to refuse the hearing of shall be sent by the court registry office to the minor by registered mail with acknowledgement of receipt with a copy sent by regular mail. Where relevant, a copy of the decision shall be sent to the minor's attorney by simple notice.

Article 338-9

The court sitting as a panel of judges may hear the minor or appoint one of its members to proceed with the hearing of the minor's testimony and to report the same thereafter.

TITLE X
WITHDRAWAL, CHALLENGE AND REFERRAL

Chapter I
Withdrawal

Article 339

The judge who considers that grounds exist to challenge him/her personally, or who thinks he/she should in all conscience abstain, must have him/herself replaced by another judge nominated by the president of the court to which he/she is attached. The replacement of a judge of the district court shall be made by the president of the regional court in default of a presiding judge.

Article 340

Where the abstention of several judges prevents the court from ruling on the case, it shall be dealt with in the same way as in matters of referral back on grounds of reasonable suspicion.

Chapter II
Challenge

Article 341

The challenge of a judge shall be allowed only on grounds provided by the law.

As provided under Article L.731-1 of the Code of Judicial Organization, and unless special provisions for certain courts exist, the challenge of a judge may be requested:

"1. Where he/she or his/her spouse has a personal interest in the dispute;

"2. Where he/she or his/her spouse is the creditor, debtor, presumed heir or donee of one of the parties;

"3. Where he/she or his/her spouse is related by blood or marriage to one of the parties, or to his/her spouse up to the fourth degree of kinship;

"4. Where there have been legal proceedings between him/herself or his/her spouse and one of the parties or his/her spouse;

"5. Where he/she has, previously, had knowledge of the matter in the capacity of a judge or arbitrator or where he/she has counseled one of the parties;

"6. Where the judge or his/her spouse is entrusted with the administration of the property of one of the parties;

"7. Where there exists a link of subordination between the judge or his/her spouse and one of the parties or his/her spouse;

"8. Where there has been a well-known friendship or enmity between the judge and one of the parties.

"The State Prosecution Service, as a joined party, may be challenged on the same grounds."

Article 342

The party who wishes to challenge a judge must, unless the challenge is to be inadmissible, do so as soon as he/she has knowledge of a ground for a challenge.

In no case may the request for a challenge be made after the close of oral pleadings.

Article 343

With the exception of actions brought before the Court of Cassation, the challenge may be made by the party him/herself or by his/her representative. The latter must be duly authorised to do so.

Article 344

The request for the challenge shall be made by a petition filed with the court registry to which the relevant judge is attached or by a declaration recorded by the clerk in an official statement.

The request for the challenge must, under penalty of it otherwise being declared inadmissible, specify precisely the grounds for the challenge and be supported by the necessary exhibits.

An acknowledgment of the request shall be issued.

Article 345

The clerk shall send to the judge a copy of the application to challenge him/her.

Article 346

As soon as he/she receives the copy of the application, the judge must withdraw from the case until the challenge has been ruled upon.

If it is urgent, another judge may be appointed, even by order of the court, to carry out the necessary procedures.

Article 347

Within eight days of receiving the application, the challenged judge must submit in writing either his/her acceptance of the challenge or the grounds on which he/she objects to it.

Article 348

If the judge accepts the challenge, he/she shall immediately be replaced.

Article 349

If the judge objects to the challenge or does respond, the challenge shall be decided at once by the court of appeal or, where it is directed against a member of a court composed of professional and lay judges, by the president of the court in question, whose ruling cannot be appealed.

Article 350

The clerk shall send the challenge application together with the judge's response or a note of his/her failure to respond, to the first president of the court of appeal or to the president of the court composed of professional and lay judges.

Article 351

The matter shall be determined without the need to call the parties or the challenged judge.

A copy of the decision shall be delivered or sent by the clerk to the judge concerned and to the parties.

Article 352

If the challenge application is granted, the judge shall be replaced.

Article 353

If the challenge application is dismissed, the plaintiff may be ordered to pay a fine of between 15€ and 1,500€ without prejudice to any damages which may be claimed.

Article 354

Any acts performed by the challenge judge before he/she had knowledge of the challenged may not be subject to any objection.

Article 355

A challenge against several judges must, if it is not to be declared inadmissible, be made in the same document, unless a ground for a challenge comes to light subsequently.

The matter is then dealt with as set out in the following Chapter, even though a referral has not been requested.

Chapter III
Referral to Another Court

Section I
Referral for Presumed Bias

Article 356

The application for referral on grounds of presumed bias shall be subject to the same conditions of admissibility and form as a challenge application.

Article 357

The application to refer the matter to another court shall immediately be sent by the clerk to the president of the court.

Article 358

Where the president considers the application well-founded, he/she shall assign the matter to another panel of the same court or refer it to another court of the same type.

Where the president considers that the matter should be referred to another court, he/she shall forward the court file to the president of the next superior court who shall designate the court of referral.

A copy of the decision shall be sent by the clerk to the parties.

The decision cannot be appealed; it shall be binding on the parties and on the referring judge.

Article 359

If the president objects to the application, he/she shall refer the matter, with the reasons of his/her refusal, to the president of the next superior court.

Such court shall, in chambers, rule within one month after having heard the State Prosecution Service and without the need to call the parties.

A copy of the decision shall be sent by the court clerk to the parties and to the president of the court which is being asked to refer the case.

Article 360

If the application is well-founded, the matter shall be referred to another panel of the court originally assigned to handle the case, or to another court of the same type.

The decision shall be binding on the parties and on the referring judge. The decision cannot be appealed.

Article 361

The proceedings shall not be stayed before the court from which the matter is being asked to be referred elsewhere.

The president of the court dealing with an application for referral may, notwithstanding the above, and according to the circumstances, order that the court suspected of bias should refrain from making any ruling until the referral application has been decided.

Article 362

Where there is a referral, the provisions of Article 97 shall be followed.

Article 363

The dismissal of the referral application may be subject to the provisions under Article 353.

Section II
Referral on Grounds of a Challenge Against Several Judges

Article 364

Where the referral is requested on grounds of a personal challenge against several judges of the court hearing the case, it shall be dealt with in the same way as in matters of referral on grounds of presumed bias after each judge has replied or the time limit for replying has expired.

Section III
Referral on Grounds of Public Security

Article 365

The referral on grounds of public security shall be ordered by the Court of Cassation on the request of the State Prosecutor attached to such court.

Article 366

The provisions of Articles 360 to 362 shall apply.

TITLE XI
INTERLOCUTORY PROCEEDINGS

Chapter I
Joinder and Disjoinder of Proceedings

Article 367

The judge may, on the application of the parties or on his/her own motion, order the joinder of several proceedings pending before him/her where there is a connection between the disputes to the extent that it would be in the interests of justice to hear or rule upon them together.

He/she may likewise order the disjoinder of proceedings into separate actions.

Article 368

The decision of joinder or disjoinder of proceedings are measures of judicial administration.

Chapter II
Interruption of the Proceedings

Article 369

The proceedings shall be interrupted by:

– the coming of age of a party;

– the discontinuance of representation by an attorney or appeal advocate where such representation is compulsory;

– the effect of a judgment which orders the receivership or compulsory sale of assets in cases where this involves the control or the dispossession of the debtor.

Article 370

After notification to the other party, the proceedings shall be interrupted by:

– the death of a party in cases where the action is transferable;

– the discontinuance of the legal representation of a person under a legal disability;

– the recovery or loss by a party of the legal capacity to appear in court.

Article 371

In no case shall the proceedings be interrupted if the event happens or is notified after the opening of oral pleadings.

Article 372

Any legal acts performed and even final judgments obtained after the termination of the proceedings, shall have no effect unless they are expressly or tacitly confirmed by the party for whose benefit the termination is intended.

Article 373

The proceedings may be restored voluntarily by means of the procedure for presenting the grounds of defense.

In the absence of voluntary restoration, they may be restored by way of a writ of summons.

Article 374

Once restored, the proceedings shall continue where they left off at the time when they were interrupted.

Article 375

Where a party who is summonsed in order to restore the proceedings fails to appear, the action shall proceed as provided under Articles 471ff.

Article 376

The interruption of proceedings shall not deprive the judge of his/her jurisdiction to hear the case.

He/she may invite the parties to inform him/her of their steps to start the proceedings afresh and may strike the case off the list if no action is taken within the time limit that he/she lays down.

He/she may request the State Prosecution Service to gather the information necessary for the restoration of the proceedings.

Chapter III
Stay of the Proceedings

Article 377

Apart from the cases provided for by law, the proceedings shall be suspended by a decision ordering a stay of judgment or that the matter should be struck from the roll.

Section I
Stay of Judgment

Article 378

The order to stay shall suspend the proceedings for the period, or until the occurrence of an event, specified in the order.

Article 379

The stay shall not deprive the judge of his/her jurisdiction to hear the case. At the expiration of the stay, the proceedings shall be resumed at the initiative of the parties or by the judge, subject to the latter's power to order a fresh stay, where necessary.

The judge may, under the circumstances, revoke the stay or shorten its length.

Article 380

The order to stay the judgment may be appealed by permission of the first president of the court of appeal where a serious and legitimate cause against it is shown.

The party who wishes to appeal shall apply to the first president, who shall decide in accordance with the rules for summary procedure. The summons must be served within one month from the order.

Where leave to appeal is granted, the first president sets the date when the matter is to be examined by the court, which assumes jurisdiction and gives its ruling as in fixed-day proceedings or as set out in Article 948, as the case may be.

Article 380-1

The order for a stay of judgment given as one of last resort, may be opposed by a petition to the Supreme Court, but only in relation to a breach of a rule of law.

Section II
Striking from the Roll

Article 381

An order striking from the Roll shall be made, under the conditions provided in law, as a result of the want of prosecution on behalf of the parties.

It shall involve the removal from the Roll of pending cases before the court.

It shall be sent by regular mail to the parties as well as to their representatives. Such notification shall state the want of prosecution.

Article 382

The striking from the Roll shall be ordered if requested by all the parties given sufficient reason.

Article 383

The striking from the Roll is a measure of judicial administration.

Unless the proceedings have become time-limit, a matter may be restored to the Roll, if it has been struck off, by showing compliance with the steps which should have been undertaken and which led to the matter being struck off, upon the application to the court by one of the parties.

Chapter IV
Termination of the Proceedings

Article 384

Apart from cases where the termination of the proceedings results from the pronouncement of a judgment, the proceedings shall terminate upon the conclusion of an amicable settlement, acceptance or withdrawal of action or, in non-assignable actions, upon the death of one of the parties.

The termination of the proceedings shall be recorded by a decision in which the court is no longer dealing with the matter.

It is for the judge to bestow enforceability on the instrument recording the agreement between the parties, whether this happened in his/her presence or not.

Article 385

The proceedings shall terminate principally by the effect of a time-limit, discontinuance of the proceedings or the lapse of the writ of summons.

In such cases, the recording of the termination of the proceedings and the withdrawal of the court's jurisdiction to hear the case shall not be a bar to the commencement of fresh proceedings where the proceedings are not otherwise terminated.

Section I
Dismissal for Want of Prosecution

Article 386

Proceedings shall be dismissed for want of prosecution where no party has prosecuted the case for a period of two years.

Article 387

Dismissal for want of prosecution may be applied for by either of the parties.

It may be raised as a plea against the party who performed an act after the expiration of the time limit.

Article 388

A plea for dismissal for want of prosecution must, if it is to be admissible, be made or raised as a defense before any other measure; a party is entitled to it.

It may not be raised by a judge on his/her own initiative.

Article 389

Dismissal for want of prosecution shall not terminate the right of action; it shall only terminate the proceedings, and shall not allow a party to object to any of the time-barred pleadings or to make use of them for his/her own benefit.

Article 390

Dismissal for want of prosecution in relation to appeals or applications to set aside shall render the judgment final even if it has not been served.

Article 391

The time limit applies for natural persons and corporate entities, even if they are under a legal incapacity, except for their right of action against their administrators or tutors.

Article 392

The interruption of proceedings shall suspend the time-limit for dismissal for want of prosecution.

The time limit shall continue to run in cases of a stay of proceedings, unless they are only for a limited period or until the occurrence of a specific event; in the latter case, a fresh period shall run from the expiration of the limited period or from the occurrence of the event.

Article 393

The costs incurring from a dismissal for want of prosecution shall be charged to the party who instituted the relevant proceedings.

Section II
Discontinuance of Proceedings

Sub-Section 1
The Discontinuance of the Claim at First Instance

Article 394

The claimant may, in all matters, discontinue his/her claim in order to terminate the proceedings.

Article 395

The discontinuance shall be effective upon the acceptance of the same by the defendant.

Notwithstanding the above, an acceptance shall not be necessary where the defendant has not filed a substantive defense or a plea seeking a summary declaration of inadmissibility at the time when the claimant applies for a discontinuance.

Article 396

The judge shall declare the discontinuance to be effective if the defendant's non-acceptance is not based upon any reasonable grounds.

Article 397

The discontinuance may be expressed or implied; the same shall apply to any acceptance.

Article 398

The discontinuance of proceedings shall not imply any waiver of right to sue, but only the termination of the proceedings.

Article 399

Discontinuance shall, unless there is an agreement to the contrary, include an undertaking to bear the costs of the proceedings that have lapsed.

Sub-Section 2
Discontinuance of an Appeal or Objection

Article 400

The discontinuance of an appeal or an objection shall be allowed in all matters except where there are provisions to the contrary.

Article 401

The discontinuance of an appeal shall only require the acceptance where it contains provisos or where the party against whom it is made has previously filed a cross-appeal or an interlocutory claim.

Article 402

The discontinuance of an objection only has to be accepted if the original claimant has already raised an additional claim.

Article 403

The discontinuance of an appeal shall imply an acceptance of the judgment. It shall be void where another party subsequently files an appeal in proper form.

Article 404

The discontinuance of an objection without provisos shall imply an acceptance of the judgment.

Article 405

Articles 396, 397 and 399 shall not apply to the discontinuance of an appeal or objection.

Section III
Invalidity of the Writ of Summons

Article 406

A writ of summons shall lapse in the cases and in the conditions prescribed by the law.

Article 407

The decision which records the lapse of the summons may be revoked, in case of error, by the judge who made the decision.

Section IV
Acceptance of a Judgment

Article 408

Acceptance of a claim implies a recognition of the merits of the opposing party's claims and a withdrawal of any challenge to it. It is only admissible with respect to rights at the free disposal of the party.

Article 409

Acceptance of a judgment shall imply an admission of its findings and a waiver of any rights of recourse unless another party has subsequently started proper proceedings for an appeal.

It shall always be allowed unless any contrary provisions apply.

Article 410

The acceptance may be expressed or implied.

The unconditional enforcement of a non-enforceable judgment shall amount to an acceptance of the same, except where such an acceptance is not recognized by the court.

TITLE XII
LEGAL REPRESENTATION AND ASSISTANCE BEFORE A COURT

Article 411

The authority to represent a party before a court of justice shall include the power and the duty to settle written pleadings on behalf of that party.

Article 412

The function of assistance before a court of law shall include the power and duty to advise the party and to present his/her defense without the same binding him/her.

Article 413

The authority to represent shall include the duty to assist unless provisions or an agreement to the contrary shall apply.

Article 414

A party may be represented only by a person, whether a natural person or a corporate entity, who is entitled to do so by law.

Article 415

The name of the representative and the capacity in which he/she acts must be given to the judge by a declaration to the clerk of the court.

Article 416

Whoever intends to represent or assist a party must demonstrate his/her authority to act or assist.

An attorney or an appeal advocate shall, however, be exempted from such an obligation.

A court bailiff is also exempt in cases where he/she is entitled to represent or assist the parties.

Article 417

The persons entitled to act as representatives before a court of justice shall be considered, as regards the judge and the opposing party, to have received special powers to request or accept a discontinuance of the action, to admit a claim, to make or accept offers, to tender admissions or agreements.

Article 418

A party who dismisses his/her representative must immediately either provide for a replacement or inform the judge and the opposing party of his/her intention to conduct his/her case him/herself, if the law so permits, failing which, the opposing party may continue the proceedings and obtain judgment while continuing to recognize only the representative who was dismissed.

Article 419

The representative who intends to terminate his/her retainer shall only be discharged where he/she has informed the party on whose behalf he/she has been acting, the judge and the opposing party of his/her intention.

Where representation is compulsory, the attorney or appeal advocate may only discharge their retainer after they are replaced by a new representative instructed by the party, or in default thereof, instructed by the chairperson of the bar or the president of the disciplinary council.

Article 420

The attorney or appeal advocate shall fulfill his/her duties pursuant to his/her instructions, without any renewal of his/her powers until the enforcement of the judgment, provided that the same shall be executed within a year after the judgment has been made final.

These provisions shall not prevent a direct payment to the party of what is due to him/her.

TITLE XIII
THE STATE PROSECUTION SERVICE

Article 421

The State Prosecution Service may act as a main party or be joined as a party to the proceedings. It shall represent such other persons as prescribed by the law.

Chapter I
The State Prosecution Service as a Main Party

Article 422

The State Prosecution Service shall act of its own motion in cases provided by the law.

Article 423

In addition to these cases, it may be the advocate to defend public policy in such cases.

Chapter II
The State Prosecution Service as a Joined Party

Article 424

The State Prosecution Service shall be deemed to be a party to the action when it intervenes to give its opinion on the application of the law in a matter which has been brought to its attention.

Article 425

The State Prosecution Service shall be notified of:

1. Matters relating to parentage, to the arrangements for guardianship, to the institutionalization of or modification of an order of protection for adults;

2. Proceedings for provisional stay of prosecution and general writing-off of debts, personal bankruptcy or other penalties and, with regard to corporate entities, proceedings relating to a court administration of insolvency and sale of property, proceedings relating to receiverships and compulsory liquidation as well those relating to the financial liability of company directors.

The State Prosecution Service must, furthermore, be informed of all matters in relation to which the law provides that it shall give its opinion.

Article 426

The State Prosecution Service may take note of such other matters in relation to which it believes that it is within its duty to intervene.

Article 427

The judge may of his/her own initiative decide to send a matter to the State Prosecution Service.

Article 428

The information to the State Prosecution Service must, unless special provisions apply, be dealt with on the initiative of the judge.

It must be given in sufficient time so as not to delay the judgment.

Article 429

Once it has been informed of a matter, the State Prosecution Service must be notified of the date of the hearing.

TITLE XIV
THE JUDGMENT

Chapter I
General Provisions

Section I
Oral Arguments, Deliberation and the Judgment

Sub-Section 1
Oral Pleadings

Article 430

The court must, if it is to be recognized as valid, be constituted in accordance with the rules governing judicial organization.

Any challenges to its regularity must be made, if they are not to be declared inadmissible, immediately at the opening of the hearing or at the time when the irregularity becomes apparent if this occurs subsequently, failing which the court cannot be declared invalid on this ground, even by the court acting on its own initiative.

The provisions of the preceding paragraph shall not apply to cases where a person has been called upon whose profession or duties are not such as entitle him/her to be a member of the court.

Article 431

The State Prosecution Service shall only be obliged to attend a hearing in cases where it is a principal party, in which it represents other persons or where its presence is required by law.

In all other cases, it may give its opinion to the court either by sending its written submissions, which are made available to the parties, or by the oral presentation of the same at the hearing.

Article 432

The oral pleadings shall be heard on the day and, to the extent that the progress of the hearing shall allow, at the time previously specified, according to the rules of each court. They may be resumed in subsequent court sittings.

Should there be a change in the composition of the court after the opening of the oral pleadings, they will have to be represented from the beginning.

Article 433

The oral pleadings shall be public except where the law requires them to be heard in chambers.

The provisions in this regard at first instance must be followed on appeal, unless otherwise provided.

Article 434

In non-contentious matters, an application is heard in chambers.

Article 435

The judge may decide that the oral pleadings shall take place or shall continue in chambers in cases where their public disclosure might adversely affect an individual's privacy or, if all the parties so request, or if there is a disturbance which might disrupt the conduct of the judicial proceedings.

Article 436

In chambers, they shall be heard with the public present.

Article 437

Where it appears, or where it is alleged either that the oral pleadings should be presented in chambers whereas they are being presented in open court, or vice versa, the president must rule on the spot and the irregularity must be disregarded.

Where the hearing is being conducted according to the proper procedure, no invalidity based on the previous conduct may subsequently be declared, even by the court itself.

Article 438

The president must ensure that the hearing is properly conducted. Any directions given for this purpose must be implemented at once.

Judges shall exercise the same powers in any court in which they may sit.

Article 439

All persons who are attending a hearing must observe a dignified attitude and show due respect to the court. They shall not be allowed to speak without having been invited to do so, to show approval or disapproval, or to cause any disturbance of any nature whatsoever.

The president may have any person who fails to comply with his/her orders expelled without prejudice to any criminal or disciplinary proceedings which might be brought against him/her.

Article 440

The president shall direct the oral pleadings. He/she shall ask the judge in charge of the case to address the court where a report is to be made.

The claimant, and then the defendant, shall be called in that order to present their contentions.

Where the court decides that it has heard enough information about the matter, the president shall order the closing speeches and the observations of the parties.

Article 441

Even in cases where legal representation is mandatory, the parties may themselves, assisted by their representatives, make oral comments.

The court may withhold this right of address from parties whose passion or inexperience prevents them from presenting their case with suitable dignity or the necessary clarity.

Article 442

The president and the judges may ask the parties to provide any legal or factual explanations necessary to clarify matters which are otherwise unclear.

Article 443

The State Prosecution Service, when joined to proceedings, shall be the last to be called to address the court.

If the State Prosecution Service does not believe that it is in a position to make submissions at that time, it may request that its testimony be deferred to a subsequent hearing.

Article 444

The president may order oral pleadings to be re-opened. He/she must do so each time that the parties have not been able to present their case on equal terms with respect to the elucidation of matters of law and fact that were required of them.

Where there is a change in the composition of the court, the oral pleadings have to be restarted.

Article 445

After the close of oral pleadings, the parties may not file any written memoranda in support of their arguments except in reply to the arguments submitted by the State Prosecution Service or at the request of the president in the circumstances provided for under Articles 442 and 444.

Article 446

The provisions of Articles 432 (second paragraph), 433, 434, 435 and 444 (second paragraph) must be complied with at the risk of a penalty of invalidity.

However, no invalidity may subsequently be declared as a result of a failure to comply with such provisions where it has not been pleaded prior to the close of the oral pleadings. A finding of invalidity may not be raised by the court of its own motion.

Sub-Section 2
The Deliberation

Article 447

It is up to the judges before whom a matter has been pleaded to decide on it. They must at least be equal in number to that set down by the rules relating to court organization.

Article 448

The deliberations of the judges shall be held “in camera”.

Article 449

The decision shall be made by a majority of votes.

Sub-Section 3
The Judgment

Article 450

If the judgment cannot be given immediately, the delivery of the judgment shall be postponed to allow greater consideration to a date that the president shall indicate.

He/she may, however, inform the parties at the end of the hearing that the judgment will be given by deposition at the court registry on the date specified by him/her.

Article 451

Decisions in contentious proceedings shall be given in open court, and in non-contentious proceedings without the public being present, subject to any special provisions relating to certain matters.

The deposition of the judgment at the court registry shall comply with the same rules on public notice

Article 452

The judgement shall be read out in court by one of the judges who decided on it, even where the other judges and the State Prosecution Service are absent.

The reading of the judgment may be limited in its operative provisions.

Article 453

The date of the judgment shall be that on which it was given in court or deposited at the court registry.

Article 454

The judgment shall be issued on behalf of the French people.

It shall state:

- the court by which it is given;
- the names of the judges who considered it;
- its date;
- the name of the representative of the State Prosecution Service if he/she attended the oral pleadings;
- the name of the court clerk;

– the names of the parties as well as their address or registered office;

– where relevant, the names of the attorneys or any person who represented or assisted the parties;

– in non-contentious matters, the name of the persons who must be notified.

Article 455

The judgment must set out succinctly the respective claims of the parties and their grounds in support. Such presentation may take the form of a reference to the pleadings of the parties with the indication of their date. Reasons for the judgment must be given.

It must state the court's decision in the form of operative provisions.

Article 456

The judgment must be signed by the president and the clerk of the court. If the president cannot do so, this fact shall be recorded in the original draft which must be signed by one of the judges who deliberated it.

Article 457

The judgment shall have the evidential value of an official document subject to the provisions of Article 459.

Article 458

The provisions of Articles 447, 451, 454, with regard to the names of the judges, 445 (first paragraph) and 456 must be complied with under penalty of otherwise being declared invalid.

However, no invalidity may subsequently be claimed or raised automatically for non-compliance with the formalities provided in Articles 451 and 452, if it was not invoked at the time the judgment was given by simple comments that are noted in the registrar's record of the hearing.

Article 459

Any omission or inaccuracy in an entry intended to prove the regularity of the judgment may not result in its invalidity where it is shown, by production of the written pleadings, the transcript of the hearing, or by any other means, that the legal requirements have, in fact, been complied with.

Article 460

The invalidity of a judgment may only be requested by the means of the rights of recourse provided in law.

Article 461

It is up to any judge to interpret his/her judgment if it is not being appealed.

An application for the interpretation of a judgment shall be made by a simple request by one of the parties or by joint application. The judge shall rule upon it with the parties being present or called to appear.

Article 462

Clerical errors or omissions which affect a judgment, even one which is a final judgment, may always be rectified by the court which issued it or by the one to which it has been referred, in accordance with the court's record, or in default thereof, with common sense.

The judge shall be empowered to hear the request by a simple request filed on behalf of one of the parties, or by joint application; he/she may also do so on his/her own motion.

The judge shall rule upon the matter after having heard the parties or having called the latter.

An entry rectifying a decision shall be made on the original and on the certified copies of the judgment. It shall be served in the same way as a judgment.

Where the rectified decision is a final judgment, it may only be opposed by an appeal to the Court of Cassation.

Article 463

The court which has failed to rule upon a ground of a claim, may likewise complete its judgment without affecting the decision in respect of the other grounds of the claim, unless, where necessary in order to re-establish the exact statements and grounds in the respective claims of the parties.

An application for this procedure must be presented no later than one year after the decision has become final, or in case of an appeal to the Court of Cassation, on this ground, after the decision on its inadmissibility.

The judge shall be empowered by way of a simple request of one of the parties or by a joint application. He/she shall rule after having heard the parties or calling the latter.

An entry of the decision shall be made in the original and on certified copies of the judgment. It shall be served in the same way as a judgment and shall allow the same rights of recourse as the latter.

Article 464

The provisions of the preceding Article shall apply where the judge has ruled upon matters not in issue, or where he/she has awarded an amount which is more than has been claimed.

Article 465

Each party shall be entitled to receive a certified copy of the judgment endorsed with a certificate of enforcement.

If necessary, a second certified copy, containing the same certificate, may be sent to the same party by the clerk of the court which has issued the judgment. If there is a difficulty, the president of such court shall rule upon it by a reasoned order.

Article 465-1

If a judgment orders any family maintenance or payment of a debt under Articles 214, 276 and 342 of the Civil Code, the parties must be informed by a document annexed to the certified copy of the judgment of the manner of the debt collection, of the rules of revision of the debt and any criminal sanctions which have been imposed.

Article 466

In non-contentious matters, a copy of the application shall be annexed to the certified copy of the judgment.

Section II
Failure to Appear

Sub-Section 1
Judgment Reached after Hearing All the Parties

Article 467

The judgment shall be defended provided that the parties appear in person or through a representative, according to the rules pertaining to the court before which the claim is brought.

Article 468

If the plaintiff does not appear, without any legitimate reason, the defendant may request a judgment on the merits of the case that shall be deemed to have been given in the presence of both parties, although the judge has the power to adjourn the case for a subsequent hearing.

The judge may also, even automatically, declare that the summons has expired. The declaration of expiration may be withdrawn if the claimant informs the clerk of the court within fifteen days of a lawful reason why he/she has not been in a position to respond. In the latter case, the parties shall be called to a subsequent hearing.

Article 469

If, after having appeared, one of the parties failed to serve the written submissions within the required time limit, the judge shall reach a decision in a defended judgment on the basis of the material before him/her.

The defendant may, however, request the judge to declare that the summons has expired.

Article 470

If none of the parties serve the written submissions within the required time limit, the judge may, of his/her own initiative, delete the matter from the roll by a decision not subject to appeal, after a final notice has been sent to the parties themselves and to their representatives if they have instructed one.

Sub-Section 2
The Default Judgment and the Judgment Deemed to Have Been Given after Hearing All the Parties

Article 471

The defendant who does not appear may, at the initiative of the claimant or by virtue of a decision made by the judge on his/her own motion, be invited to appear again if the summons to appear has not been served on him/her personally.

The summons to appear shall, subject to special rules applicable to certain courts, be re-issued in the same form as the original one. The judge may order that it shall be served by a court bailiff if the first summons was served by the clerk of the court. The new summons must contain, where relevant, the provisions of Articles 472 and 473 or those of the second paragraph of Article 474.

The judge may also inform the interested party by regular mail of the consequences of his/her failure to appear.

Article 472

Where the defendant fails to appear, a ruling shall nevertheless be made on the merits of the case.

The judge shall uphold the claim only to the extent that he/she considers it is valid, admissible and well-founded.

Article 473

If the defendant does not appear, the judgment shall be given in default where the decision is given in the last instance and where the summons to appear has not been served on the defendant in person.

The judgment shall be deemed to be defended if the decision is subject to appeal or if the summons has been served on the defendant in person.

Article 474

If there are several defendants summonsed in the same matter, where at least one of them does not appear, the judgment shall be deemed to be defended with regard to all of them where the decision is subject to appeal or where those who did not appear have been summonsed in person.

Where the decision applied for is not subject to appeal, the defaulting parties who have not been served personally must be served again. The judge may, nevertheless, decide, where service has been carried out in the accordance with the procedure laid down in Article 659, that there is no need for a new service. The judgment given after the parties have served anew shall be deemed to have been given in the presence of all the parties, provided that one of the defendants has appeared or has been served personally a first or second time; otherwise, the judgment shall be given in default.

Article 475

The judge may not rule prior to the expiration of the longest time limit for appearing, under the first or second summons.

He/she shall decide upon the matter with regard to all the defendants in one single judgment, unless circumstances require that a ruling be made with regard to some of them only.

Article 476

The judgment given in default may be opposed by an application to set it aside, except in cases where this recourse is unavailable by virtue of an express legal provision.

Article 477

The judgment deemed to be defended may only be opposed by the means available against defended judgments.

Article 478

A judgment given in default or a judgment deemed to be defended on the sole ground that it is subject to an appeal shall be invalid if it has not been served on the defendant within six months from its date.

The proceedings may be recommenced after the re-issue of the original writ of summons.

Article 479

A judgment in default or a judgment deemed to be defended served upon a party residing abroad must expressly state the efforts made to inform the defendant of the originating process.

Chapter II
Special Provisions

Section I
Judgment on the Merits

Article 480

A judgment which deals in its wording with all or part of the main issue, or one which rules upon a procedural plea, a plea seeking a declaration of inadmissibility or any other interlocutory application, shall from the time of its issue, become final regarding the dispute which it is settling.

The main issue shall mean the subject-matter of the litigation as specified under Article 4.

Article 481

A judgment, once given, shall release the judge from ruling on the dispute before him/her.

However, the judge shall have the power to rescind his/her decision where a third party application is made to set it aside or there is an appeal on a question of law.

He/she may likewise interpret or amend it in accordance with Articles 461 to 464.

Section II
Other Judgments

Sub-Section 1
Interlocutory Orders

Article 482

A judgment whose operative provisions are limited to a procedural measure or an interlocutory measure does not have the authority of a final judgment of the main issue.

Article 483

An interlocutory order shall not release the judge from ruling on the dispute before him/her.

Sub-Section 2
Summary Orders

Article 484

A summary order shall be a provisional order made at the request of one party, the other party being present or called to be present, in cases where the law confers upon a judge who is not empowered to rule upon the main issue, the power to immediately give the necessary orders.

Article 485

The request shall be made by a summons to a hearing held for that purpose on the usual day and time for dealing with summary proceedings.

If, nevertheless, the case is urgent, the judge in charge of the summary proceedings may issue a summons with a particular return day, even if that day might fall on a public holiday, to appear either at a hearing, or at his/her private domicile, open to the public.

Article 486

The judge shall ensure that sufficient time has elapsed between the summons and the hearing date, to enable the party summonsed to prepare his/her case.

Article 487

The judge in charge of the summary proceedings shall have the right to refer a matter dealt with under a summary procedure to a panel of judges of the court for a hearing whose date he/she shall specify.

Article 488

A summary order shall not become final regarding the main substantive issue.

It may only be amended or withdrawn by summary proceedings is there are new supervening circumstances.

Article 489

Summary orders shall be provisionally enforceable. The judge may, however, make this provisional enforcement conditional on the provision of a security under the conditions provided in Articles 517 to 522.

Where necessary, the judge may order the enforcement to take place upon the simple production of the original judgment.

Article 490

A summary order may be opposed by an appeal unless it is made by the first president of the court of appeal or it has been given in the last resort because of the amount at stake or the subject-matter.

The order given in default as a last resort may be subject to an objection.

The time limit for appealing or to applying to set it aside shall be fifteen days.

Article 490-1 - *Repealed.*

Article 491

The judge may impose a fine by a summary order. He/she may fix the amount thereof provisionally.

He/she shall rule upon taxable expenses.

Article 492

The originals of summary orders shall be kept at the court registry.

Sub-Section 3
Ex Parte Orders

Article 493

An *ex parte* order shall be a provisional order given without the other party being heard in cases where the plaintiff is justified in not calling the other party.

Article 494

The application shall be made in duplicate. It must contain the reasons for the application. It must contain a precise indication of the exhibits relied upon in its support.

Where it is presented in the course of the proceedings, it must indicate the court which is hearing the matter.

In urgent cases, the application may be made to the judge's domicile.

Article 495

The *ex parte* order shall contain reasons.

It shall be enforceable upon simple production of the original.

A copy of the application and the order shall be given to the person against whom it is enforceable.

Article 496

If the application is not complied with, an appeal may be lodged unless the order was made by the first president of the court of appeal. The time limit for the appeal is fifteen days. The appeal must be lodged, handled and decided as in non-contentious matters.

If the application is complied with, any interested party may refer back to the judge who has given the order.

Article 497

The judge shall have the right to amend or withdraw his/her order even if the trial judge is dealing with the matter.

Article 498

The duplicate of the order shall be kept at the court registry.

Chapter III
Final Provision

Article 499

The provisions of the above Title shall not apply to orders of judicial administration.

TITLE XV
ENFORCEMENT OF JUDGMENTS

Article 500

A judgment which is not subject to any right of recourse which might stay its execution shall become final.

A judgment which is subject to such a right of recourse shall have the same force on the expiration of the time limit for such a right of recourse when it has not been exercised within the prescribed time limit.

Article 501

The judgment shall be enforced, under the following conditions, after it becomes final, unless the debtor enjoys the benefit of a period of grace or the creditor has been granted the benefit of a provisional enforcement.

Chapter I
General Conditions for Enforcement

Article 502

A judgment or an instrument may be enforced only upon the production of a certified copy bearing a certificate of enforcement, unless the law provides otherwise.

Article 503

Judgments may not be enforced against the parties who are liable unless they have been served upon them, except where the enforcement is voluntary.

In the event of an enforcement on demand, the simple production of the original court entry shall amount to service.

Article 504

The proof of its enforceable nature shall appear from the judgment itself if it is not subject to any right of recourse which might stay its enforcement, or if it is vested with provisional enforcement.

Otherwise, such proof arises:

- either from the acceptance of the judgment by the unsuccessful party;
- or, from the notification of the judgment and a certificate allowing it to be established, in conjunction which this notification, that, within the time limit, there was no objection, appeal or appeal to the Court of Cassation where such an appeal would suspend its enforcement.

Article 505

Any party may obtain from the clerk of the court before which the right of recourse could be exercised a certificate confirming the absence of any objection, appeal or appeal to the Court of Cassation, or indicating the date of the remedy if any has been applied for.

Article 506

The releases, canceling of guarantees, entries in court records, transcripts or publications, which shall have to be made pursuant to a judgment may be validly carried out upon the production by any interested party of a duplicate or certified copy of the judgment or of an abstract thereof and, where it is not provisionally enforceable, upon proof of its enforceable nature. The proof may be given in a certificate drafted by an attorney or an appeal advocate.

Article 507

The delivery of the judgment or the instrument to a court bailiff shall constitute an authority to enforce any judgment which does not require specific authority.

Article 508

No enforcement may be carried out before 6 a.m. or after 9 p.m. nor on public holidays and non-working days except by permission of the judge in case of necessity.

Chapter II
Cross-border Recognition

Article 509

Judgements made by foreign courts and instruments received from foreign officials shall be enforced in the territory of the Republic in the manner and under the circumstances set down by law.

Article 509-1

Requests for certification of enforceable French instruments for the purpose of their recognition and enforcement abroad shall be addressed to the chief registrar of the court which gave the decision or approved the agreement.

Requests for the certification of enforceable French instruments for the purpose of their recognition and enforcement abroad, pursuant to Articles 41 and 42 of (EC) Council Regulation 2201/03 of November 7, 2003 concerning jurisdiction and the recognition and enforcement of judgments in matrimonial matters and in matters of parental responsibility, are addressed to the judge who made the decision or approved the agreement. They do not need to be presented by an attorney.

Article 509-2

Requests for the recognition or a record of the enforceability, on the territory of the Republic, of enforceable foreign instruments, pursuant to (EC) Regulation 44/2001 of December 22, 2000 on jurisdiction and the recognition and enforcement of judgments in civil and commercial matters, shall be addressed to the chief registrar of the Regional Court.

Requests for the recognition or a record of the enforceability, on the territory of the Republic, of enforceable foreign instruments, pursuant to (EC) Regulation 2201/03 of November 27, 2003 concerning jurisdiction and the recognition and enforcement of judgments in matrimonial matters and in matters of parental responsibility, are addressed to the President of the Regional Court or his/her representative. They do not need to be presented by an attorney.

Article 509-3

In derogation from Articles 509-1 and 509-2, requests for the certification, recognition or a record of the enforceability of notarised instruments, pursuant to the aforesaid Regulation of December 22, 2000, shall be addressed to the President of the Chamber of Notaries or, in cases of absence or impediment, to a substitute appointed by the members of the Chamber.

Where this Regulation requires it, the election of residence is made within the judicial district of the court of appeal in which the Chamber of Notaries is situated.

Article 509-4

The request shall be presented in duplicate. It must contain precise details of the documents concerned.

Article 509-5

A decision rejecting a request for a record of enforceability must contain reasons.

Article 509-6

The certificate or decision on a request for recognition or a record of enforce ability is issued to the applicant in return for a signature or receipt or is sent to him/her by registered mail with acknowledgement of receipt.

A copy of the request as well as of the certificate or decision are kept at the registry.

Article 509-7

If it is not issued by a judge, a refusal to issue a certificate may be referred to the president of the Regional Court. The latter shall make a final decision upon application after the applicant and the authority concerned have been heard or called to appear.

Chapter III
The Period of Grace

Article 510

Subject to the following paragraphs, the period of grace may only be granted in the decision the execution of which is intended to be delayed.

In urgent cases, the summary procedure judge shall have the same power to grant the period of grace.

Following the service of an order authorizing seizure, as the case may be, the enforcement judge has jurisdiction to grant a period of grace. Such power shall be exercised by the district court in matters of attachment of earnings.

The grant of the period of grace shall be reasoned.

Article 511

The period shall run from the day of the judgment where it is defended; in other cases, it shall only run from the service of the judgment.

Article 512

A period of grace may not be granted to a debtor whose property is seized by other creditors nor to one who is under administrative receivership or subject to a forced sale of assets or who has, by his/her actions, reduced the value of the securities which he/she has provided in his/her agreements with his/her creditors.

In such cases, the debtor shall lose the benefit of the period of grace previously granted.

Article 513

The period of grace shall not prevent the enforcement of any protective measures.

Chapter IV
Provisional Enforcement

Article 514

Provisional enforcement may not be made without having been ordered unless it is available as of right.

In particular summary orders, decisions containing provisional orders for the conduct of proceedings, orders providing for protective measures as well as directions of the pre-trial judge granting an interim payment to a creditor, shall be provisionally enforceable as of right.

Article 515

In addition to cases where it is obtainable as of right, provisional enforcement may be ordered at the request of the parties or of his/her own initiative whenever the judge shall deem it proper and appropriate to the subject matter, provided that it is not prohibited by law.

It may be ordered for all or part of the judgment. In no case may it be ordered in relation to taxable costs.

Article 516

Provisional enforcement may only be ordered in relation to a decision which is to be enforced, subject to provisions of Article 525 and 526.

Article 517

Provisional enforcement may be made subject to the provision of undertakings relating to real or personal property sufficient to cover all restitutions or damages.

Article 518

The nature, extent and conditions of the undertakings shall be specified in the decision which orders them.

Article 519

If the undertakings consists of the payment of a sum of money, the same shall be paid into the Bank for Official Deposits;[11] it may also, at the request of one of the parties, be paid into the hands of a third party appointed for that purpose.

In the latter case, the judge, if he/she accedes to the request, must state in his/her decision the conditions of such a deposit.

If the third party refuses to accept such a deposit, the sum shall be deposited, without further decision at the Deposits and Consignation Office.

Article 520

If the value of the security cannot immediately be determined, the judge shall invite the parties to appear before him/her, at a date which he/she shall specify, with their supporting evidence.

It shall be determined without any right of review.

A note of the decision shall be made on the original, and on the certified copies of the judgment.

Article 521

The party ordered to pay a sum other than maintenance, compensatory annuities or interim payment may avoid provisional execution, by leave of the judge, by depositing cash or securities of sufficient value to guarantee the amount of the award in respect of the principal claim, interest and costs.

In the case of a judgment ordering the payment of a lump-sum in cases of personal injury, the judge may also order that the lump-sum be paid to a receiver on condition that he/she pays the victim such installments as the judge shall specify.

11 The French term is "caisse des dépôts et consignations". This body is an administrative department that is responsible for receiving, investing and lending public money.

Article 522

The judge may, at any time, authorize the substitution of the original security for one of equal value.

Article 523

Requests relating to the application of Articles 517 to 522 may only be made in cases of appeal before the first president who shall issue a summary order or, in the circumstances provided under Articles 525 to 526, before an appeal court judge entrusted with the management of the case as soon as he/she is empowered to do so.

Article 524

Where provisional enforcement has been ordered, it may be stopped, in cases of appeals, only by the first president, who shall make a summary order in the following cases:

1. Where it is forbidden by law;
2. Where it is likely to lead to consequences which are clearly excessive; in the latter case, the first president may also prescribe the measures referred to under Articles 517 to 522.

The same powers may be exercised, on an objection, by the judge who has given the said decision.

Where provisional execution is obtainable as of right, the first president may order any direction specified in the second paragraph of Article 521 and Article 522.

Article 525

Where provisional execution has been refused, it may be requested, in cases of appeal, only before the first president who shall rule upon it as by way of summary procedure or, from the time when he/she is empowered, by the judge entrusted with the management of the case, and provided it is urgent.

Article 526

Where provisional execution has not been requested, or, where a judge has failed to rule upon it, the same may be requested, in cases of appeal, only before the first president ruling upon it by way of summary procedure or, where he/she is involved, the judge entrusted with the management of the case.

TITLE XVI
RIGHTS OF RECOURSE

Article 527

The normal rights of recourse are the appeal[12] and the objection;[13] special rights of recourse are the third party objection,[14] the application for reconsideration[15] and the appeal to the Court of Cassation.[16]

SUB-TITLE I
COMMON PROVISIONS

Article 528

The time limit after which a right of recourse may no longer be exercised, shall run from the notification of the judgment, unless the time limit has, as provided by law begun to run, from the day of the judgment.

The time limit shall run even as regarding party who proceeds with the notification.

Article 528-1

If the judgment has not been notified within two years from its issue, the party who appeared shall not be allowed to exercise a right of recourse on the substantive issue after the expiration of the said time limit.

Such provision shall only apply to judgments which rule wholly on the substantive issue and to those which, ruling on a procedural issue, a plea seeking a sum-

---

12 The French term "appel" refers to an appeal as of right to a court of appeal on points of law or fact. The appeal takes the form of a trial *de novo*. Appeals have suspensive effect.

13 The French term "opposition" in this context refers to an appeal by a party who was not present at the hearing that gave judgment against him/her. It may be made as of right on points of law and fact. It takes the form of a trial *de novo*. I have translated the term as "objection". It has suspensive effect.

14 A third party objection ("tierce opposition" in French) may normally be made by third parties with a legitimate interest in a case. It is one of the special appeals that do not have suspensive effect.

15 The "recours en revision" allows a party to request that a judgment be reviewed on factual and legal grounds as the judgment itself is tainted or fresh evidence is available. It does not have suspensive effect. I have translated it as "an application for reconsideration".

16 The French term is "pourvoi en cassation" (or "recours en cassation") and must be distinguished from an "appel". The "pourvoi en cassation is an appeal to the Court of Cassation (*see* note 8) on a point of law alone, notably: the inconsistency of the judgment, the lack of formal requirements and the lack of a legal basis due to a change in the law. Unlike an appeal to a court of appeal, it does not have suspensive effect.

mary declaration of inadmissibility and on any other interlocutory pleas, bring the proceedings to a close.

Article 529

Where judgment has been given jointly and severally or severally against several parties, a notification given to one of them starts the time limit running only against that party.

Where the judgment is made in favor of several parties jointly or indivisibly, each of them may take advantage of the notification made by one of them.

Article 530

The time limit shall run only against a person placed under guardianship from the day the judgment has been notified to his/her legal representative as well as to the deputy guardian and, if necessary, even though the latter has not been joined to the proceedings.

The time limit shall run only against an adult under temporary guardianship from the date when the notification is given to the temporary guardian.

Article 531

If, during the time limit for rights of recourse, there is a change in the legal capacity of the party to whom the judgment is notified, the time limit shall be suspended.

The time limit shall continue to run after a notification is given to the person who has thereafter attained the legal capacity to receive it.

Article 532

The time limit shall be suspended by the death of the party to whom the judgment has been notified.

It shall continue to run after a notification is given to the domicile of the deceased person, to be calculated from the expiration of the time limit for the making of an inventory in the succession and deliberation, if this further notification took place before the preceding time limits expired.

Notification may be given to the heirs and representatives, collectively and without indication of names and descriptions.

Article 533

Where the party who has been notified of the judgment has died, any recourse may be notified to the domicile of the deceased person, his/her heirs and representatives collectively and without indication of names and descriptions.

However, a judgment may only be requested against the heirs and representatives if each of them has been summonsed to appear.

Article 534

The person who legally represents a party may, if he/she no longer acts for that party and if he/she has a personal interest, exercise the right of recourse in his/her own name. The right of recourse may similarly be exercised against him/her.

Article 535

The party to whom a recourse has been notified shall be deemed, for the purposes of the notification, to live at the address which he/she indicated in the notification of the judgment.

Article 536

An incorrect characterization of the judgment by the judges has no effect on the right to exercise a remedy.

If the right of recourse is declared to be inadmissible by reason of such incorrectness, the decision on inadmissibility shall be notified by the court registry to all the parties affected by the judgment. This notification shall re-activate the running of the time limit for exercising the appropriate right of recourse.

Article 537

Measures of judicial administration shall not be subject to any right of recourse.

SUB-TITLE II
THE ORDINARY RIGHTS OF RECOURSE

Article 538

The time limit for exercising ordinary rights of recourse is one month in contentious matters; it is fifteen days in non-contentious matters.

Article 539

The time limit for exercising ordinary rights of recourse shall suspend the enforcement of the judgment. The filing of an application for right of recourse within the time limit shall likewise suspend the enforcement.

Article 540

If a judgment has been given in default or where it is deemed to be defended, the judge shall have the power to waive the time bar against the defendant resulting from the expiration of the limitation period, if the defendant, without any fault on his/her part, did not have knowledge of the judgment in time to file an application for recourse or if he/she was unable to act.

A declaration waiving the time-limit shall be requested from the president of the court competent to hear an objection or an appeal. The president shall be empowered in the same way as in a summary procedure.

The request shall only be allowed if it is filed within a reasonable time from the moment the defendant had knowledge of the judgment, but it can never be made later than one year from the notification of thereof; such time shall not suspend the enforcement.

The president shall rule without any right of review of his/her decision.

If he/she grants the request, the time limit for an objection or appeal shall run from the date of his/her decision, subject to the president's right to reduce the limitation period or to order that the summons should be made on a date which he/she shall specify.

Article 541

If an interested party has been unable, without any fault on his/her part, to exercise within the prescribed time limit, the right of recourse available against a non-contentious decision, he/she may be granted a declaration waiving the time-limit in the manner set out in the preceding Article.

Chapter I
The Appeal

Article 542

The purpose of an appeal shall be the overturning or annulment by the court of appeal of a judgment given by a court of first instance.

Section I
The Right of Appeal

Sub-Section 1
Judgments Subject to Appeal

Article 543

Rights of appeal shall be available in all matters, even non-contentious ones, against judgments at first instance, unless otherwise provided.

Article 544

Judgments which, in their terms rule on part of the principal issue and give a direction or make a provisional order, may immediately be appealed in the same way as judgments decided upon the whole of the principal issue.

The same shall apply where a judgment which rules upon a procedural issue, a plea seeking a summary declaration of inadmissibility or on any other interlocutory pleas has the effect of terminating the proceedings.

Article 545

An appeal may only be made against other judgments, independently of the judgments on the merits where provided for by the law.

Sub-Section 2
The Parties

Article 546

The right of appeal shall be exercised by any party who has an interest if he/she has not waived the same.

In non-contentious matters, rights of appeal shall also be available to third parties to whom a judgment has been notified.

Article 547

In contentious matters, an appeal shall be made against those who were the parties at first instance. All those who were parties may be the respondents to an appeal.

In non-contentious matters, the appeal may be allowed even in the absence of other parties.

Article 548

A cross-appeal may be made by a respondent against the appellants as well as against the other respondents.

Article 549

A cross-appeal, against the main appeal may also be made by any person, even if they were not sued, who was a party at first instance.

Article 550

The cross-appeal, may be brought at any stage of the proceedings even though the person making it may be precluded from acting as an original appellant. In the latter case, the appeal will not be allowed; however, if the main appeal is not itself admissible.

The court may award damages against those persons who, with an intention to delay, have refrained from making a cross-appeal or an appeal by a person other than a respondent who is caused to join issue in due time.

Article 551

The cross or third-party appeal as above shall be brought in the same way as interlocutory claims.

Article 552

Where several parties are found jointly or severally liable, the appeal made by one shall preserve the rights of appeal of the others, subject to the latter joining themselves as parties to the appeal proceedings.

In the same situation, an appeal made against one of the parties shall preserve the appellant's right to join the others in the proceedings.

The court may of its own motion order the issue of proceedings against all interested parties.

Article 553

Where several parties stand as an indivisible entity, an appeal by one shall apply to the others, even though they have not been joined to the proceedings; an appeal brought against one of them shall not be admissible unless all of them are joined to the proceedings.

Article 554

Where they have an interest, persons who have neither been parties nor been represented at first instance or who appeared in those proceedings in another capacity, may join an appeal.

Article 555

The same persons may be called to appear before the court even for the purpose of having a judgment entered against them, where the progress of the case requires that they should be joined to the same.

Article 556

Persons entitled to arbitrate may waive the right to appeal. They may only do so in cases where they have an unfettered right to do so.

Article 557

A right of appeal may not be waived prior to the commencement of the litigation.

Article 558

A waiver must be expressed or may be implied from the unchallenged enforcement of a non-enforceable judgment.

The waiver shall have no effect where, subsequently, another party duly lodges an appeal.

Sub-Section 3
Miscellaneous Provisions

Article 559

In cases where the main appeal is dilatory or abusive, the appellant may be ordered to pay a civil fine of 15€ to 1,500€, without prejudice to any claim for damages which may be brought against him/her.

Such a fine, collected separately from the costs of registration of the decision ordering the same, may not be collected from the respondents. The latter may obtain a certified copy of the enforceable decision without being deprived thereof by the non-payment of the fine.

Article 560

The appeal court judge may award damages against the person lodging an appeal on the main issue who fails to appear before the court of first instance without providing any lawful excuse.

Section II
The Legal Effect of an Appeal

Sub-Section 1
Transfer to a Higher Court

Article 561

An appeal shall refer a matter already determined before a court of appeal, so that it may be ruled upon afresh after consideration of the facts and the law.

Article 562

An appeal shall only refer to the court those grounds of the judgment which are expressly or impliedly challenged and those which are subsidiary to them.

The referral shall relate to all matters where the appeal is not limited to specific grounds of the judgment, or where it seeks the annulment of the judgment or where the subject-matter in issue cannot be considered except by reference to the whole case.

Article 563

In order to support, on appeal, the claims submitted to the judge at first instance, parties may raise new grounds, produce new exhibits or offer new evidence.

Article 564

The parties may not submit to the court new claims except to plead set-off, to defeat an opponent's claims, or to obtain a ruling on issues arising from the intervention of a third party, or in relation to a new relevant fact which has come to light.

Article 565

Claims shall not be considered to be new where they have the same object as those submitted to the judge at first instance, even where their basis in law might be different.

Article 566

The parties may also clarify any claims that were included by implication in the pleadings submitted to the judge at first instance, and they may add to them any other claims which are collateral, consequential upon or complementary to them.

Article 567

Counterclaims shall likewise be admissible on appeal.

Sub-Section 2
Decision of Higher Court

Article 568

Where the court of appeal is considering a judgment containing an order, or a judgment which, ruling on a procedural plea, has closed the proceedings, it may decide any points which were left undecided if it deems it to be in the interests of justice to dispose of the matter finally, after having given a directive, where appropriate.

The decision shall not prevent the application of Articles 554, 555 and 563 and 567.

Section III
Final Provisions

Article 569

The enforcement of judgments improperly designated as being in the last resort may be stayed by the appeal court judge at any time during the proceedings.

Article 570

The enforcement of the judgment on appeal shall be conducted by the court which ruled at first instance or, where the latter is unable to enforce its own decisions, by the regional court.

However, the appellate court may, even on its own motion, decide in its judgment to supervise its enforcement unless by law another court should do so; under the same reservation, the appellate court may also indicate the court which will supervise the enforcement of its judgment, provided that the latter court has jurisdiction to enforce judicial decisions.

Chapter II
The Objection

Article 571

An objection shall be intended to quash a judgment given in default.

It shall only be available to the party in default.

Article 572

The objection shall bring back, before the same judge, the points which were decided in default, so that a new decision may be given on the facts and law.

The judgment subject to an objection shall only be rendered invalid by the judgment which quashes it.

Article 573

An objection shall be made according to the procedure for commencing proceedings before the court which gave the decision.

It may be made by way of a notification by and between attorneys before courts where legal representation is not compulsory.

Where an objection is intended to quash a decision of a court of appeal given by default in a matter governed by the procedure under which representation by a lawyer is not mandatory, it is made by a declaration of the party or an agent that is made or sent by registered mail to the registry office of the court that gave the judgment. The objection is considered and determined in accordance with the rules applicable to a court of appeal in cases where representation by a lawyer is not required.

Article 574

The objection must contain the grounds relied upon by the party in default.

Article 575

In cases where an objection is made in the manner set out in the second paragraph of Article 573, it must, at the risk of being held inadmissible, be filed at the registry of the court that made the decision, by the attorney or appeal advocate instructed by the party in default, within one month from the date when it was drafted.

Article 576

The matter shall be managed and decided in accordance with the rules applicable to the court which gave the decision subject to the objection.

Article 577

In the re-opened proceedings, the admissibility of the respective claims of the claimant and the defendant shall be determined upon consideration of the original contentions, according to the ordinary rules of procedure.

Article 578

A person who has a second judgment entered against him/her by default shall be precluded from making a new objection.

SUB-TITLE III
THE EXTRAORDINARY RIGHTS OF RECOURSE

Article 579

Extraordinary rights of recourse and the time limits for exercising the same shall not have the effect of staying the enforcement, unless the law provides otherwise.

Article 580

Extraordinary rights of recourse shall be available only where specified by the law.

Article 581

In cases of dilatory or abusive recourse proceedings, the party concerned may be subjected to a civil fine of 15€ to 1,500€, without prejudice to any claim for damages which might be made to the court considering the application.

Chapter I
The Third-Party Objection

Article 582

A third-party objection shall be intended to quash or vary a judgment in favor of the third-party who challenges it.

It challenges with respect to the third party objector the parts of the judgment that it criticizes so that a new judgment may be given on the facts and the law.

Article 583

A third-party objection may be made by any person who may have an interest in the matter, provided that he/she was neither a party nor was represented at the judgment that he/she is challenging.

The creditors and other assigns of a party may, however, file a third-party objection of a given judgment which evades their rights or where they can raise grounds which pertain to them in particular.

In non-contentious matters, a third-party objection is only available to third parties who have not been notified of the court's decision; it is also available against judgments given in the last resort even where they have been notified of the decision.

Article 584

Where liability is indivisible as regards several parties in respect of the challenged judgment, a third-party objection shall only be allowed where all the parties are summonsed in the proceedings.

Article 585

All judgments may be subject to a third-party objection unless the law provides otherwise.

Article 586

A third-party objection is available principally for thirty years from the date of the judgment unless the law provides otherwise. It may be made without any time bar against a judgment given in the course of proceedings relating to another case by the person against whom enforcement is being sought. However in contentious matters, it is only allowable to a third party who has been notified of the judgment, within two months from the date of notification, provided that the judgment clearly indicates the time limit applicable to him/her, as well as the means whereby a right of recourse may be commenced. The same shall apply in non-contentious matters where notification of a decision in the last resort has been made.

Article 587

A third-party objection made principally shall be filed at the court which gave the judgment being challenged.

The decision on the application may be given by the same judges.

Where a third-party objection is made against a judgment given in a non-contentious matter, it shall be filed, managed and determined in accordance with the rules relating to contentious procedure.

Article 588

A third-party objection, which is interlocutory in a dispute that a court is hearing, shall be decided by the latter where it is a court superior to the one which has given the original judgment or, where it is a court of the same level, there is no rule of public policy which prohibits the same. The third-party objection shall therefore be made in the same way as for interlocutory claims.

Otherwise, an incidental third-party objection shall be brought, by way of a main claim, before the court that has delivered the decision.

Article 589

The court before which the challenged judgment is produced may, depending on the circumstances, pass or defer its judgment.

Article 590

The judge hearing a third-party objection on the principal issue or as an interlocutory matter may stay the execution of the judgment being challenged.

Article 591

The decision which upholds a third-party objection shall only quash or vary the judgment on the points which are prejudicial to the third-party making the application. The original judgment shall remain in effect as regards the other parties, even on the issues which have been set aside.

However, a third-party objection shall be deemed to be final as regards all the parties called to the proceedings in application of Article 584.

Article 592

The judgment given on a third-party objection shall be subject to the same rights of recourse as the decisions of the court which has made it.

Chapter II
The Application for Reconsideration

Article 593

An application for reconsideration is intended to quash a judgment which has become final, so that a new decision may be given on the facts and law.

Article 594

The reconsideration may only be requested by the persons who were parties to or represented in relation to the judgment.

Article 595

An application for reconsideration shall be available only on the following grounds:

1. Where it has come to light, subsequent to judgment, that the decision has been obtained by fraud by the party in whose favor it was given;
2. Where, since the judgment, decisive exhibits have been discovered, which have been withheld owing to another party's conduct;
3. Where the judgment has been decided on the basis of exhibits which, since the judgment, have been acknowledged or legally declared to be false;
4. Where the judgment has been decided on the basis of statements, testimonies or oaths which, since the judgment, have legally been declared to be false.

In all these cases, the application shall only be allowed where the appellant has been unable, without any fault on his/her behalf, to raise the ground on which he/she is relying before that the judgment became final.

Article 596

The time limit for making an application for reconsideration shall be two months.

It shall run from the date on which the party has knowledge of the ground upon which he/she relies for seeking the reconsideration.

Article 597

All the parties to a judgment under review must be called to the proceedings for reconsideration by the appellant, at the risk of their arguments being declared inadmissible.

Article 598

An application for reconsideration must be filed by way of a summons.

However, where it is filed against a judgment given in the course of other proceedings between the same parties before the court which issued the judgment, the reconsideration may be requested in the way provided for the filing of grounds of defense.

Article 599

Where a party has filed or declares his/her intention to file an application for reconsideration against a judgment given in proceedings pending before a court other than the one which has delivered the same, the court hearing the matter on which it was given may, depending on the circumstances, pass or defer its judgment until the application for reconsideration has been determined by the court that has jurisdiction.

Article 600

An application for reconsideration shall be sent to the State Prosecution Service.

Article 601

Where the judge rules that application is allowed, he/she shall decide in the same judgment the substantive issues, unless there is need for a further hearing.

Article 602

Where the reconsideration is justified in respect of only one issue in the judgment, such issue alone shall be revised unless the issues are related to it.

Article 603

A party shall not be allowed to apply for a reconsideration of a judgment that he/she has already challenged by this same procedure, unless upon grounds which subsequently came to light.

The judgment ruling upon an application for reconsideration may only be challenged by means of this procedure.

Chapter III
The Appeal to the Court of Cassation

Article 604

An appeal to the Court of Cassation shall ask the court to quash a judgment owing to an error on a point of law.

Section I
The Commencement of an Appeal to the Court of Cassation

Article 605

The appeal to the Court of Cassation is only available against judgments given in the last resort.

Article 606

Any judgments in the last resort which rule, in their findings, on part of the main issue in dispute and give directions or give a provisional direction, may be subject to an appeal to the Court of Cassation in the same way as judgments which rule in the last resort on all of the main issues.

Article 607

Judgments in the last resort which, by ruling on a procedural plea, a plea seeking a summary declaration of inadmissibility, or any other interlocutory plea, put an end to the proceedings, may similarly be subject to an appeal to the Court of Cassation.

Article 608

Judgments in the last resort other than the above may not be subject to an appeal to the Court of Cassation independently of the judgments on the merits, unless it is provided by law.

Article 609

Any party who has an interest shall be allowed to file an appeal to the Court of Cassation, even if the decision that is unfavorable to him/her does not benefit his/her opponent.

Article 610

In non-contentious matters, the appeal shall be allowable even in the absence of an opponent.

Article 611

In contentious matters, the appeal shall be admissible even if a judgment has been given in favor or against a person who was not a party to the proceedings.

Article 611-1

Apart from those cases where the notification of the decision that is subject to appeal is the responsibility of the registry of the court that issued it, an appeal to the

Court of Cassation is only allowed where the decision that it challenges has been notified beforehand.

Article 612

The time limit for filing an appeal to the Court of Cassation is two months, unless contrary provisions apply.

Article 613

The time limit shall run, with regard to a judgment in default, from the date at which an objection is no longer admissible.

Article 614

The admissibility of a cross-appeal, even a forced appeal filed by a party other than a respondent who is joined in due time, must follow the rules governing cross-appeals, subject to the provisions of Article 1010.

Article 615

In the case of indivisibility of a judgment with regard to several parties, the appeal by one of them shall affect the others, even where the latter have not been joined to the proceedings before the Court of Cassation.

Likewise, an appeal filed against one of the parties is only admissible if all of them are made party to the proceedings.

Article 616

Where a judgment may be amended by virtue of Articles 463 and 464, an appeal to the Court of Cassation is only available against a judgment ruling on the amendment in the way provided in these Articles.

Article 617

The inconsistency of judgments may be raised where a plea of inadmissibility on the grounds of the finality of judgment has been argued without success before the trial judges.

In that case, an appeal to the Court of Cassation shall be made against the judgment later in time; where the contradiction has been recorded, it shall be resolved in favor of the first judgment.

Article 618

Inconsistencies of judgments may, as an exception to Article 605, be further relied upon where two decisions, albeit not in the last resort, are incompatible with each other and where neither of them is subject to any ordinary right of recourse; the appeal to the Court of Cassation shall therefore be admissible, even when one of the decisions has already been challenged by way of a previous appeal to the Court of Cassation and was dismissed.

In the latter case, an appeal may be filed even after the expiration of the time limit under Article 612. It must relate to the two decisions concerned; where an inconsistency has been established, the Court of Cassation shall quash one of the decisions or, where necessary, both of them.

Article 618-1

The State Prosecutor attached to the Court of Cassation may, on a referral of a judgment to the latter with a view to clarifying the law, invite the State Prosecution Service attached to the court that delivered the judgment to notify the parties concerned of the referral. The notification shall be given by the clerk of the relevant court, by registered mail with acknowledgment of receipt.

Section II
The Consequences of an Appeal to the Court of Cassation

Article 619

No new grounds shall be admissible before the Court of Cassation.

However, new grounds may be raised for the first time if, subject to any contrary provision on such issue, they are:

1. grounds of pure law;
2. grounds arising out of the decision being challenged.

Article 620

The Court of Cassation may dismiss the appeal by substituting a ground strictly based in law for an erroneous ground; it may do the same in relation to a ground which is wrong in law, but which is superfluous.

It may, unless contrary provisions apply, quash the decision being challenged by raising of its own motion a point of pure law.

Article 621

Where the appeal to the Court of Cassation is dismissed, the party who brought it shall lose his/her *locus standi* to bring a fresh appeal against the same judgment, except in the cases referred to Article 618.

The same shall apply where the Court of Cassation declares its withdrawal or its refusal to allow the appeal, or declares the appeal to be time-barred.

The respondent who has not filed a cross-appeal or third party appeal within the time limit in Article 1010 shall not be allowed to file an appeal in principal against the judgment being challenged.

Article 622

Judgments given by the Court of Cassation may not be subject to objections.

Article 623

The quashing may relate to the whole or part of a judgment. It in part, it may only apply to certain heads of the judgment which are severable from the others.

Article 624

The criticism contained in a Court of Cassation judgment shall be limited to the grounds upon which the appeal was based except in the case of indivisibility or dependent grounds.

Article 625

On the points with which it deals, a quashed judgment shall place the parties in the position in which they found themselves before the judgment being quashed was given.

It shall include, without any need for a new decision, the annulment of all decisions given subsequent to the quashed judgment, decisions relating to the application or enforcement of the preceding judgment or such other decisions which are linked to it.

Article 626

As provided under Article L. 131-4 of the Code of the Judicial Organization:

> "On a successful appeal to the Court of Cassation, the matter must be referred, subject to any contrary provisions, to a court of the same type as that from which the decision or judgment that has been quashed was issued, or it must be referred back to the same court, but made up of different judges".

Article 627

As provided under Article L. 131-5 of the Code of the Judicial Organization:

> "The Court of Cassation may quash a judgment without further referring the matter to a court where the granting of the appeal does not imply any need to determine the main issue.
>
> "It may, furthermore, in quashing without a referral, put an end to the dispute where the facts, as found by the trial judge on the merits, allow the Court to apply the appropriate rule of law.

"In the latter case, the Court must consider the issue of taxable costs incurred in proceedings before the judges on the merits.

"The judgment shall be compulsorily enforceable."

Article 628

The appellant to the Court of Cassation who is unsuccessful or whose appeal is not allowed, may, where his/her appeal is considered to constitute an abuse, be ordered to pay a fine in an amount that may not exceed 3000€ and, within the same limit, to pay damages to the respondent.

Article 629

Without prejudice to the application of the provisions of Article 700, the Court of Cassation may order all or part of the taxable costs to be borne by a party other than the one who is unsuccessful.

Article 630

The judgment shall be compulsorily enforceable as regards a payment of the fine, indemnity and taxable costs.

Article 631

Before the court to which the matter is referred back, the proceedings shall be resumed at the stage in the proceedings that were not affected by the appeal to the Court of Cassation.

Article 632

The parties may refer to new grounds in support of their claims.

Article 633

The admissibility of new grounds is subject to the rules which apply to the court decision that has been quashed.

Article 634

The parties who do not raise any new grounds or new claims shall be deemed to confine themselves to the points and claims which they have submitted to the court whose decision has been quashed. The same shall apply to those parties who do not appear.

Article 635

The intervention of a third party shall be subject to the same rules as those which apply to the court whose decision has been quashed.

Article 636

The persons who, having been a party before the court whose decision has been quashed, and who were not parties before the Court of Cassation, may be joined in the new proceedings or may join them voluntarily, where the cassation might affect their rights.

Article 637

Such persons may, under the same conditions, take the initiative themselves to empower the court to which the matter has been referred.

Article 638

The matter shall be heard again on the facts and based on the law by the court to which the matter has been referred, except in relation to those issues not affected by the granting of the appeal.

Article 639

The court to which the matter has been referred shall consider the issues of taxable costs incurred before the trial courts as well as those relating to the quashed decision.

TITLE XVII
TIME LIMITS, PROCEDURE OF COURT BAILIFFS AND NOTIFICATIONS

Chapter I
Calculation of Time Limits

Article 640

Where an act or formality must be performed before the expiration of a time limit, the latter shall run from the date of the act, the event, the decision or the notification that causes time to run.

Article 641

Where a time limit is expressed in days, the date of issue of the document, event, decision or notification shall not be counted for the purpose of calculating the time limit.

Where the time limit is expressed in months or years, it shall expire on the day of the last month or year bearing the same date as the date of the issue of the document, of the event, of the decision or of the notification which begins the time limit. In the absence of such a date, the time limit shall expire on the last day of the month.

Where a time limit is expressed in months and in days, the months shall be counted first, then the days.

Article 642

All time limits shall expire on the last day at midnight.

The time limit which would normally expire on a Saturday, Sunday or a public or bank holiday shall be extended to and shall include the next working day.

Article 642-1

The provisions of Articles 640 and 642 shall likewise apply to time limits within which registration and other formalities of publication must be effected.

Article 643

Where a claim is brought before a court sitting in metropolitan France, the time limits for entering appearances, or lodging an appeal, an objection, an application for reconsideration or an appeal to the Court of Cassation shall be extended by:

1. One month in relation to persons living in an overseas department or an overseas territory;
2. Two months in relation to persons living in a foreign country.

Article 644

Where the claim is brought before a court sitting in an overseas department, the time limit for entering appearances, or lodging an appeal, an objection, an application for reconsideration or an appeal to the Court of Cassation shall be extended by:

1. One month in relation to persons not living in that department, as well as those who have established their residence in the localities of such department, as specified by the Order of the first president;
2. Two months in relation to persons living in foreign countries.

Article 645

The extension of the time limits provided under Articles 643 to 644 shall apply in all cases where they have not been specifically excluded.

The time limits for review before a court in electoral matters shall be extended only in cases specified by the law.

Article 646

The preceding provisions shall not affect the judges' power, in case of urgency, to shorten the time limits for entering an appearance or allowing a summons for a specific return date.

Article 647

Where a document, to be served on a party whose place of residence would allow him/her the benefit of an extended time limit, is served on him/her in person in a place not conferring such benefits, the notification shall only be subject to the time limits granted in the latter case.

Chapter II
The Form of the Documents of the Court Bailiff

Article 648

Every document of a court bailiff must, in addition to other particulars otherwise required, indicate:

1. Its date;

2. a) Where the plaintiff is a natural person: his/her family name, first names, occupation, address, nationality, date and place of birth;

b) Where the plaintiff is a corporate entity: its type, name, address of its registered office and the body which shall represent it;

3. The family name, first names, address and signature of the court bailiff;

4. If the document must be served, the family name and place of residence of the addressee, or, when it is a corporate entity, its family name and registered office.

These particulars are necessary, at the risk of the document otherwise being found invalid.

Article 649

The invalidity of the documents of a court bailiff shall be governed by the provisions relating to the invalidity of written submissions.

Article 650

The costs relating to any unnecessary document shall be borne by the court bailiff who served them, without prejudice to any damages which might be claimed. The same shall apply to costs relating to written pleadings rendered void by reason of their errors.

Chapter III
The Formalities of Notification

Article 651

Documents must be brought to the knowledge of the parties concerned by notification made to them.

Any notification made through a court bailiff must be by way of service.

A notification may always be made by way of service even where the law has provided for another method.

Article 652

Where a party has appointed a person to represent him/her in court, his/her representatives shall be notified of any documents that are directed to him/her, subject to special rules for notification of judgments.

Section I
Service

Article 653

The date of service of a document by a court bailiff shall, without prejudice to Article 688-9, be the date when it has been served on the person, at his/her domicile or residence, on the State Prosecutor's office[17] or, in the case specified in Article 659, the date of issue of the official document.

Article 654

Service must be made in person.

Service on a corporate entity must be effected personally, where the documents must be delivered to its legal representative, to its authorized recipient, or to any other person empowered to do the same.

Article 655

Where service in person proves to be impossible, the documents may be delivered either at the place of residence or, in default of a known place of residence, at a place of residence.

A copy may be delivered to any person present, or in default thereof, to the caretaker of the building, or as a last resort, to any neighbor.

17 The French term is "parquet" and denotes the authorities of the State Prosecutor's office.

A copy may be only be left on condition that the person present, the caretaker or the neighbor, will agree to take possession of the documents, state his/her family name and first names, status and, in the case of a neighbor, indicate his/her place of residence and shall thereby acknowledge receipt thereof.

The court bailiff must, in any case, leave at the place of domicile or residence of the addressee, a notice showing the date of his/her visit, stating the delivery of the copy, and indicating the nature of the document and the family name of the claimant, as well as providing information relating to the person upon whom the copy has been served.

Article 656

Where no one is able or willing to receive the copy of the document, and where it appears from the investigations made by the court bailiff, which shall be noted on the document to be served, that the addressee has in fact made his/her home at the address indicated, the service shall be deemed to have been made at the place of domicile or residence.

In the latter case, the court bailiff shall be bound to deliver a copy of the documents to the municipality on the same day, or, no later than the first day on which the municipality's services are open to the public. The mayor, his/her deputy or the town clerk shall make a note in the delivery register and shall issue an acknowledgment of the same.

The court bailiff shall leave at the place of domicile or residence of the addressee a notice of visit pursuant to the provisions of the preceding Article. Such notice shall state that a copy of the document should be collected as soon as possible from the municipality, upon the issue of an acknowledgment or upon a margin note being made in the registers, by the interested party or by any person specially authorized to act.

The copy of the documents shall be kept at the municipality for three months. Thereafter, it shall be discharged from having to retain the same.

The mayor, his/her deputy or the town clerk may, at the request of the addressee, shall send a copy of the document to another municipality where it may be collected under the same conditions.

Article 657

Where the document is not delivered in person, the court bailiff must indicate on the copy either the particulars of the person with whom the copy was left or those of the municipality to which it was delivered.

A copy of a served document must be placed in a sealed envelope bearing only the family name and address of the addressee and the stamp of the court bailiff affixed to the flap of the envelope.

Article 658

In all the cases referred to under Articles 655 and 656, the court bailiff must advise the party concerned of the service, on the same day, or no later than the first working day by regular mail, providing the same information as the notice of the visit, and when a copy of the document has been given to the municipality, reminding him/her of the provisions of the last paragraph of Article 656; the letter must furthermore enclose a copy of the official document of service.

The same shall apply in case of service on a chosen place of residence or where the service has been made on a corporate entity.

The stamp of the court bailiff must be affixed to the envelope.

Article 659

Where the person on whom the document has to be served does not have any known domicile, residence or place of employment, the court bailiff shall draft an official document in which he/she shall narrate in details the steps which he/she took to look for the person on whom the document should be served.

On the same day, or no later than the first following working day, at the risk of it otherwise being declared invalid, the court bailiff shall send to the addressee, at the last known address, by registered mail with acknowledgment of receipt, a copy of the official document to which is annexed a copy of the documents which are the subject of the service.

On the same day, the court bailiff shall notify the addressee, by regular mail, of the formality which he/she has carried out.

The provisions of this Article shall apply to the service of a document relating to a corporate entity which has no office known at the place indicated as the registered office in the corporate and commercial register.

Article 660

Where a document is destined for a person living in an overseas territory, service must be made on the State Prosecutor's office.

A prosecutor will stamp the original with a seal and shall send a copy thereof to the head of the local legal services in order for it to be delivered to the party concerned, in accordance with the formalities applicable to the territory where he/she lives.

The court bailiff must, on the same day as the service on the State Prosecutor's office, or no later than the first working day, send to the addressee, by registered letter, a certified copy of the document.

The provisions of the present Article shall not apply where it has been possible to effect service in person.

Article 661

Where service is made on the State Prosecutor's office, a prosecutor must inform the court bailiff of the steps taken; he/she must send him/her, where applicable, the official document of service or acknowledgment recording the delivery of the copy, which is to be attached to the first original. These documents shall be held by the court bailiff attached to the relevant court.

Article 662

Where, in the cases specified under Articles 659 and 660, it is not proven that the addressee has in fact been notified, the judge may order, of his/her own initiative, any additional steps, unless he/she gives provisional or protective directions necessary to safeguard the rights of the claimant.

Article 663

The originals of the documents of the court bailiff must contain a note of the formalities and steps carried out in accordance with the provision of this section with an indication of the dates when they were carried out.

Where the service has not been made in person, the originals of the documents must state the name and occupation of the person with whom the copy has been left. The same shall apply to the case specified in the second paragraph of Article 654.

Article 664

No service may be made before six o'clock in the morning or after nine o'clock in the evening or on Sundays, public or bank holidays except by permission of the judge in urgent matters.

Section II
Notification of Documents in Ordinary Form

Article 665

The notification must contain all the particulars relating to the family name and first names or to the corporate or firm name of the person who issues it, and to the place of residence or registered office of that person.

It must describe the addressee in the same manner.

Article 666

The other particulars which must be included in the notification shall be determined, according to the nature of the legal process, by the special rules governing each case.

Article 667

The notification is given in a sealed envelope or letter, either by post or by its physical delivery, against a marginal entry on the papers or on the receipt.

Article 668

Without prejudice to Article 688-10, the date of the notification by post shall be, as regards the sender, the date it was posted, or as regards the person to whom it is sent, the date when he/she receives the letter.

Article 669

The date of sending a notification by post shall be that which appears on the postmark of the post office which sends it.

The date of delivery shall be that of the acknowledgment or the marginal entry.

The date of receipt of a notification made by registered mail with acknowledgment of receipt shall be that which is stamped by the postal service when delivery of the letter is made to its addressee.

Article 670

The notification shall be deemed to have been made in person where the delivery receipt is signed by the addressee.

Article 670-1

Where a letter of notification is returned to the court registry office and has therefore not been delivered, the clerk shall ask the parties to proceed by way of service.

Article 670-2

A notification made by the clerk of a court to a person living in an overseas territory shall be made by the delivery or sending of the notification to the State Prosecutor's office.

A prosecutor shall then proceed as in matters of service.

Article 670-3

In cases where, for the purposes of a notification abroad by the court registry, the translation of the document or any other paper appears to be necessary, a translator is requested by the chief registrar or the person in charge of the court registry.

The translation shall be remunerated in accordance with Article R.122 of the Code of Criminal Procedure.

The costs incurred by the notification of a document abroad by the court registry shall be taxed, advanced and recovered as expenses provided for in Article R.93 (16°) of the Code of Criminal Procedure.

Section III
Notification Between Attorneys

Article 671

The provisions of Sections I and II shall not apply to notification of documents between attorneys. This is done by means of service or direct notification.

Article 672

The service is recorded by affixing the seal and the signature of the court bailiff to the document and a copy thereof with an indication of the date and the name of the attorney to whom it is addressed.

Article 673

Direct notification shall be made by delivery of two copies of the document to the attorney to whom it is addressed, who shall immediately return one of the copies to his/her opponent after having dated and stamped the same with a seal.

Article 674

The notification between appeal advocates in appeal court is subject to the same rules.

Section IV
Special Rules for the Notification of Judgments

Article 675

Notification of judgments must be served by way of service unless the law provides otherwise.

In non-contentious matters, the clerk of the court must make notification of judgments by registered mail with acknowledgment of receipt.

Article 676

Valid notifications of judgments may be made by the delivery of a certified copy.

Article 677

The parties themselves must be notified of judgments.

Article 678

Further, where legal representation is compulsory, the representative must first be notified of a judgment in the same way as for notification between attorneys, failing which the notification to the party shall be invalid. A note confirming that such formality has been carried out must be made after notification has been given to the party.

However, where the legal representative has died or has ceased to practice, notification must only be given to the party, with a note of the death or of the cessation of his/her practice.

The time limit for exercising any right of recourse shall run from date of the notification to the party himself/herself.

Article 679

In non-contentious matters, the parties and third parties whose interests may be affected by the decision must be notified of a judgment, as well as the State Prosecution Service, if a recourse to the judgment is open.

Article 680

The written notification of a judgment to a party must indicate very clearly the time limits for an objection, appeal, or appeal to the Court of Cassation where one of these rights of recourse is available, as well as the manner in which such recourse may be exercised; it shall, further, indicate that the person who exercises rights of recourse in an abusive or dilatory way may be ordered to pay a fine and damages to the other party.

Article 681

Notification, even without reservation, shall not imply any acceptance of it.

Article 682

Notification of a judgment may validly be given to the chosen place of residence in France of a party residing abroad.

Section V
Special Rules for International Notifications

Sub-Section 1
Notification of Documents in Foreign Countries

Article 683

Notifications in foreign countries must be made by way of service.

Where a notification is effected by the clerk of the court, it must follow the procedure set out in Article 670-2. The clerk of the court must then perform the same duties as a court bailiff.

The provisions of this Article shall not prejudice the application of any treaties providing for another form of notification.

Article 684

The service of a document addressed to a party resident in a foreign country must be made through the State Prosecutor's office.

The State Prosecutor's officer on which the service is made must, as the case may be, be the one that is attached to the court before which a claim has been brought, or the one attached to the court which has given a ruling on the matter, or which is competent within the claimant's place of residence. Where there is no State Prosecutor's office attached to the court, the service must be made to the State Prosecutor's office of the regional court within whose judicial district the court sits.

Article 685

The court bailiff must deliver two copies of the documents to a prosecutor who must stamp the original with a seal.

The prosecutor shall forward the copies of the documents to the Minister of Justice with a view of its transmission, except in cases where the transmission may be made from one State Prosecutor's office to another.

He/she shall attach to them an order of the judge providing for the transmission of the documents, when the intervention of a judge is required by the country of designation.

Article 686

The court bailiff must, on the same day of the service on the State Prosecutor's office or no later than the first working day, send a certified true copy of the documents which have been served on the addressee by registered mail with acknowledgment of receipt.

Article 687

Where it is not proved that the addressee of the document has had knowledge thereof in due time, the judge dealing with the matter of his/her own initiative may order any further measures of service, unless he/she gives provisional or protective directions to safeguard the rights of the claimant.

The judge may delegate any competent authority to ensure that the addressee has had knowledge of the document and informing him/her of the consequences of default on his/her part. In the latter event, the delegated service shall be sent by the State Prosecutor's office, as set out in Article 685.

Article 688

The documents intended to be served on a foreign State or a foreign diplomatic representative in France or on any other person benefitting from a legal immunity, shall be served on the State Prosecutor's office and sent via the Minister of Justice, unless where, by virtue of a Treaty, the service may be made by any other means.

Sub-Section 2
Notification of Documents Originating in Foreign Countries

Article 688-1

Documents originating in a foreign State whose authorities request service must be notified by means of a simple delivery or service.

Article 688-2

The documents addressed to the Minister of Justice are sent by him/her to the State Prosecution Service attached to the regional court within whose judicial district they must be served, or to the National Chamber of Court Bailiffs, unless by virtue of a treaty, the transmission may be made by the foreign authorities directly to the State Prosecution Service or to the National Chamber of Court Bailiffs subject to any other means of service.

Article 688-3

Where the service is made on the State Prosecution Service, it may be made by means of simple delivery and at no cost.

Article 688-4

The documents addressed to the National Chamber of Court Bailiffs must be sent to a court bailiff who is territorially competent to serve it.

Article 688-5

The requesting party must advance the costs of the service, subject to any existing international conventions.

Article 688-6

The document must be served in the language of the State of origin.

However, the addressee who does not know the language in which the document is drafted may refuse to accept service and ask that it should be translated or have attached to it a translation in the French language to be made by and at the expense of the claimant.

Article 688-7

Documents proving the compliance or non-compliance with any requests for notification or service must be returned by the same method as that in which the requests were sent originally from a foreign country.

Article 688-8

The compliance with a request for notification or service may be refused by the French authority where it would adversely affect the sovereignty or the security of the State. It may similarly be refused where the request is not made in accordance with the provisions of this Code.

Section V-1
Regulations Specific to the Service and Notification of Judicial and Extra-judicial Documents in Civil and Commercial Matters in Another State Within the European Union

Article 688-9

Where a document is destined for a public official, a public authority or another person of a Member State of the European Community, the date of service of judicial and extra-judicial documents in civil and commercial matters is, with respect to the plaintiff, that of the date when the court bailiff sends it.

Article 688-10

Where a document is destined for a public official, a public authority or another person of a Member State of the European Community, the date of notification of judicial and extra-judicial documents in civil and commercial matters is, with respect to the plaintiff, that of the date when the court bailiff sends it.

Article 688-11

Articles 688-9 and 688-10 do not apply to documents sent to the Kingdom of Denmark, which continue to be governed by Section V of the present Chapter.

Section VI
The Place for Notifications

Article 689

In relation to a natural person, the notification must be given at the place where the addressee lives.

However, where it is given in person, the notification shall be valid wherever it is given, including a place of employment.

The notification shall also be validly given at the chosen place of residence where the law so allows or requires.

Article 690

The notification on a private law corporate entity of or a public corporation of a commercial and industrial nature must be given at its place of business.

In the absence of such a place, it shall be given personally to one of its members authorized to receive it.

Article 691

Notifications given to the State Prosecution Service and those which have to be given to the State Prosecutor's office, must, as the case may be, be given to the State Prosecutor's office attached to the court before which the matter is brought, or to that of the court which has given a ruling on the matter, or to that of the court which has jurisdiction over the last known place of residence of the addressee.

Where no State Prosecutor's office is attached to a court, the notification must be given to the State Prosecutor's office attached to the regional court within whose judicial district that court sits.

Section VII
Miscellaneous Provisions

Article 692

Notifications given to local authorities and public corporations must be given at the place where they are located or to any person authorized to receive them.

Article 693

The provisions of Article 654 to 659, 663 to 665, 672, 675, 678, 680, 683, 684, 686, 689 to 692 must be complied with, or the actions have no validity.

The provisions of Articles 4, 6 and 7 of Council Regulation (EC) 1348/2000 of 29 May 2000 must be complied with in the case of a document sent to another Member State of the European Community, with the exception of the Kingdom of Denmark, or the actions have no validity.

Article 694

The invalidity of a notification is governed by the provisions which determine the invalidity of written submissions.

TITLE XVIII
COSTS AND EXPENSES

Chapter I
The Burden of Costs

Article 695

Taxable costs relating to proceedings, court documents and enforcement procedures shall include:

1. The fees, taxes, government fees or expenses charged by the court registry offices or by the tax administration except fees, taxes and penalties which may be due in respect of documents and documentary evidence produced in support of the claims of the parties;

2. The costs of translating documents when this is made necessary by law or an international commitment;

3. Payments for witnesses;

4. Expert's fees;

5. Fixed disbursements;

6. Fees of public officers;[18]

7. Fees of attorneys in so far as they are regulated, including fees for the closing speeches;

8. The costs incurred in notifying a document abroad;

9. The costs of interpretation and translation made necessary by procedural steps taken abroad at the request of a court within the framework (EC) Council Regulation 1206/01 of May 28, 2001 on co-operation between the courts of the Member States in the taking of evidence in civil or commercial matters.

---

18 The French has two terms—"officier public", which means a member of certain professions, such as a notary, who is entitled to make officially recorded documents, and "officier ministériel", which means a member of certain professions, again like a notary, who are officially appointed. I have translated both terms as "public officer".

Article 696

Costs shall be paid by an unsuccessful party unless the judge orders them, either in part or in full, against another party pursuant to reasoned decision.

Article 697

The attorneys, appeal advocates and court bailiffs may be personally liable for costs relating to proceedings, documents and enforcement proceedings issued or conducted outside the scope of their authority.

Article 698

The costs relating to unjustified proceedings, documents and enforcement proceedings shall be paid by the officers of the court who conducted them without prejudice to any damages which might be claimed. The same shall apply to costs relating to proceedings, documents and enforcement proceedings which are declared invalid by reason of the fault of those officers.

Article 699

Attorneys may, in matters where their representation is mandatory, request that the taxation of their recoverable costs shall include, for their benefit, the right to recover directly from the party against whom they have been assessed those expenses which they may have advanced, without having been placed in funds by that party.

The party against whom the recovery is claimed may, however, deduct, by legal set-off, the amount from the legal costs owed to him/her by way of recoverable costs.

Article 700

As provided in I of Article 75 of Act No. 91-647 of 10 July 1991, in all proceedings, the judge shall order the party bearing the burden of taxable costs or, in default, the unsuccessful party, to pay to the other party the amount which he/she shall fix on the basis of the sums expended and not included in the taxable costs. The judge must take into consideration the rules of equity and the economic situation of the party against whom it is ordered. He/she may, of his/her own initiative, rule that there is no need for such order, for reasons based on the same considerations.

Chapter II
Assessment of Costs to be Recovered by the Court Registry

Article 701

The costs provided for in Article 695 (paras. 1 and 3) must be assessed in the judgment ordering them, or in a note made on the original judgment by one of the judges of the court.

Official copies of the judgment may be delivered before the assessment is carried out.

Article 702

Where the amount of the assessed costs does not appear in the certified copy of the judgment, the clerk shall issue an enforceable order.

Article 703

The assessment may be challenged in accordance with the procedure set out in Articles 708 to 718.

Chapter III
Verification and Recovery of Costs

Article 704

In cases of difficulty, the parties may, by virtue of Article 52, informally ask the clerk of the court that has jurisdiction to verify the amount of the costs stated under Article 695.

The same shall apply where an officer of the court wishes to recover the costs; his/her request shall then have annexed to it a breakdown which he/she is bound to give to the parties in accordance with the fixed fee regulations. The breakdown must set out any interim payments received.

Article 705

The clerk of the court will check the amount of the costs after having made, where applicable, the necessary corrections so that the account of costs complies with the fee scales. He/she shall give or send by regular mail a certificate of verification to the interested party.

Article 706

The party applying for their costs shall notify the verified account of costs to the opposing party who has one month within which to challenge it. This notification implies acceptance by the plaintiff of the verified account.

Such notification must indicate the time limit for making a challenge and the manner in which it may be made, and must specify that in default of any challenge within the specified time-limit, the certificate of verification may become enforceable.

Article 707

In the absence of any challenge by the opposing party within the time limit, the party applying for costs may request the verifying clerk to state this on the certificate of verification. Such a statement shall be enforceable.

Article 708

The person who wishes to challenge the verification may, at any time, file a request for an order for taxation; he/she may also do so through his/her legal representative.

The request may be made orally or in writing to the clerk of the court which has verified the costs account. It must contain reasons and enclose the certificate of verification.

Article 709

The president of the court or the judge assigned thereto shall, after having received or requested observations from the opponent, make a ruling in the form of an order in respect to the verified account and any other relevant documents.

Article 710

The judge shall rule upon the request for an order for taxation as well as on the other requests relating to the recovery of costs.

Article 711

The judge may make, of his/her own initiative, all necessary corrections so as to make the costs accounts conform with the fee scales. He/she must indicate, where necessary, the sums already paid by way of interim payment.

Article 712

The judge shall have the power to refer the request, as it stands, to a court for a hearing on a date specified by him/her. The parties shall be called by the clerk of the court to appear at least fifteen days before the hearing.

Article 713

The clerk shall attach a certificate of enforcement to the original of the taxation order.

Where it is subject to an appeal, notification of the order must, at the risk of it otherwise being declared invalid, include:

1. A statement that the order will become enforceable where no recourse against it is brought within the time limit and in the manner provided in Articles 714 and 715;

2. A summary of Articles 714 and 715.

Article 714

The taxation order made by the president of a court of first instance may be challenged by any interested person by way of recourse to the first president of the court of appeal.

The time limit for exercising the recourse shall be one month; it shall not be extended by reason of distance.

The time limit for the exercising the recourse and its conduct within the time limit shall not stay the execution.

Article 715

The recourse shall be commenced by giving or sending to the registry of the court of appeal a memorandum setting out the grounds for the review.

A copy of such memorandum shall be sent simultaneously to all parties to the main dispute at the risk of the review being held inadmissible.

Article 716

The parties shall be called to appear at least fifteen days before, by the registrar of the court of appeal.

The president or his/her deputy shall hear each side's arguments.

He/she shall conduct or have conducted, where necessary, all useful investigations.

Article 717

The first president or his/her deputy shall have the power to refer the request for a review as it stands to a court for a hearing, the date of which he/she shall specify.

Article 718

The notifications and summonses shall be made by registered mail with acknowledgment of receipt.

Where they are made by the clerk of the court, they may be done so by a simple memorandum if they are sent to the attorneys or appeal advocates.

Chapter IV

Requests or Disputes Relating to Expenses, Fees and Disbursements Not Included in the Costs

Article 719

Requests or disputes relating to expenses, fees and disbursements which are not included in the costs specified in Article 695, made by or against the officers of the court and public officers, shall be subject to the rules set out in Articles 704 to 718.

Article 720

Disputes relating to the fees of assistants to the court and public officers in relation to which method of calculation is not set by any regulatory provisions, shall rcmain subjcct to thosc spccial rulcs which govcrn thcm.

Article 721

In the case of Article 720, the judge shall decide according to the nature and the extent of the activities of the court assistant or the public officer, the difficulties they were faced with and the responsibility they undertook. He/she shall indicate, where necessary, the amounts already paid as interim payment, costs or fees.

Article 722

Repealed.

Article 723

Repealed.

Chapter V

Disputes Relating to the Payment of Experts

Article 724

The decisions stated in Articles 255, 262 and 284 given by a judge of a court of first instance or the court of appeal may be challenged by a review brought before the first president of the court of appeal in the manner set out in the second paragraph of Article 714 and Articles 715 and 718. Where the decision has been given by the first president of the court of appeal, it may be amended by the latter under the same conditions.

The time limit runs as against each of the parties from the date when the notification was given to him/her by the expert.

The review and the time limit for bringing it do not stay execution of the decision. The application for the review must, at the risk of it being declared invalid, be filed against all the parties and against the expert where it is not made by him/her.

Article 725

The notification must, at the risk of it being declared invalid, provide a summary of the preceding Article as well as that of the second paragraph of Article 714 and Article 715.

Chapter VI

Disputes Relating to Expenses, Fees and Disbursements of the Registrars of the Commercial Courts[19]

Article 725-1

As an exception to Articles 704 through 708, the demands and disputes relating to expenses, fees and disbursements, whether or not included or in the costs of the registrars of the Commercial Courts, must be made directly to the president of the regional court within whose judicial district the registrar of the Commercial

---

19 The French term is "tribunal de commerce". There are several commercial courts in each department and they are staffed by judges ("juges" in French) elected by the local business community. The commercial courts constitute, together with the other specialized courts (e.g. administrative and industrial relations courts) and the district courts, the second rung of the French judicial hierarchy for civil matters. The commercial courts hear all cases between commercial persons and companies as well as other matters relating to commerce, except where the district court has jurisdiction (*see* note 5). An appeal lies as of right from a commercial court to a court of appeal on matters of fact and law.

Court conducts his/her business, without any need to issue first a certificate of verification.

TITLE XIX
THE COURT REGISTRY

Article 726

The court registry shall maintain a general register of the cases brought before the court.

The general register shall indicate the date the case is filed, the folio number, the names of the parties and the nature of the matter, where necessary, the number of the court to which the matter is assigned, and the nature and date of the decision.

Article 727

For every case entered on the general register, the clerk shall open a file in which is shown, in addition to the information appearing on the docket, the name of the judge or judges who will hear the case and, where necessary, the name of the persons who represent or assist the parties.

After having been stamped with a seal by the judge or the clerk of the court, the originating process, notes and documents relating to the case shall be placed and recorded in the file.

Decisions resulting from the case, notices and letters sent by the court, or copies thereof shall be placed on record.

Where the procedure is oral, the claims of the parties or the references they make to claims submitted in writing shall be noted on the file or set out in an official document.

Article 728

The clerk of the court who shall keep a register in which shall be entered for each hearing:

- the date of the hearing;
- the names of the judges and of the clerk;
- the names of the parties and the nature of the case;
- the particulars of the parties who appear in person, in cases where representation is not mandatory;
- the names of the persons who represent or assist the parties at the hearing.

The clerk shall likewise state whether the hearing is public or not, what happened at the hearing, and the decisions given.

Information as to the judgments made must be entered in the register, which must be signed after each session of the hearing by the president and the clerk.

Article 729

Where there is a reconsideration or a referral after a hearing of the Court of Cassation, the clerk shall send the file to the court that has jurisdiction either within fifteen days of the request made to him/her or within the time limit provided by any particular provisions.

TITLE XX
LETTERS ROGATORY

Chapter I
Domestic Letters Rogatory

Article 730

Where the remoteness of parties from the court or of persons who have to take part in the proceedings, or the remoteness of the court itself might make travel too difficult or too onerous, the judge may, at the request of the parties or of his/her own initiative, appoint a court at an equal or inferior level, which appears to him/her to be best placed in the territory of the Republic, to implement all the legal functions which he/she shall deem necessary.

Article 731

The judge's decision shall be sent, with all the relevant documents, by the registry of the appointing court to the designated one. Upon receipt, the prescribed procedure shall be implemented on the initiative of the court or by the judge who the president of that court has appointed for that purpose.

The parties or persons who have to participate in the proceedings shall be summoned or notified directly by the designated court. The parties shall not be obliged to retain an attorney or appeal advocate before such a court.

Article 732

As soon as the proceedings are completed, the registry of the court which carried out the delegated functions shall send to the appointing court the record thereof, together with the documents and objects annexed or deposited.

Chapter II
International Letters Rogatory

Section I
Letters Rogatory Destined for a Foreign State

Article 733

The judge may, at the request of the parties or of his/her own initiative, give directives in a foreign state and take such other judicial acts as he/she shall deem necessary in connection with granting letters rogatory to any judicial authority in the state in question that has jurisdiction to French diplomatic or consular authorities.

Article 734

The clerk of the commissioning court shall send a certified copy of the decision granting the letters rogatory, together with a translation made by the parties, to the State Prosecution Service.

Article 735

The State Prosecution Service shall send the letters rogatory immediately to the Minister of Justice in order for them to be forwarded accordingly, except where by virtue of a treaty the transmission may be made directly to the foreign authority.

Section II
Letters Rogatory Coming from a Foreign State

Article 736

The Minister of Justice shall send the letters rogatory transmitted to him/her by foreign states to the State Prosecution Service in whose judicial district they must be implemented.

Article 737

The State Prosecution Service shall remit the letters rogatory immediately to the court with jurisdiction to implement them.

Article 738

Upon receipt of the letters rogatory, the prescribed procedures shall be implemented on the initiative of the commissioned court or by the judge appointed by the president of that court for that purpose.

Article 739

The letters rogatory shall be implemented in accordance with French law, unless the foreign State has requested that it should be implemented in a particular way.

Where so requested in the letters rogatory, the questions and answers shall be transcribed or recorded in full.

Article 740

The parties and their representatives, even when they are foreigners, may, where authorized by the judge, put forward questions; these must be formulated in, or translated into, French; similar provisions shall apply to the answers given thereto.

Article 741

The commissioned judge shall be bound to inform the commissioning court, which requests it, of the place, date and time at which the letters rogatory have been implemented; the foreign commissioning judge may attend the proceedings.

Article 742

The judge may not refuse to implement letters rogatory on the sole ground that French law claims exclusive jurisdiction over the matter, or that it does not recognize the legal remedy sought pursuant to the claim brought before the commissioning court, or that it does not approve of the purposes of the letters rogatory.

Article 743

The commissioned judge may refuse, either of his/her own initiative or at the request of any interested party, to implement the letters rogatory where he/she considers that they do not fall within his/her competence. He/she must refuse the same where it is such that they adversely affects the sovereignty or security of the French State.

Interested parties may similarly, in the same cases, ask the commissioned judge to withdraw the direction he/she has already given and to annul the documents recording the implementation of the letters rogatory.

Article 744

The State Prosecution Service must ensure compliance with the fundamental principles of procedure in implementing the letters rogatory.

Where there is a breach of these principles, the State Prosecution Service or an interested party may request the commissioned judge to withdraw the directions which he/she has already given and to annul the documents recording the implementation of the letters rogatory.

Article 745

Where the letters rogatory have been irregularly transmitted, the commissioned judge may, on his/her own motion or at the request of the State Prosecution Service, refuse to implement them; likewise, he/she may, at the request of the State Prosecution Service, cancel the directions which he/she has already given and annul the instruments recording the execution of the letters rogatory.

Article 746

The judge must give reasons for the decision in which he/she refuses to implement the letters rogatory, annuls the documents recording their implementation, and withdraws the directions which he/she has already given, or where he/she refuses to withdraw the latter.

The parties and the State Prosecution Service may file an appeal against the decision.

The time limit for the appeal shall be fifteen days; it may not be extended on grounds of remoteness.

Article 747

The documents recording the implementation of letters rogatory, or the decision whereby a judge refuses to implement the same, shall be sent to the commissioning court in the same way as the letters rogatory were remitted to the appointed court.

Article 748

The implementation of the letters rogatory shall be conducted without any costs or fees.

However, the sums due to witnesses, experts, interpreters as well as to any person participating in the implementation of letters rogatory shall be at the expense of the foreign authority. The same shall apply to the costs arising from the application of a particular form of procedure at the request of the commissioning court.

TITLE XXI
FINAL PROVISION

Article 749

The provisions of the present Book shall apply to all courts of the general-court system hearing any civil, commercial, social security, agricultural or labor matter, subject to the special rules governing each matter and to the specific provisions relating to each court.

BOOK TWO
SPECIFIC PROVISIONS RELATING TO EACH COURT

TITLE I
SPECIFIC PROVISIONS RELATING TO THE REGIONAL COURT

SUB-TITLE I
THE PROCEDURE BEFORE THE COURT

Chapter I
The Procedure in Contentious Matters

Article 750

An application to the court shall be made by way of a writ or by the filing of a joint application at the court registry office, except in cases whereby the court may be empowered by way of an *ex parte* application or declaration.

Article 751

Parties are obliged to retain an attorney, unless contrary provisions apply.

The appointment of an attorney shall include an election of domicile.

Article 752

Further to the particulars prescribed under Article 56, the writ must contain, at the risk of it otherwise being declared invalid:

1. the appointment of the plaintiff's attorney;
2. the time limit within which the defendant must appoint an attorney.

Article 753

The pleadings must expressly set out the claims of the parties as well as the issues of law and fact which are the basis of each claim. A memorandum listing the documents in support of these claims must be annexed to the pleadings.

In their most recent pleadings, the parties must refer to the claims and points submitted or referred to in earlier ones. In default thereof, they shall be deemed to have been abandoned and the court shall only rule upon the last pleadings filed.

Pleadings must be notified and documents must be exchanged by the attorney of each of the parties with the other one; where there is a multiplicity of plaintiffs or defendants, this shall be done in relation to each attorney on record.

Copies of the pleadings shall be filed at the court registry with the proof of their notification.

Article 754

The court shall be empowered and a matter shall be conducted in accordance with the rules relating to ordinary procedure, except for urgent matters.

Section I
The Ordinary Procedure

Sub-Section 1
Commencement of Proceedings

Article 755

The defendant is obliged to appoint an attorney within a period of fifteen days from the date of the writ.

Article 756

Once appointed, the attorney for the defendant informs the plaintiff's attorney of his/her appointment; a copy of the appointment is filed at the court registry.

Article 757

The court shall be instructed, at the suit of one or the other party, by the filing at the court registry of a copy of the writ.

The said filing must be made within four months of the writ, failing which the writ lapses.

The lapse of the writ shall be put on record automatically by an order of the president or a judge dealing with the matter.

In default of being filed, an application may be made to the president to put the lapse of the writ on record.

Article 758

The president of the court shall fix the date and the time at which the case shall be called for a hearing; where it appears necessary, he/she shall specify the court to which it shall be assigned.

Article 759

On the appointed day, the matter must be called before the president of the court to which it has been assigned.

The latter shall confer with the attorneys present on the current position of the matter.

Sub-Section 2
Setting Down for Trial

Article 760

The president shall schedule actions for trial where, based on the submissions of the attorneys and on an examination of the pleadings served and documents exchanged, they appear to him/her to be in good order and ready for a substantive consideration.

He/she shall schedule similarly for trial actions in which the defendant has not entered an appearance where they are ready for a substantive consideration, unless he/she orders a new service of the writ on the defendant.

In all cases, the president shall declare the closure of the pre-trial management of the matter and shall set the date of the trial. The latter may be conducted on the same day.

Article 761

The president may equally decide that the attorneys shall appear again before him/her, on a date that he/she shall specify, in order to confer on the action for a last time, where he/she forms the view that a final service of pleadings or a final exchange of documents would bring the action under a proper case-management or that the pleadings of the parties should comply with the provisions of Article 753.

In the latter case, he/she shall specify to each of the attorneys the appropriate time limit for the service of the pleadings and, where necessary, for the exchange of documents. His/her directions shall be recorded by a simple notes on the court file.

On the date specified by him/her, when proper management has been complied with within the specified time limit, or at the request of one of the attorneys, the president shall set down the cause for trial, in which case he/she shall declare the close of the pre-trial management of the action and shall specify the date of the trial. The latter may be conducted on the same day.

Article 762

All actions which the president does not schedule for trial shall be managed in accordance with the provisions as hereinafter set out.

Sub-Section 3
Preparation of the Case Before the Pre-Trial Judge

Article 763

An action must be prepared under the supervision of a judge of the court to which it has been assigned.

The judge shall supervise the proper conduct of the proceedings, particularly as to the timely service of pleadings and exchange of documents.

He/she may hear the attorneys and bring to their attention any appropriate observations.

He/she may equally, where required, give them instructions.

He/she may order the removal of the case from the list of cases in the cases and under the conditions set out in Articles 382 and 383

Article 764

Having considered the nature, urgency and complexity of the matter, and after having requested the opinion of the attorneys, the pre-trial judge shall set, as the case progresses, the time limits within which the matter is to be prepared.

He/she may grant extensions of time.

He/she may adjourn the matter for another conference with a view to resolving dispute.

Article 765

The pre-trial judge may invite the attorneys to address him/her in relation to such grounds as pleaded, to provide such arguments in fact and in law as may be necessary for the resolution of the dispute, and, where appropriate, to make their pleadings comply with the provisions of Article 753.

He/she may request the originals of the documents on record or request the filing of a copy thereof.

Article 766

The pre-trial judge shall deal with joinders and disjoinders of proceedings.

Article 767

The pre-trial judge, may, even, hear the parties of his/her own initiative.

The testimony of the parties shall be heard in the presence of all parties, unless one of the parties, duly summoned, has not appeared.

Article 768

The pre-trial judge may put on record a conciliation of the parties, even in part.

Article 768-1

The pre-trial judge may invite the parties to join any other interested party as a third party whose joinder to the action shall appear necessary to him/her for the resolution of the dispute.

Article 769

The pre-trial judge shall put on record the lapse of the proceedings.

Article 770

The pre-trial judge shall exercise all his/her powers necessary for the service, receipt and production of documents.

Article 771

Where an application is made after he/she has been appointed, the pre-trial judge shall until such time as the matter is withdrawn from his/her jurisdiction and to the exclusion of any other panel of the court be the only judge who has the power to:

1. rule upon procedural pleas and applications to dismiss the case;
2. provide for an advance for costs;
3. provide for an advance payment to a creditor where the existence of the claim is not seriously contested. The pre-trial judge may make the enforcement of his/her decision conditional on the provision of a security under the conditions provided in Articles 517-522;
4. order any other interim measures, including protective measures, except for attachments and interim legal charges and pledges, as well as varying or supplementing measures already ordered if a new fact arises;
5. order, even on his/her own motion, any procedural steps.

Article 772

The pre-trial judge may rule upon costs.

Article 773

Directions given by the pre-trial judge shall be recorded by simple notes in the court file; the attorneys shall be advised of the same.

However, in the case set out in Articles 769 to 772, the pre-trial judge shall decide by a reasoned order, subject to the specific rules applicable to pre-trial procedures.

Article 774

Orders are given, immediately, where necessary, after the attorneys have been heard or summoned.

The attorneys are summoned by the judge to appear before him/her.

In matters of urgency, a party may, by notification between attorneys, invite the other party to appear before a judge at a date, time and place specified by the judge.

Article 775

Orders of the pre-trial judge, in relation to the main issue, shall not have the authority of a final decision.

Article 776

Orders of the pre-trial judge shall not be subject to an objection or an appeal.

They may be subject to an objection relating to jurisdiction where they rule on jurisdiction or *lis alibi pendens.*

However, they are subject to appeal in the cases and under the conditions that apply for expert opinions or suspensions of proceedings in the conditions laid down for expert opinions for deferment of judgments. They are equally subject to appeal if, within fifteen days from service:

1. they have the effect of terminating the proceedings or if they establish the termination of the proceedings;

2. they relate to interim measures ordered with respect to a matter involving divorce or judicial separation;

3. in cases where the value of the claim exceeds the limit of jurisdiction at last instance, they concern interim payments that may be granted to a creditor where the existence of the claim is not seriously contested.

Article 777

The pre-trial judge shall oversee the implementation of the orders which he/she has given, subject to the provisions of the third paragraph of Article 155.

Article 778

Where the directives have been complied, the conduct of the matter shall be continued at the chambers of the pre-trial judge.

Article 779

As soon as the pre-trial management of the matter permits, the pre-trial judge shall schedule the case for trial to be argued at the date specified by the president or by him/herself where he/she was delegated for that purpose.

The pre-trial judge shall declare the closure of the pre-trial management. The closing date must be as near as possible to the one fixed for the closing speeches.

The pre-trial judge shall exercise his/her jurisdiction up to the opening of the oral pleadings.

Article 780

Where one of the attorneys has failed to implement the procedural steps within the specified time-limit, the judge may schedule the case for trial and close the pre-trial management, either of his/her own initiative or at the request of one of the parties, except that, in the latter case, he/she may refuse the request upon making a reasoned order which shall not be subject to appeal.

Article 781

Where the attorneys have failed to take the procedural steps within the specified time-limit, the pre-trial judge may, of his/her own initiative, and after notifying the attorneys of the same, make an order for the dismissal of the action, which shall not be subject to a review.

A copy of that order shall be sent to each of the parties by regular mail to their actual address or residence.

Sub-Section 4
Common Provisions

Article 782

The closure of the pre-trial management, as set out in Articles 760, 761, 779 and 780, shall be declared by way of an order without reasons, which shall not be subject to appeal. A copy of that order must be given to the attorneys.

Article 783

After declaring such closure, no further pleadings may be filed nor any new document be produced in the course of the oral pleadings, at the risk of them being declared inadmissible automatically.

However, applications to revoke declarations of closure, third party applications to join the proceedings by way of voluntary joinder, pleadings relating to rents, arrears, interest and other interlocutory costs that are due, and, where a breakdown thereof cannot seriously be challenged, disbursements incurred up to the opening of the oral pleadings shall be admissible.

Pleadings for the resumption of proceedings from the time when they were suspended shall be equally admissible.

Article 784

The order for closure shall only be revoked where a serious matter has come to light subsequent to its making; the appointment of an attorney after to the closure does not constitute, per se, a ground for revocation.

Where an application to be joined as third parties by way of voluntary joinder has been filed after the closure of the pre-trial management, the order for closure shall only be revoked where the court cannot immediately rule upon the whole matter.

The order for closure may be revoked by the court or at the suit of the parties, either by the making of a reasoned decision by the pre-trial judge, or, after the opening of oral pleadings, by a decision of the trial court.

Article 785

Where he/she deems that the matter so requires, the president of the court may assign the pre-trial judge to draft a written report; exceptionally, he/she may assign any other judge or do it him/herself.

The report shall set out the subject-matter of the claim and the grounds put forward by the parties, it shall specify the issues of fact and law that are raised by the dispute and shall mention any things that might clarify the arguments.

The judge assigned to draft the report shall present the same at the hearing, before the closing speeches, without giving his/her opinion.

Article 786

The pre-trial judge or the judge assigned to draft the report may, if the attorneys do not raise any objection to the same, sit alone at the trial to hear the closing speeches. He/she shall quote the same to the court in his/her discussions.

Article 787

Trial court orders shall be implemented under the supervision of the pre-trial judge.

Once an order has been complied with, the president of the court to which the matter has been assigned shall set it down for trial or shall refer it back to the pre-trial judge, as referred to under sub-section 2 below.

Section II
Fixed Date Proceedings

Article 788

In urgent matters, the president of the court may grant leave to a plaintiff, upon his/her request, to summon the defendant to appear on a set return date. He/she shall specify, where the same appears necessary, the court number to which the matter shall be assigned.

The request must set out the grounds of urgency, include the pleadings of the plaintiff and identify the supporting documents.

A copy of the request and the supporting documents shall be sent to the president to be placed in the court's file.

Article 789

The writ must indicate, subject to it otherwise being declared invalid, the date and time specified by the president on which the matter shall be called as well as the court number to which it has been assigned. A copy of the application shall be annexed to the writ.

The writ shall inform the defendant that he/she may examine the copy of the documents identified in the request at the court registry and gives him formal notice that he/she must indicate before the date of the hearing the documents that he/she intends to rely upon.

Article 790

The defendant is obliged to instruct counsel before the date of the hearing.

Article 791

The court shall be empowered by the filing of a copy of the writ at the court registry office.

This filing must take place before date fixed for the hearing, failing which the writ shall lapse.

The lapse is recorded, of his/her motion, by the president of the chamber to which the matter has been assigned.

Article 792

On the date of the trial, the president must be satisfied that sufficient time has elapsed since the service of the writ so that the party summoned has been able to prepare his/her defense.

If the defendant has instructed counsel, the matter is argued immediately and shall be argued as is, even in the absence of any pleadings by the defendant or on simple oral submissions.

Where necessary, the president of the court may exercise the powers referred to under Article 761 or may remit the matter to the pre-trial judge.

Where the defendant has not instructed counsel, the matter shall proceed in accordance with the provisions of Article 760.

Section III
The Joint Application

Article 793

In addition to the particulars prescribed in Article 57, a joint application must include, at the risk of it being inadmissible, the appointment statement of the parties' attorneys.

It shall be signed by the appointed attorneys.

Article 794

The plaintiffs may, from the date of the joint application, request that the matter be assigned to a single judge, or may renounce the right to request that the matter be referred to a panel of judges.

Article 795

The court shall be empowered by the filing of the joint application at the court registry office.

Article 796

The president of the court shall specify the time and date on which the matter shall be heard; where necessary, he/she shall specify the court-room to which it shall be assigned.

Notice of the same shall be given to the attorneys of record, by the court registry office.

The matter shall then proceed as set out in Articles 759, 760 and 762, except for matters referred to under Article 794, where the matter would have been assigned to a judge sitting alone.

Chapter II
Procedure in Non-Contentious Matters

Article 797

The application must be brought by an attorney or by a public officer in cases where he/she is empowered to act under the legal provisions in force.

Article 798

The State Prosecution Service must be informed of non-contentious matters.

Article 799

A reporting judge[20] shall be designated by the president of the particular court to which the matter has been assigned.

He/she shall be entrusted with the same powers, as regards the pre-trial management of a matter, as that of the court.

Article 800

If there are oral pleadings, the State Prosecution Service is obliged to attend.

Chapter III
The Single Judge

Article 801

The assignment of a matter to a single judge may be decided upon up to the fixing of a date for the hearing.

The assignment of actions to be considered by a single judge shall be made by the president of the court or by the president of the particular court to which they shall be assigned.

Article 802

Where a matter is assigned to a single judge, he/she exercises the same powers as those conferred on the court or the pre-trial judge.

Where the matter is subsequently brought before a panel-judge, its pre-trial management shall be handled, where it appears necessary, either by the judge exercis-

20 The French term is "juge rapporteur". It means the judge who prepares a report on a case for a court, hence the English translation "reporting judge". However, in the Commercial Courts, the juge rapporteur has a different function—*see* note 22.

ing the powers of the pre-trial judge, or by the pre-trial judge, in accordance with the decision of the president of the court.

Article 803

The assignment of a matter to a single judge or its referral to a panel of judges shall be recorded by a simple entry in the court's file. Notice of the same shall be given to the attorneys of record.

In matters where the instruction of an attorney is dispensed with, notice of the same shall be sent to the parties by registered mail with acknowledgment of receipt.

Article 804

The application to have a matter, which has been assigned to a single judge, brought before a panel of judges must be made, at the risk of it being time-barred, not later than fifteen days from the date of the notice referred to in the aforementioned Article, or from the date of its receipt where it is addressed to the parties themselves.

The referral of a matter to a panel of judges by the president of the court or his/her deputy may be decided upon at any stage.

Article 805

The provisions laid down under the second paragraph of Article 803 and the first paragraph of Article 804 shall cease to be applicable if the right to request for a referral to a panel of judges has been waived.

Chapter IV
Miscellaneous Provisions

Article 806

Where the court is empowered pursuant to a request, in contentious and non-contentious matters, the parties must be advised of the trial date by the registrar.

Article 807

Notice must be given either to the attorneys by simple memorandum, or, where legal representation is not mandatory, transmitted to the parties by registered mail with acknowledgment of receipt. A copy of the request shall be attached to the notice sent to the attorneys or the parties.

SUB-TITLE II
THE POWERS OF THE PRESIDENT

Chapter I
Summary Orders

Article 808

In all urgent matters, the president of the regional court may order, by way of summary proceedings, such measures to which no serious objections are raised or to which ought to be given by reason of a dispute.

Article 809

The president may always, even where faced with a serious objection, order in summary proceedings the protective or preparatory measures that are required either to prevent imminent injury or to stop a nuisance that is clearly illegal.

Where a liability resulting from a contractual obligation cannot seriously be challenged, the president may award an interim payment to the creditor or order the specific performance of the obligation even where it is an obligation to do something.

Article 810

The powers of the president of the regional court as set out in the aforementioned two Articles shall extend to all matters where there are no particular summary proceedings available.

Article 811

At the request of one or the other party and where it is justified by the urgency of the matter, the president handling summary proceedings may schedule the matter for a hearing, the date of which he/she shall specify, in order to decide on the merits.

He/she shall pay special attention to the fact that the defendant must be given ample time to prepare his/her defense. The order shall imply the instruction of the court. The matter shall then proceed in accordance with the provisions of Article 790 and the last three paragraphs of Article 792.

Chapter II
Orders upon Application

Article 812

The president of the court shall assume jurisdiction on an application in the cases provided by the law.

He/she may also give such urgent orders, on request, where the circumstances require that they are not dealt with *ex parte*. Interlocutory requests relating to a pending proceeding must be made to the president of the court to which the matter has been assigned or to the judge already handling the same.

Article 813

The application must be presented by an attorney, or by a public officer in cases where he/she is empowered to act under the legal provisions in force.

Where the application is presented in the course of a proceeding, it must state the court that is hearing the matter.

SUB-TITLE III
MISCELLANEOUS PROVISIONS

Chapter I
Instruction of Attorneys and Pleadings

Article 814

The instruction of an attorney by the defendant or by any other person who shall be joined as a party to a pending proceeding shall be disclosed to the other parties by way of notification between attorneys.

The document shall specify:

a) where the defendant is a natural person: his/her family name, first names, occupation, place of residence, nationality, date and place of birth;

b) where the defendant is a corporate entity: its type, name, registered office and the officer that shall represent it legally.

Article 815

Pleadings on behalf of the parties must be signed by their attorneys and must be served by way of notification between attorneys. They shall only be admissible when the particulars referred to under the second paragraph of Article 814 have been provided.

The service of documents produced shall be validly acknowledged by the attachment of the signature of the attorney being served with them to the statement drafted by the attorney effecting the service.

Article 816

The filing at the court registry office of a copy of the notice of acting and of the pleadings shall be done either when they are being notified, or, where that has been done before the court was empowered, with the filing of a copy of the writ.

Chapter II
Judicial Administration

Article 817

The appointment of pre-trial judges and judges sitting alone shall be made in accordance with the manner prescribed for the allocation of judges in the different courts of the regional court.

The president of the regional court and the presidents of the various courts may exercise these specific powers.

Article 818

More than one judge may be entrusted with the pre-trial management of a matter before the same court; in that case, the matters shall be divided between them by the president of that court.

Article 819

The pre-trial judges may be replaced at any time when there are any circumstances which prevent them from sitting.

Article 820

The president of the regional court may delegate to one or more judges part or all of his/her powers conferred upon him/her by sub-titles I and II.

The presidents of the particular courts may similarly delegate to other judges of their courts all or part of the functions attributed to them under sub-title I.

Chapter III
The Court Registry Office

Article 821

The filing at the court registry office of a copy of written submissions or of any document shall be entered on the record by stating the date of filing and by the stamp of the registrar on the copy, as well as on the original, which shall be returned to its holder forthwith.

Article 822

A copy of the writ, of the application and of the joint application shall, as soon as it is filed at the court registry office, be presented by the registrar to the president of the court who can then schedule and assign the case.

The decision of the president shall be recorded by simple notes on the court file.

Article 823

The court record must be retained and updated by the registrar of the court to which it is assigned.

A properly organized case file shall be created. The status of any case can be tracked through this case file at any time.

Article 824

With reference to Article 788, copies of the application and documents brought to the president shall be, as well as a copy of his/her order, placed by the registrar on the court's record, as soon as such record is created.

If on the day the matter ought to be called, a copy of the writ has not been filed at the court registry office, the registrar shall of his/her own initiative return those copies which he/she has in his/her possession, to the attorney concerned.

Article 825

The registrar shall immediately advise the attorneys whose appointments are known to him/her, of the case number of the matter on the general register, of the dates and time fixed by the president of the court for the hearing of the matter and the particular court to which it has been assigned.

This notice is given to those attorneys whose appointments are not yet known once a copy of their instrument of appointment is filed with the court registry office.

Article 826

The attorneys for each of the parties shall be called or advised of the duties incumbent upon them by the president or by the pre-trial judge, according to the method of court management of the matter; they shall be called or advised orally, with a marginal note and a record made on the court's file.

Where they are not present, they shall be so advised by way of a simple memorandum, dated and signed by the registrar, and served or left by him/her at the office of the court where notifications between attorneys are exchanged.

Injunctive decrees must always be issued in a memorandum.

SUB-TITLE IV
THE PROCEDURE ON A REFERRAL FROM A CRIMINAL COURT

Article 826-1

Where a matter has been referred to the regional court in the manner prescribed under the second paragraph of Article 470-1 and under Article R-41-1 of the Code of Criminal Procedure, the court registry office shall, by registered mail with acknowledgment of receipt, summon to a hearing, at least a month before its date, the parties to the civil proceedings who appeared before the criminal court as well as third parties who are liable in the referral decision. The court registry office shall on the same day send to the same individuals a copy of the summons by regular mail. The summons to which is annexed a copy of the referral decision, shall be the same as a summons to appear before a court of law.

The summons shall state that legal representation at the hearing by an attorney shall be obligatory and that, where they fail to appear, provisionally enforceable judgments may be entered against any party other than the victim who suffered loss and damage, and against third parties who are so liable under in the referral decision.

The social security bodies and the motor insurance fund, where they have made an appearance before the criminal court, shall be called to appear at the same hearing by way of registered mail with acknowledgment of receipt sent by the court registry office. A copy of the referral decision shall be annexed to the summons.

At the hearing, matters shall be dealt with as set out in Articles 759 to 762. The president of the court may, further to summary proceedings, order interim payments in the manner provided under the second paragraph of Article 809.

TITLE II

SPECIFIC PROVISIONS RELATING TO THE DISTRICT COURT AND LOCAL COURT

Article 827

The parties shall plead their actions themselves.

They shall have the right to be assisted or represented.

Article 828

The parties may be assisted or represented by:

- an attorney;
- their spouse;
- their direct relations or relations by marriage;
- their collateral relations or relations by marriage;
- persons exclusively attached to their personal service of their undertaking.

The State, departments, municipalities and public bodies may be represented or assisted by a civil servant or an officer of their body.

The representative, where he/she is not an attorney, must demonstrate specific authority to act.

SUB-TITLE I
THE ORDINARY PROCEDURE

Article 829

The application to the court in the case of a district court and a local court is made in the form of a writ to appear with the aim of mediation and, failing that, judgment, except for the right of the plaintiff to undertake an attempt at conciliation before issuing the writ.

The application may also be brought either by filing a joint application at the court registry or by a voluntary appearance before the judge, or, in the case referred to in Article 847-1, by a declaration made to the registry.

In the absence of an agreement by the parties to attempt a conciliation, the judge, by a decision that is not open to appeal, may enjoin them to meet with a conciliator that he/she appoints for this purpose and who is charged with informing them about the purpose and conduct of a conciliation proceeding.

Chapter I
The Pre-Action Attempt at Conciliation

Article 830

An application for a pre-action attempt at conciliation may be made orally or by regular mail, to the court registry office.

The plaintiff must specify the family name, first names, occupation and address of the parties, as well as the subject-matter of his/her claim.

Article 831

The pre-action attempt at conciliation may be chaired by the judge or by a conciliator satisfying the conditions contained in Decree No. 78-381 of 20 March 1978 as amended relating to conciliations, appointed for that purpose.

In all cases, the parties must appear in person.

Article 832

The initial time period for the conciliator's duties shall not exceed one month. His/her duties may be renewed once, for a similar period, at the request of the conciliation.

Article 832-1

Where a judge is considering the appointment of a conciliator, he/she shall advise the parties by registered mail with acknowledgment of receipt and shall invite them to advise him/her of their acceptance within fifteen days.

He/she shall notify the parties that, in the absence of an acceptance on their behalf, matters shall proceed in accordance with Articles 833 and 834.

The letter states that each party may appear before the conciliator with a person allowed by law to assist him/her before a judge, and shall quote the provisions of Article 832.

The letter sent to the defendant must state the family name, first names, occupation and address of the plaintiff and the subject-matter of the claim.

Article 832-2

Once the parties communicate their acceptance, the judge shall appoint a conciliator and shall fix a time limit within which to undertake his/her duties.

Notice of the same shall be given to the conciliator and to the parties. A copy of the application shall be sent to the conciliator.

Article 832-3

The conciliator shall summon the parties, to the place, date and time which he/she shall decide, to proceed with the pre-action attempt at conciliation.

Article 832-4

The conciliator may visit the premises.

He/she may, with the consent of the parties, hear the testimony of any person, which he/she deems useful to him/her, provided that they agree.

Article 832-5

The conciliator shall keep the judge informed of any obstacles encountered by him/her in the conduct of his/her duties.

Article 832-6

The judge may at any stage bring an end to the conciliation at the request of a party or the conciliator.

The judge may also of his/her own initiative bring the proceedings to an end where the conciliation appears to have been compromised.

Notice of the same must be given to the conciliator.

The court registry shall notify the parties of the decision of the judge, by registered mail with acknowledgment of receipt, which shall further remind them that they have the right to instruct the court that has jurisdiction with a view to obtaining a judgment.

Article 832-7

At the end of his/her duties, the conciliator must inform the judge in writing of the success or failure of the attempt at the pre-action conciliation.

Where a conciliation has been effected, even partially, the conciliator shall draft an agreement in relation to the same, signed by the parties.

Where there is a failure to effect a conciliation, the court registry shall send the parties registered mail with acknowledgment of receipt reminding them that they have the right to bring the matter before a court with jurisdiction to hear it with a view to obtaining a judgment.

Article 832-8

The application for court approval of the agreement reached between the parties shall be sent to the judge by the conciliator; a copy of the agreement shall be attached thereto.

The approval by the court is treated as a non-contentious matter.

Article 832-9

The findings of the conciliator and the statements that he/she has recorded may not be produced nor be referred to in subsequent proceedings without the agreement of the parties, nor may be produced in any other proceedings.

Article 832-10

There is no appeal against a decision ordering or renewing the attempt at conciliation or terminating it.

Article 833

When the judge him/herself undertakes the pre-action attempt at conciliation, the court registry shall advise the plaintiff by regular mail of the place, date and time where it shall be held.

The defendant shall be summoned by regular mail. The summons must state the family name, first names, occupation and address of the defendant as well as the subject-matter of the application.

The notice and summons must specify that each party may be assisted by one of the persons listed under Article 828.

Article 834

Failing conciliation before the judge, the matter may proceed immediately to judgment if the parties agree. In this case, the matter proceeds according to the rules for voluntary appearance of the parties.

Article 835

The application for a pre-action attempt at conciliation shall only suspend the running of the time limit if the writ has been served within two months calculated from the date of the attempt at conciliation conducted by the judge, or from the notification referred to under the fourth paragraph of Article 832-6, or from the one referred to under the third paragraph of Article 832-7 or from the expiration of the time limit granted by the plaintiff to the debtor to perform his/her obligation.

Chapter II
The Procedure by Way of a Writ for All Purposes

Article 836

The writ must, at the risk of it being declared invalid, further specify the particulars prescribed under Article 56:

1. the place, date and time of the hearing at which the conciliation shall be attempted where that has not already taken place, and where relevant, the matter shall be decided.

2. where the defendant resides outside the jurisdiction, the family name, first names and address of the person at whose place he/she has chosen his residence in France.

The originating process shall furthermore specify the conditions under which the defendant may be assisted or represented, as well as, where necessary, the name of the defendant's representative.

Article 837

The writ must be served at least fifteen days before the hearing date.

Article 838

The judge takes jurisdiction, on the initiative of one or the other party by the filing of a copy of the writ at the court registry office.

The filing must be at least eight days before the hearing date.

Article 839

In urgent cases, the time limit for appearance and filing the writ may be shortened by leave of the judge.

Article 840

The judge shall attempt to effect a conciliation between the parties. The attempt at conciliation may be held in his/her chambers.

It may also be conducted by a court conciliator appointed by the judge without any specific formality, with the agreement of the parties.

Article 841

In the absence of a conciliation, the matter shall be decided immediately or, where it is not in sufficient order to be considered, it shall be scheduled for trial on another date. In the latter case, the registrar must advise the parties who would not have been advised verbally, of the date of the hearing by regular mail.

Article 842

The prosecution of the proceedings after the implementation of an order or on the expiration of a time limit for suspension of a judgment, shall take place following the notice which is given to the parties orally or by regular mail sent by the registrar.

Article 843

The procedure shall be conducted orally.

The claims of the parties or the references they make to any claims which they submitted in writing shall be noted in the court records or in the form of a memorandum.

Article 844

The judge may invite the parties to provide such explanations as he/she deems necessary for the resolution of the dispute or may put them on notice to produce, within such time as he/she shall decide, such relevant documents or supporting exhibits as might provide him/her with guidance, failing which, he/she may disregard them and rule upon the matter, drawing any inference which he/she chooses from the abstention or refusal of a party to comply with the same.

Chapter III
The Joint Application and the Voluntary Appearance of the Parties

Article 845

The parties may present their claim by joint application; they may also appear voluntarily before a judge in order to decide the matter.

Article 846

The judge obtains jurisdiction either by the filing of the joint application or by the signing of an official document in which it shall be recorded that the parties have appeared voluntarily to have their claims decided.

The official document must include the particulars in relation to the joint application as set out in Article 57.

Article 847

The judge shall endeavor to expect a conciliation between the parties.

He/she may with their agreement and without any specific formalities, appoint a court conciliator to proceed with the attempt at conciliation.

Where attempts at conciliation fail the judge shall rule upon their contentions.

Chapter IV
The Declaration to the Court Registry

Article 847-1

Where the value of the claim does not exceed the limit of the district court, as a court of last resort, the court assumes jurisdiction on a declaration made by, sent or addressed to the court registry, whereupon it shall be entered in the record.

The declaration must specify the family name, first names, occupation and address of the parties, or, in relation to corporate bodies, their name and their registered office. It must include the subject-matter of the claim and a brief summary of the grounds for it.

Time limits for prosecuting the action shall be suspended by the recording of the declaration.

Article 847-2

The parties shall be summoned to a hearing by the registrar by registered mail with acknowledgment of receipt. On the same date, he/she shall forward a copy of the summons by regular mail. The claimant may also be summoned orally on the making of a marginal note in the court file.

The summons addressed to the defendant shall be the same as a summons to appear before a court of law. It shall state that, where he/she fails to appear, he/she shall run the risk that a judgment may be entered against him/her based solely on the facts alleged by his/her opponent. A copy of the declaration shall be attached to the summons.

Article 847-3

The judge shall attempt to effect a conciliation between the parties.

He/she may with their agreement and without any specific formalities, appoint a court conciliator to proceed with the attempt at conciliation.

When a conciliation fails, the judge shall rule upon their contentions.

Chapter V
Referral to Another Court

Article 847-4

Where a local judge is confronted with a serious legal difficulty involving the application of a rule of law or the interpretation of a contract that is binding on the parties, he/she, having heard the parties, refers the matter to a district court judge by forwarding the file to him/her.

His/her decision is a judicial administrative measure. It may take the form of a simple note in the file.

The district court judge takes on the proceedings in the state that the local judge has left them, except for hearing the parties again if they have already presented their cases.

Article 847-5

A local judge refers all objections in his/her jurisdiction to a district court judge. His/her decision may take the form of a simple note in the file.

The local judge may raise the issue of his/her lack of jurisdiction, and the district court as well for the benefit of the local judge.

The district court judge's ruling is without appeal if it concerns his/her jurisdiction to deal with the matter and that of the local judges of his/her judicial district.

Articles 96 and 97 apply.

SUB-TITLE II
SUMMARY ORDERS BEFORE A DISTRICT COURT JUDGE

Article 848

In all urgent cases, a judge of the district court may, within the limits of his/her powers, issue summary orders regarding matters not subject to serious objections or which ought to be made because of a dispute.

Article 849

A judge of the district court may at any time, even when faced with serious objections, order in summary proceedings such protective measures or such measures as are necessary to maintain the status quo of matters or to protect against any impending damage, or to stop a clearly illegal nuisance.

In cases where the existence of the claim is not seriously contested, the judge may grant an interim payment to the creditor or order the specific performance of the obligation even where it is an obligation to do something.

Article 849-1

At the request of one of the parties, and if justified by urgency, a judge in chambers may send a matter to a hearing on a date that he/she sets so that a decision may be made on the substantive issue. He/she shall ensure that the defendant has sufficient time to prepare his/her defence. The order constitutes the jurisdiction of the court.

Article 850

A judge of the district court shall exercise the same powers over disputes arising out of employment contracts when they fall within his/her jurisdiction.

SUB-TITLE III
EX PARTE ORDERS BEFORE A DISTRICT COURT JUDGE

Article 851

A judge of the district court assumes jurisdiction by way of an *ex parte* application in the circumstances as prescribed by law.

Further to an *ex parte* application he/she may equally provide for, within the confines of his/her powers, any such urgent orders where the circumstances so demand that they are not handled with all the parties present.

Article 852

The *ex parte* application shall be remitted or addressed to the court registry office by the plaintiff or by any person acting on his/her behalf.

SUB-TITLE IV
THE PROCEDURE ON A REFERRAL FROM A CRIMINAL COURT

Article 852-1

Where a matter has been referred to a judge under the conditions prescribed under the second paragraph of Article 470-1 and under Article R-41-1 of the Code of

Criminal Procedure, the court registry office shall, by registered mail with acknowledgment of receipt, summon to a hearing, at least a month before its date, the parties to the civil proceedings who appeared before the criminal court as well as third parties who are liable in the referral decision. The court registry office shall on the same day send to the same individuals a copy of the summons by regular mail. The summons, to which is annexed a copy of the referral decision, shall be the same as a summons to appear before a court of law.

The summons shall state that, even if the parties fail to appear, provisionally enforceable decisions may be entered against them except for the victim of the injury as well as against third parties mentioned in the decision to refer.

The social security bodies and the motor insurance fund, where they have made an appearance before the criminal court, shall be called to appear at the same hearing by way of registered mail with acknowledgment of receipt sent by the court registry office. A copy of the referral decision shall be annexed to the summons.

At the hearing, matters shall be dealt with as set out in Articles 840 to 844. The president of the court may, further to summary proceedings, order interim payments in the manner provided under the second paragraph of Article 849.

TITLE III
SPECIFIC PROVISIONS RELATING TO THE COMMERCIAL COURT

Article 853

The parties shall plead their cases themselves.

They shall have the right to be assisted or represented.

The representative, where he/she is not an attorney, must demonstrate a specific authority to act.

Chapter I
The Procedure Before the Commercial Court

Section I
Commencing the Proceedings

Article 854

The action is brought by writ, the filing of a joint application at the court registry or by the voluntary appearance of the parties before the court.

Sub-Section 1
The Writ

Article 855

The writ must, at the risk of it being declared invalid, further specify the particulars prescribed under Article 56:

1. the place, date and time of the hearing at which the conciliation shall be attempted where that has not already taken place, and where relevant, the matter shall be decided.

2. where the defendant resides outside the jurisdiction, the family name, first names and address of the person at whose place he/she has elected to reside in France.

The originating process shall furthermore specify the conditions under which the defendant may be assisted or represented, as well as, where necessary, the name of the defendant's representative.

Article 856

The writ must be served at least fifteen days before the hearing date.

Article 857

The court assumes jurisdiction, at the request of one or the other party, by the filing of a copy of the writ at the court registry.

The filing shall take place at least eight days before the hearing date.

Article 858

In urgent cases, the time limit for appearing and filing the writ may be shortened by leave of the president of the court.

In maritime or aviation matters, the writ may be served, even contemporaneously, without the leave of the president when there are parties not resident within the jurisdiction or where the writ concerns urgent and interlocutory matters.

Sub-Section 2
The Joint Application and the Voluntary Appearance of the Parties

Article 859

The parties may present their claim by a joint application; they may also appear voluntarily before the court in order to decide the matter.

Article 860

The court assumes jurisdiction either by the filing of the joint application or by the signing of an official document recording that the parties have appeared voluntarily in order to have their claims determined.

The official document shall include the particulars required in relation to joint application under Article 57.

Section II
The Court Proceedings

Article 861

Where the matter is not ready for trial, the panel of judges shall schedule the matter for trial on a later date or shall request that one of its members prepare it for trial as a preparing judge.[21]

Sub-Section 1
The Preparing Judge

Article 862

The preparing judge may meet with the parties.

He/she may invite them to provide such explanations as he/she deems necessary for the resolution of the dispute or order them to produce, within such time as he/she shall decide, such relevant documents or exhibits as would provide guidance to the court, failing which, they may be disregarded and the matter may be scheduled before the bench which may draw any inferences it chooses in relation to the abstention or refusal by a party to provide explanations or to produce relevant documents or exhibits.

Article 863

The preparing judge shall enter on record any conciliation between the parties, even where the same is partial.

Article 864

The preparing judge may order a joinder or a disjoinder of proceedings.

---

21 The French term is "juge rapporteur". In the Commercial Court, this is the judge who directs preparations for the trial of a case. Thus, in this instance, I have translated the term as "preparing judge" but *see note* 21.

Article 865

The preparing judge may even of his/her own initiative make any directions he/she deems necessary.

He/she shall rule on any difficulties regarding the service of documents.

He/she shall record the termination of the proceedings. In that case, he/she shall, where necessary, rule upon any taxable costs.

Article 866

The directions provided for by the preparing judge shall be recorded by simple notes on the court's file. A notice of the same shall be given to the parties.

However, in the cases referred to in the preceding Article, the preparing judge rules by an order giving reasons, subject to the specific rules that are particular to procedural direction.

Article 867

The orders of a preparing judge are not the final authority, with reference to the main issue.

Article 868

The orders of a preparing judge shall not be subject to appeal independently of the substantive judgment on the matter.

However, they may be subject to appeal, either in the cases and under the conditions set down for expert opinions or within fifteen days from the date on which they record the termination of the proceedings.

Article 869

The preparing judge may, where the parties do not object, sit alone to hear the closing speeches. He/she must report them to the court in his/her summing up.

In other cases, he/she refers the matter back to the court as soon as the pre-trial management of the same will permit.

Sub-Section 2
General Provisions

Article 870

Unless the matter has been tried at a first hearing, the registrar shall advise the parties who have not been advised of the date of the subsequent hearings verbally, by regular mail.

Article 871

The procedure shall be conducted orally.

The claims of the parties or the references which they may make to any written submissions shall be noted down on the court's record or taken down in the form of an official document.

Chapter II
The Powers of the President

Section I
Summary Orders

Article 872

In all urgent cases, the president of a Commercial Court may, within the limits of the court's jurisdiction, order in summary proceedings any measures that do not meet with a serious objection or which are justified by the existence of a dispute.

Article 873

The president may within the same limits, even where faced with serious objections, order in summary proceedings such protective measures or such measures as are necessary to maintain the status quo of matters or to protect against any impending damage, or to stop a clearly illegal nuisance.

Where liability deriving from an obligation cannot seriously be challenged, the judge may award an interim payment to the creditor or order specific performance of the obligation.

Section II
Ex Parte Orders

Article 874

The president of the Commercial Court shall assume jurisdiction on an *ex parte* application in these cases as provided by law.

Article 875

He/she may also, pursuant to an *ex parte* application, and within the limits of the powers of the court, order any urgent directions where the circumstances require that they should not be made in the presence of all the parties.

Article 876

In urgent cases, the *ex parte* application may be presented at the president's residence or at the place where he/she practices professionally.

Chapter III
Miscellaneous Provisions

Article 877

The Commercial Courts do not have jurisdiction to enforce their judgments.

Article 878

The president of a Commercial Court may delegate to one or more members of the court part or all of the powers that are conferred upon him/her under this Title.

TITLE IV
SPECIFIC PROVISIONS RELATING TO INDUSTRIAL RELATIONS TRIBUNALS

Article 879

The specific provisions relating to industrial relations tribunals are the following Articles of the Labor Code:

"BOOK 5
INDUSTRIAL DISPUTES

Chapter VI
Procedure Before the Industrial Relations Tribunal

Article R.516-0

Court procedures dealing with employment matters shall be governed by the provisions of Book I of the New Code of Civil Procedure subject to the provisions of the present Code.

Section I
Admissibility of Claims

Article R. 516-1

Any claim arising out of a contract of employment must, whether it is made by the applicant or the defendant, be joined into one single action, unless the basis of the claims arose or became apparent after the industrial relations tribunal assumed jurisdiction.

Article R. 516-2

New claims arising out of the same contract of employment shall be admissible at any stage of the proceedings, even on appeal, notwithstanding the fact that there has been no attempt at conciliation.

Industrial relations tribunals matters shall recognize any counter-claim or pleas for compensation which, by their nature, are within their jurisdiction, even when raised on appeal.

Article R. 516-3

In employment matters, the proceedings shall only be time barred where the parties fail to implement, within a time limit of two years as referred to in Article 386 of the New Code of Civil Procedure, the steps which are expressly assigned to them by the court.

Section II
Assistance and Representation of Parties

Article R. 516-4

The parties are obliged to appear in person unless a representative is legally acting on their behalf.

They may be assisted.

Article R. 516-5

The persons empowered to assist or represent parties in employment matters shall be:

- employees or employers in the same type of work;
- delegates, whether permanent or non-permanent, of trade unions or of employers' association;
- spouses;
- attorneys.

An employer may also be assisted or represented by a member of the undertaking or establishment.

Before the court of appeal, the parties may also be assisted or represented by an appeal advocate.

Article R. 516-6

The proceedings shall be oral.

Article R. 516-7

The claims of the parties or references they make to written submissions shall be noted in the court record or in the form of an official document.

Section III
Assumption of Jurisdiction by the Industrial Relations Tribunal

Article R. 516-8

The industrial relations tribunal assumes jurisdiction either by an application, or by the voluntary presentation of the parties to the conciliation office.

The assumption of jurisdiction by the industrial relations tribunal, even where it lacks jurisdiction, shall suspend the running of limitation periods.

Article R. 516-9

An application shall be brought to the registry of the industrial relations tribunal. It may be sent by registered mail.

It must specify the family names, occupations and addresses of the parties as well as the various grounds at issue. The registry shall immediately send an acknowledgment of the same to the applicant.

The acknowledgment, or a document attached to it, shall quote relevant sections of Articles R.516, R.516-5 and R.516-13 to R.516-20-1.

Article R. 516-10

The registry, either orally on the presentation of the application or by pre-paid regular mail, shall advise the applicant of the place, date and time at the office for conciliation on which the matter shall be heard and shall invite him/her to bring along useful documentation.

Article R. 516-11

The registry shall summon the defendant to the office for conciliation by registered mail with acknowledgment of receipt. On the same day, he/she shall send a copy of that summons by regular mail.

The summons to the defendant must indicate the name, occupation and place of residence of the defendant, the place, date and time on which the matter shall be heard, as well as the grounds of the claim. It shall also inform the defendant that decisions which are provisionally enforceable may, in his/her absence be pronounced against him/her by the office for conciliation on the examination of only the exhibits advanced by his/her opponent. The summons shall invite the defendant to bring along any useful documentation. This summons, or any document attached to it, shall quote relevant sections of Articles R. 516-4, R. 516-5 and R. 516-13 to R. 516-20-1.

Article R. 516-12

The summons of the defendant to the office for conciliation shall be the same as a summons to appear before a court of law, subject to the provisions of the second paragraph of Article R. 516-8.

Section IV
The Office for Conciliation

Article R. 516-13

The office for conciliation shall hear the parties' submissions and shall endeavor to conciliate them. A report shall be drawn up.

Article R. 516-14

Where there is total or partial conciliation, the report shall mention the terms of the agreement. When a conciliation has taken place, it shall specify that the agreement has been the subject in whole or in part of an immediate enforcement before the office for conciliation.

Article R. 516-15

In the absence of a complete conciliation, the issues that are still in dispute and the declarations of the parties in relation to these issues must be noted in the file or in the report drawn by the registrar under the supervision of the president.

Article R. 516-16

If on the date set for the attempt at conciliation, the applicant does not appear without having providing a lawful excuse in due time, the office for conciliation shall declare that the application and summons have lapsed. The application may only be presented again once, unless the office for conciliation, instructed without any formality, states that the applicant has been unable to appear at the second summons owing to an event beyond his control.

Article R. 516-17

If, on the date set for the attempt at conciliation, the defendant does not appear, the office for conciliation shall proceed as indicated under Article R. 516-20, acting under the powers conferred upon it by virtue of Article R. 516-18.

However, where the defendant has within the allotted time demonstrated a lawful impediment excusing his/her absence, he/she shall be summoned by regular mail to a subsequent session of the office for conciliation.

Where it appears that the defendant has not been properly served at the first hearing, the office for conciliation shall decide that he/she shall be called again to a subsequent session, either by registered mail with acknowledgment of receipt from the registry, or by the process of a court bailiff at the request of the applicant. This process must be served within six months of the decision of the office for conciliation, or the application will lapse.

Article R. 516-18

The office for conciliation may, notwithstanding any procedural defenses or the failure of the defendant to appear may order:

- the provision, where relevant and subject to a fine, of a certificate of employment, pay slips and such other items that the employer shall be bound legally to provide;
- when the existence of the obligation cannot seriously be challenged, the office for conciliation may order interim payments in respect of salaries and other incidental payments, commissions and paid holidays, indemnities on termination of a contract provided in Article L. 122-3-5, the indemnity provided in IV of Article L. 122-3-8, the indemnity provided in Article L. 122-32-6- an unemployment indemnity as provided in Article L, 124-4-4. The total amount of these sums, which must be quantified by the office for conciliation, cannot exceed six months' salary based on the average of the three last salaries;
- any direction, on its own motion;
- any direction necessary for the preservation of items of evidence or objects in dispute.

The office for conciliation may quantify, provisionally, the fine that it has ordered.

Where this Article is applied, and in derogation from the provisions of the last sentence of Article R. 515-1, the sittings of the office for conciliation are open to the public.

Article 516-19

Decisions made under Article R. 516-18 shall always be provisional; they shall have the effect of being final as regards the main action. They shall be enforceable, where this is provided for and where appropriate, in the minutes. They shall not be subject to an objection. They may be appealed or be petitioned to the Court of Cassation at the same time as the judgment on the merits, subject to the specific rules in relation to expert opinions.

Article 516-20

When the applicant and the defendant are present or are represented and the matter is ready for trial without the appointment of one of the two chairman or the need for a direction, the office for conciliation shall set the matter before the trial office. The parties may be convened before this office orally with a marginal note of the same having been entered on the file; in the latter event, a memorandum indicating the date of the hearing shall be remitted to them by the registrar.

When the matter is able to be determined immediately, and when the court calendar so allows, the office for conciliation may, subject to the approval of all parties, ask them to appear at a hearing which the trial office shall hold immediately.

When the defendant has not appeared and the need for an investigation or a direction does not appear necessary beforehand, the office for conciliation shall refer the matter to the trial office. The applicant may be called before the latter office verbally, a marginal note of the same having been entered on the file; in the latter case, a notice indicating the date of the hearing shall be sent to him/her by the registrar.

Article R. 516-20-1

The office for conciliation may fix the time limit for exchanges documents or notes that the parties intend to submit in support of their contentions.

Section V
The Rapporteur[22]

Article R. 516-21

For the purpose of putting the matter in good order for trial, the office for conciliation or the trial office may, by virtue of a decision which shall not be subject to appeal, appoint one or more rapporteurs in order to compile the information needed for the industrial relations tribunal to make a ruling.

One or two rapporteurs may equally be appointed by the summary proceedings panel, in order to compile the information necessary for a decision by this panel.

The decision appointing one or two rapporteurs shall fix a time limit for the completion of their assignment.

Article R. 516-22

A rapporteur is an adviser to the industrial relations tribunal. He/she may be part of the panel making a judgment.

Where two rapporteurs are appointed in the same matter, one must be an employer, and the other an employee. They work together on their assignment.

22 The French term “rapporteur” refers to the person, who may under certain circumstances be a judge, who is in charge of a particular matter before a court, tribunal or commission. The term is now usually translated as “rapporteur”.

Article R. 516-23

A rapporteur may hear the parties.

He/she may invite them to submit any explanations that he/she deems necessary for the resolution of the dispute and put them on notice to produce any documents or explanations appropriate to help the industrial relations tribunal within a time limit which he/she shall decide, failing which he/she may disregard them and refer the matter to the trial office which may draw whatever inference it chooses from the abstention or refusal by a party.

He/she may hear any person whose testimony appears useful to the establish the truth, as well as implement him/herself or order the implementation of such directions as are necessary.

Article R. 516-24

Where the parties are conciliated, even partially, the rapporteur shall, in a report record the terms of the agreement reached.

Article R. 516-25

Decisions made by the rapporteur shall always be provisional and shall not be final as regards the main action. They shall be immediately enforceable, and can only be subject to an appeal of the judgment on the merits, subject to the rules specific to expert opinions.

Section VI
The Judgment

Article R. 516-26

Unless they have been summoned orally, with a marginal note having been entered on the file, the parties must be summoned to the trial office by registered mail with acknowledgment of receipt addressed by the registry which on the same date shall send the parties a copy of the summons by regular mail.

The summons must indicate the names, occupations and addresses of the parties, the place, date and time of the hearing, as well as the point in issue.

If on the date set for the hearing, the defendant does not appear, the matter shall be considered on its merits.

However, when the defendant, within the allotted time frame, has excused his/her absence due to a lawful impediment, he/she shall be summoned to a subsequent session of the trial office by registered letter.

When it appears that the defendant has not been properly served in the first hearing, the trial office must decide that he/she shall be summoned again to a subsequent hearing either by registered mail with acknowledgment of receipt, or by the process of a court bailiff at the request of the applicant.

Article R. 516-26-1

In the case where the trial office declares that the summons has lapsed by virtue of the application of Article 468 of the New Code of Civil Procedure, the request may be renewed once.

It shall be made directly to the trial office in the manner prescribed in Article R. 516-26.

Article R. 516-27

If the parties are conciliated, even partially, the trial office shall record the terms of the agreement reached in a report.

When it appears necessary, the report must specify that the agreement shall be the subject in part or in whole to immediate enforcement by the trial office.

Article R. 516-28

Decisions of the trial office must be reached by a majority vote.

When a majority cannot be reached, the matter shall proceed as in cases of equality of votes. Oral pleadings must be resumed.

Article R. 516-29

At the end of oral arguments and when a decision has not been given immediately, the date on which the judgment shall be given must be indicated to the parties either by way of a marginal note entered on the file or by the registrar sending a notice of the same.

Section VII
Summary Orders of Industrial Relations Tribunals

Article R. 516-30

In all urgent cases, the summary procedure panel may, within the scope of its powers as advisers to the industrial tribunal, order any directions that may not be seriously objected to or that may be necessary by virtue of a dispute.

Article R. 516-31

The summary procedure panel, even if faced with serious objections, may order protective measures in order to maintain the status quo, either by preventing an impending damage, or by stopping a nuisance which is obviously illegal.

When the existence of an obligation cannot seriously be challenged, it may award an interim payment to the creditor or order the performance of an obligation even when it is an obligation to do something.

Article 516-32

An application for a summary order must be brought, at the applicant's discretion, either by process through a court bailiff, or under the conditions provided in Article R. 516-8. Where the application is made through a court bailiff, a copy of the writ must be filed at the registry of the industrial tribunal no later than the day before the hearing; when the application is made in the manner set out in Article R. 516-8, the provisions of Articles R. 516-9 to R. 516-11 shall apply.

The internal rules of the industrial relations tribunal shall set the days and hours of business for summary proceedings. Provisions must be made for at least one hearing per week. When the circumstances require, the president of the industrial tribunal, shall, after having asked the vice-president to give his/her advice, fix one or more supplementary hearings or change the dates and times for the hearing or hearings during the week.

Article R. 516-33

Articles 484, 486 and 488 to 492 of the New Code of Civil Procedure shall apply in summary proceedings regarding employment matters.

When it appears that the summary procedure panel lacks jurisdiction in relation to the claim brought before it, and when the application is urgent, it may, with the agreement of all the parties and after having itself attempted a conciliation behind closed doors and in accordance with the rules laid down under Articles R. 516-13 to R. 516-15, refer the matter to the trial office. The notification to the parties of the summary procedure order stating the date of the hearing before the trial office, shall be equivalent to a summons to appear before a court of law.

Article R. 516-34

The time limit for an appeal is be fifteen days.

Article R. 516-35

The appeal must be brought, managed and decided as set out in Articles R. 517-7 to 517-9.

Section VIII
The Enforcement of Judgments

Article R. 516-36

Industrial relations tribunals cannot enforce their judgments.

Article R. 516-37

The following are provisionally enforceable:

- judgments which shall only be subject to appeal pursuant to a counter-claim;
- judgments ordering the issue of a certificate of employment, salary slips or such documents which the employer is bound to provide;
- judgments ordering the payment of sums by way of remuneration and indemnity stated in Article R. 516-18, up to nine months salary, to be calculated on the average of the last three salaries. This average shall be stated in the judgment.

Section IX
Common and Miscellaneous Provisions

Article R. 516-38

Procedural defenses must, at the risk of otherwise being inadmissible, be raised before any defense on the merits or a plea seeking a summary declaration of inadmissibility. They may still, subject to this proviso, be raised before the trial office.

Article R 516-39

The rapporteur or the trial office may give such directions as are necessary for the protection of items of evidence or in relation to objects in dispute.

Article R. 516-40

In the case of an equality of votes, the matter shall be scheduled to a subsequent hearing before the office for conciliation or the trial office, presided by the decision judge with a casting vote, which must be held within the month of the setting down.

In the case of an equality of votes from the summary procedure panel, the matter must be scheduled for a hearing presided by the decision judge, which hearing must be held without any delay and no later than fifteen days from being scheduled.

When an adviser to the industrial relations tribunals is prevented from sitting at a decision hearing, he/she shall provide for his/her replacement with another adviser to the industrial relations tribunals of the of the same department, and attached, where applicable, to his/her section, particular court or summary procedure panel.

If he/she does not provide for his/her replacement, the president or vice-president with jurisdiction over his/her section or his/her particular court or of his/her body, may provide for the replacement under the same conditions.

An adviser to the industrial relations tribunal or, if circumstances require, the president or vice-president shall immediately advise the registry of this replacement.

Before the trial office, replacements are only possible within the same branch of the industrial relations tribunal to which the adviser was assigned.

If, at the hearing that renders the decision, the bench does not sit in full, the judge rendering the decision, at the end of oral argument, decides alone regardless of the number of members of the industrial relations tribunal present and even in the absence of any such members, after having heard the opinion of the advisers present.

The provisions of Article R.516-29 shall apply to judgments given where the panel is presided by the decision judge.

Article R. 516-41

When a conciliation has been reached, extracts of the official record which state whether there has been any immediate partial or total enforcement of the agreement, may be published. This document is enforceable.

Article R. 516-42

Decisions in employment matters shall be sent to the parties' actual addresses by the registry office of the industrial relations tribunal or the court of appeal, by registered mail with acknowledgment of receipt without prejudicing the right of the parties to be served by a court bailiff.

The parties shall be advised of judicial administrative directions verbally with a marginal note entered on the file, or by regular mail.

Article R. 516-43

In all cases where, by virtue of the legislative provisions in force, the district court is asked to hear an employment matter, an applications must be brought, managed and decided in accordance with the rules provided herein. In the case of an appeal, the matter shall proceed as for employment matters.

Article R. 516-44

If a general renewal of the advisers to the industrial relations tribunal makes it impossible refer a matter, which, in accordance with the provisions in first paragraph of Article L. 515-3, has produced an equality of votes prior to said renewal, the matter shall be resumed before the office for conciliation, the trial office or the summary procedure panel, newly constituted, under the presidency of the decision judge.

Section X
Specific Provisions for Disputes in Cases of Dismissal for Redundancy

Article 516-45

In case of appeals on a dismissal for redundancy, the employer must, within eight days of the receipt of the summons to appear before the office for conciliation, lodge or send by registered mail with acknowledgment of receipt to the registry of the industrial relations tribunal, the particulars referred to under Article L. 122-14-3 so that they may recorded on the file of the industrial relations tribunal. The summons sent to the employer shall remind him/her of this obligation.

Article R. 516-46

The session for conciliation referred to in Article R. 516-13 must be held within the month in which the industrial relations tribunal has been informed of the appeal.

Article R. 516-47

The office for conciliation shall specify the time limit and directions necessary for the management of the case or to provide such information to the advisers, after having asked the parties to submit their views, and shall fix the time limit for the exchange of documents or notes upon which the parties intend to rely in support of their contentions. Directions and investigations must be implemented within three months. This time limit may only be extended by the trial office when the appointed person or the rapporteur requests it by means of a reasoned application.

The office for conciliation shall fix the date of the hearing before the trial office, which will rule upon the matter within a time limit not exceeding six months from the date on which the matter was referred it.

Article R. 516-48

If, at the session for conciliation, a section of the industrial relations tribunal is informed by more than one applicant challenging the procedure by which they have been made redundant when the dismissal was on a collective basis, the office for conciliation shall order the joinder of these applications.

Chapter VII
Jurisdiction of Industrial Relations Tribunals and Rights of Recourse Against Their Decisions

Section I
Jurisdiction

Article R. 517-1

The industrial relations tribunal which is territorially competent to hear a dispute is the one within whose judicial district the commercial premises are situated or the employment carried out.

When employment is carried out outside any commercial premises or at home, the application must be brought before the industrial relations tribunal where the employee resides.

An employee's application may always be brought before the industrial relations tribunal within whose jurisdiction the employment contract was entered into or the place of employment located.

Any clause that directly or indirectly deviates from the preceding provisions shall be deemed to be unwritten.

Article R. 517-2

Matters shall be distributed among the branches of the industrial relations tribunal according to the rules set out in Article L. 512-2 and which govern the designation of employees to the various branches.

In cases of an obstacle or challenge to the recognition by a section, and irrespective of the stage of the procedure when this obstacle is met or this challenge is made, the file shall be sent to the president of the industrial relations tribunal, who, after the vice-president has given his/her opinion, shall allocate the matter to a branch which he/she shall designate by an order not open to appeal.

Section II
Exercising Rights Of Recourse

Article R. 517-3

The industrial relations tribunal shall rule in the last resort:

1. When the amount of the claim does not exceed a sum fixed by decree.

2. When the claim seeks the issuance, even under a fine, of a certificate of employment, of salary slips and of such other documents that an employer shall be bound to provide, unless the judgment shall be of first resort by reason of the amount of the other claims.

Article R. 517-4

A judgment is not be subject to appeal where none of the grounds of the original or additional claims exceeds in itself the sum up to which the industrial relations tribunal has jurisdiction as a court of last resort.

Where one of the grounds of the claim is only susceptible of judgment subject to appeal, the industrial relations tribunal rules on all the heads of the claim as a court of first instance.

A judgment is not subject to appeal where only the counter-claim for damages, where it is based exclusively on the original claim, exceeds the sum up to which the tribunal has jurisdiction as a court of last resort.

Article R. 517-5

When a counter-claim which has been considered to be groundless and which has had the effect of rendering the judgment subject to appeal, the court may order a fine of 15€ to 500€ against the party concerned without prejudice to any damages which might be claimed.

Section III
Objections

Article R. 517-6

Objections must be made directly to the trial office.

The provisions of Articles R. 516-8 to R. 516-11 shall apply.

Objections shall lapse if the party making them does not appear. Objections cannot be renewed.

Section IV
Appeal

Article R. 517-7

The time limit for appeals shall be one month.

Appeals shall be filed by a declaration made by the party or any representative, or sent by registered letter, to the court registry office which rendered the judgment.

The declaration must indicate the family name, first name, occupation and address of the appellant as well as the name and address of the parties against whom the appeal is brought. It must specify the judgment against which the appeal is made and must state, where appropriate, the issues of the judgment to which it is limited, as well as the name and address of the appellant's representative before the court.

Article R. 517-8

Appeals must be brought before the social chamber of the court of appeal.

Article R. 517-9

Appeals must be brought, managed and decided in accordance with the procedure for non-mandatory representation.

Section V
Appeal to the Court of Cassation

Article R. 517-10

In employment matters, appeals to the Court of Cassation must be brought, prepared and determined in accordance with the procedure for dispensing with the assistance of an attorney at the Council of State[23] and at the Court of Cassation.

Chapter VIII
Challenges

Article R. 518-1

The procedure for challenging an adviser to the industrial relations tribunal shall be governed by Articles 341 to 355 of the New Code of Civil Procedure.

Article R. 518-2

Where the application for a challenge is brought before the court of appeal, it shall be determined before the social chamber."

---

23 The Council of State vets proposed legislation and gives its opinion on it to the government. It is also the highest administrative court in the French judicial hierarchy, to which appeals may be made from the administrative courts in the same way as other courts appeal to the Court of Cassation—*see* note 8.

TITLE V
SPECIFIC PROVISIONS RELATING TO THE JOINT TRIBUNAL FOR RURAL LEASES

Chapter I
The Ordinary Procedure

Article 880

The competent Joint Tribunal for Rural Leases shall be the one in whose locality the property is situated.

Article 881

Where the Joint Tribunal for Rural Leases consist of two sections, the matter shall be brought before the competent section in consideration of the type of contract binding the parties.

However, where a section of the court cannot sit or conduct its business, the matter shall be brought before the other section.

Article 882

The applicable procedure before the Joint Tribunal for Rural Leases shall be the one applicable for the district court subject to the provisions that follow.

Article 883

The parties are bound to appear in person, but may be represented where there is legitimate reason.

However, they may be assisted.

Article 884

Individuals entitled to assist or represent the parties are:

– an attorney

– a court bailiff

– a member of their family

– a member of a professional agricultural organization.

Article 885

An application must be brought and a court informed by a registered mail with acknowledgment of receipt or by a document from the court bailiff addressed to the court registry office.

Applications which must be recorded in the property registry must be made through a document from the court bailiff.

Article 886

The clerk of the court shall summon the parties by registered mail with acknowledgment of receipt, fifteen days before the date fixed by the president of the court. He/she shall on the same day send them a copy of the summons by regular mail.

Article 887

On the specified date, an attempt at conciliation shall be made before the court, a transcript of which shall be recorded.

In cases of non-conciliation, the transcript must specify the ways of resolving the contention as proposed on a majority vote.

In cases of non-appearance by one of the parties, his/her absence shall be recorded in the transcript.

Article 888

Where the conciliation fails, or in cases of a non-appearance of one of the parties, the matter is scheduled for a hearing, the date of which shall be specified by the president to the parties present.

The parties who have not been advised verbally must be summoned in the manner and within the time set out in Article 886. The summons must state that where they fail to appear, a judgment may be entered against them based on the evidence produced by their opponent.

The court shall have the powers set out in Article 844.

Article 889

The nominated assessors, and where applicable, their deputies shall be called in accordance with Article 886.

Article 890

In the case of an absence or challenge of one of the assessors, he/she shall be immediately replaced by a substitute member of his/her team in the order of the votes obtained during the poll.

Article 891

The decisions of the Joint Tribunal for Rural Leases shall be sent in their entirety to the parties within three days by the clerk of the court, by registered mail with acknowledgment of receipt.

Article 892

The decisions of the Joint Tribunal for Rural Leases shall not be subject to an objection.

If they are subject to appeal, they shall be brought, managed and determined in accordance with the procedure for non-mandatory representation.

Chapter II
Summary Orders

Article 893

In all urgent cases, the president of the Joint Tribunal for Rural Leases may, within the limits of his/her powers, give by way of summary proceedings such directions to which no serious objections may be raised or which should be given by reason of a dispute.

Article 894

The president may, within the same limits and even where faced with serious objections, order by way of summary proceedings such protective measures or such directions to maintain the status quo of the matters, as necessary, either to protect against an impending damage, or to stop a clearly illegal nuisance.

Where the existence of the obligation may not seriously be contested, he/she may award an interim payment to the creditor or provide for the specific performance of the obligation even where it shall be in the nature of an obligation to do something.

Article 895

Repealed.

Article 896

The time limit for filing an appeal shall be fifteen days.

The appeal must be brought, managed and decided in the manner set out in Article 892.

Chapter III
Ex Parte Orders

Article 897

The president of the Joint Tribunal for Rural Leases assumes jurisdiction by way of an *ex parte* application in cases specified by law.

He/she may also order, by means of an *ex parte* application, within the confines of the jurisdiction of the court, any necessary urgent measures orders where the circumstances require that they should not be taken with all parties present.

Article 898

Where an *ex parte* application has not been successful, an appeal shall be brought, prepared and decided in the manner set out in Article 892.

The time limit for filing an appeal shall be fifteen days.

TITLE VI
SPECIFIC PROVISIONS RELATING TO THE COURT OF APPEAL

SUB-TITLE I
THE PROCEDURE BEFORE THE FULL COURT

Chapter I
The Procedure in Contentious Matters

Article 899

Parties are bound to retain an appeal advocate unless this is not required.

The appointment of the appeal advocate shall include the election of a place of residence.

Section I
The Procedure Where Representation by Counsel Is Mandatory

Article 900

An appeal may be brought by a unilateral declaration or by a joint application.

Sub-Section 1
The Ordinary Procedure

Article 901

A declaration of appeal must be made in a document which specifies, at the risk of it otherwise being invalid:

1. a) where the appellant is a natural person: his/her family name, first names, address, nationality, date and place of birth;

b) where the appellant is a legal person: its type, name, its registered office and the organ which will legally represent it;

2. the family name and first names of the respondent or where it is in relation to a legal person its name and its registered office;

3. the appointment of the appeal advocate for the appellant;

4. particulars of the judgment;

5. particulars of the court to which the appeal is being made.

The declaration must specify, where appropriate, the grounds of the judgment to which the appeal is limited and the name of the attorney appointed to assist the appellant before the court.

It shall be signed by the appeal advocate. It shall be accompanied by a copy of the decision. It has the same effect as a request to be put on the list.

Article 902

The declaration must be filed at the court registry office in as many copies as there are respondents, plus two.

The filing is recorded by the registration of its date and the stamp of the registrar of the court on each of the copies, one of which shall be immediately returned to the appellant.

Article 903

The registrar shall immediately send, by regular mail, to each of the respondents, a copy of the declaration with the statement that he/she needs to appoint an appeal advocate.

Where this copy is returned by the postal service, the registrar shall forward the same to the appeal advocate of the appellant, who shall proceed in the manner set out in Article 908.

Article 904

As soon as he/she is appointed, the appeal advocate of the respondent shall inform the appeal advocate acting for the appellant; a copy of the notice of acting shall be filed at the court registry office.

Article 905 - *Repealed.*

Article 906 - *Repealed.*

Article 907

The first president shall specify the particular chamber to which the matter shall be assigned.

Notice of the same shall be given by the court registry office to the appeal advocates of on record.

Article 908

Where, pursuant to a letter sent by the registrar, a party has not appointed any appeal advocate, the appellant shall summon him/her in order to serve upon him/her the declaration of appeal.

The summons must at the risk of it otherwise being invalid, state that where the respondent fails to appoint an appeal advocate within fifteen days, he/she shall be at risk that a judgment may be entered against him/her based purely on the grounds raised by his/her opponent.

Article 909

The pleadings must be served and documents exchanged between the appeal advocates of the parties; where there are several appellants or respondents, this must be done for all of the appeal advocates on record.

Copies of the pleadings must be filed at the court registry office with proof that they have been notified.

Article 910

The matter shall be prepared under the supervision of a judge of the particular court to which it has been assigned, in the manner prescribed in Articles 763 to 787 and with the following provisions.

Where a matter appears to be urgent or is ready to be heard or where the appeal relates to a summary order, the President of the court to which is has been assigned shall as soon as possible, on his/her own initiative or at the request of a party, fix the date and time when it shall be heard; on that day, the matter shall be handled in accordance with the procedure set out in Articles 760 to 762.

Article 911

The judge directing the preparations for trial is empowered to find that the appeal is inadmissible and to rule at the same time upon any question regarding the admissibility of the appeal.

Article 912

A judge directing the preparations for trial, where he/she has been informed of a matter, shall have exclusive jurisdiction to order stays of execution of judgments which have been wrongly described as final, or to exercise the powers conferred upon him/her in relation to provisional enforcement.

Article 913

Only appeal advocates shall be entitled to represent the parties and to submit pleadings on their behalf.

Notices or injunctive orders shall be validly served where they are addressed to the appeal advocates.

Attorneys shall be heard at their request.

Article 914

The orders of the judge directing the preparations for trial are not subject to any appeal independently of the judgment on the merits.

However, they may be referred to the court by way of a simple request within fifteen days of their date when they are intended to terminate the proceedings, where they record the termination of the proceedings, where they relate to interim measures in divorce or judicial separation proceedings, or where they rule upon pleas challenging jurisdiction, pleas of *lis alibi pendens* and of pleas against duplication.

Article 915

The appeal advocate for the appellant must, within four months of the declaration of appeal, file at the court his/her pleadings, unless the pre-trial judge has granted him/her a shorter period.

In default thereof, the matter shall be struck off the register by an order not subject to appeal, a copy of which must be sent to the appellant by regular mail addressed to his/her real domicile or residence. Such striking out shall remove any suspensive effect of the appeal, except where interim enforcement is prohibited by law.

The matter may be restored either by demonstrating that the pleadings have been filed on behalf of the appellant, whilst the appeal shall not operate any stay of execution, or at the request of one the respondents who may ask that the proceedings should be closed and that the matter should be scheduled for trial based on the pleadings in the trial at first instance.

Notwithstanding the preceding provisions, the time limit of four months granted for pleading a matter may be extended by the pre-trial judge in circumstances where an appeal advocate has been appointed under legal aid or appointed by an appellant to whom legal aid has been refused.

Article 916 - *Repealed.*

Sub-Section 2
Fixed Date Proceedings

Article 917

Where the rights of a party are at risk, the first president may, on request, fix a date where the matter shall be heard as a priority. He/she shall specify the particular court to which the matter shall be assigned.

The provisions of the preceding paragraph may also be invoked by the first president of the court of appeal or by the judge directing the preparations for trial pursuant to their powers conferred upon them in relation to summary proceedings or provisional enforcement.

Article 918

The application must indicate the nature of the risk, include the substantive plea and identify the exhibits. A certified copy of the decision or a certified true copy by the appeal advocate must be attached to it.

A copy of the application and the exhibits must be filed with the first president to be entered on the court file.

Article 919

The declaration of appeal must refer to the order of the first president.

Copies for the respondent shall be returned to the appellant.

The application may also be presented to the first president at latest within eight days of the declaration of appeal.

Article 920

The appellant shall summon the opposing party by writ to appear on the date specified.

Copies of the application, the order of the first president, and a copy of the declaration of appeal stamped by the clerk or a copy of the declaration of appeal in the manner prescribed in the third paragraph of Article 919, must be attached to the writ.

The writ informs the respondent that, in the event of a failure by him/her to appoint an appeal advocate before the date of the hearing, he/she shall be deemed to rely on the grounds which he/she argued at first instance.

The writ indicates to the respondent that he/she may examine a copy of the exhibits referred to in the application at the court registry office and gives him/her formal notice to make known before the date of the hearing, the new exhibits upon which he/she intends to rely.

Article 921

The respondent shall be bound to appoint an appeal advocate before the date of the hearing, failing which he/she shall be deemed to rely on the grounds he/she argued at first instance.

Article 922

The court acquires jurisdiction by the filing of a copy of the writ at the court registry office.

The filing must be done before the date fixed for the hearing, failing which the declaration shall lapse.

The lapse is recorded of his/her own initiative by an order of the president of the particular chamber to which the matter has been assigned.

Article 923

On the day of the hearing, the president shall ensure that sufficient time has elapsed since the writ for the party who is summoned to have be able to have prepared his/her defense. Where appropriate, he/she shall make an order for a fresh service of the writ.

Where the respondent has appointed an appeal advocate, the oral pleadings shall given immediately or at the next available hearing, at the stage the matter has reached.

Where the respondent has not appointed an appeal advocate, the court shall make an order that is deemed to have been made in the presence of all the parties, relying, where necessary on the grounds raised at first instance.

Article 924

The application for the setting of a hearing date may be presented by the respondent as long as the court of appeal has not assumed jurisdiction.

Article 925

Where necessary, the president of the court may refer the matter to the judge directing the preparations for trial.

Sub-Section 3
Appeal by Joint Application

Article 926

A joint application shall only be admissible where it is made by all the parties at first instance.

Article 927

In addition to the particulars prescribed in Article 57, the joint application must include, at the risk of it being otherwise inadmissible:

1. a certified true copy of the judgment;
2. where appropriate, the particulars of the head of judgments to which the appeal is limited;
3. the appointment of the appeal advocates of the parties.

The joint application must, where relevant, state, the name of the attorneys instructed to assist the parties before the court.

It shall be signed by the appeal advocates of record.

Article 928

The court acquires jurisdiction by the filing of the joint application at the court registry office. The filing must be made within the time-limit for an appeal.

Article 929

The first president shall set the date and time when the matter shall be heard; where necessary, he/she shall designate the particular chamber to which it shall be assigned.

Notice of the same shall be given to the appeal advocate of record.

Article 930

The matter shall be prepared and decided as in a shortened form of procedure.

Section II
The Procedure Where Representation by Counsel Is Not Mandatory

Article 931

The parties shall plead their cases by themselves.

They shall have the right to be assisted or represented in accordance with the rules applicable before the court which issued the judgment; they may also be assisted or represented by an appeal advocate.

The representative must, where he/she is not an attorney or appeal advocate, provide evidence of specific authority to act.

Article 932

The appeal is made by a declaration that the party or his/her agent must give, or sent by registered letter, to the court registry.

Article 933

The declaration must specify the family name, first names, occupation and address of the appellant as well as the name and address of the parties against whom the appeal is brought. It must specify the judgment against which the appeal is made and state, where appropriate, the name and address of the representative of the appellant before the court. It must be accompanied by a copy of the decision.

Article 934

The clerk shall record the date of the appeal; he/she shall issue, or send by regular mail, a simple receipt of the declaration.

Article 935 - *Repealed.*

Article 936

As soon as the formal steps have been complied with by the appellant, the clerk must by regular mail, advise the opponent of the appeal by informing him/her that he/she would eventually be summoned by the court.

Article 937

As soon as a hearing date has been set, the registrar of the court shall summon the parties to a hearing for the oral pleadings, notifying them fifteen days in advance by registered mail with acknowledgment of receipt and on the same day shall send by regular mail a copy of the summons.

The summons shall be the equivalent to a summons to appear before a court of law.

Article 938

Where it has become necessary to re-summon a party who has not been joined by the first summons, it may be ordered that the new summons shall be effected by done by a court bailiff.

Article 939

Where the matter is not in position to be heard, its preparation shall be given to a member of the chamber. The latter may have been designated before the hearing fixed for the oral pleadings.

Article 940

The judge entrusted to prepare the matter may hear the parties.

He/she may invite them to provide such explanations as he/she shall deem necessary for the resolution of dispute, and may order them to produce within such period as he/she shall decide such relevant documents or exhibits as might guide him/her, failing which, he/she may disregard them and refer the matter to the court which may draw any inference it may choose from the abstention or refusal by a party in relation to the above.

Article 941

The judge entrusted with the preparation of the matter shall enter on record any conciliation by the parties, even partial. He/she must enter on record the termination of the proceedings.

Article 942

The judge entrusted with the preparation of the matter shall rule upon any difficulties in relation to the service of documents.

He/she shall proceed with a joinder and a disjoinder of proceedings.

Article 943

The judge entrusted with the preparation of the matter may:

- give any procedural directions, even of his/her own initiative;
- where necessary and under the threat of a fine, order the production of documents which are in the possession of a party, or a third party where there is no lawful impediment to the same.

Article 944

The judge entrusted with the preparation of the matter may award an interim payment to the creditor where the existence of the debt is not seriously contestable, as well ordering any other interim direction.

Article 945

The decisions of the judge entrusted with the preparation of the matter shall not have the effect of being final as regards the main issue.

They shall not be subject to any appeal independently of the judgment on the merits.

They may however, be referred to the court by a simple request within fifteen days of their date where they have ruled on the termination of the proceedings.

Article 945-1

The judge entrusted with the preparation of the matter may, where the parties do not so object, sit alone to hear the oral pleadings. He/she shall report on his/her deliberations to the court.

Article 946

The procedure shall be carried out orally.

The claims of the parties or the references which they may make to any written submissions shall be recorded in the court's file or in the form of an official document.

Article 947

Unless the matter has been decided at the first hearing, the registrar shall advise by regular mail those parties who would not have been advised orally of the date of the subsequent hearings.

Article 948

A party whose rights are imperiled may, even when a date for the hearing has been set, request the first president to give the matter high priority for the next available date.

Where the request is granted, an plaintiff shall immediately be advised of the new date.

Unless the first president has decided that it should be done through service by a court bailiff at the request of the appellant, the registrar shall summon the opposing party by registered letter return receipt requested and on the same date shall send a copy of the summons to him/her by regular mail.

The court shall ensure that sufficient time has elapsed from the date of the summons and the hearing so that the summoned party has been able to prepare his/her defense.

Article 949

The notice and summons prescribed in Articles 936, 937, 947 and 948 shall be dispatched in the manner provided for in these provisions to the organizations which should be kept informed of the procedure by virtue of the law.

Chapter II
Procedure in Non-Contentious Matters

Article 950

An appeal against a non-contentious judgment must be made by a declaration delivered or sent by registered letter to the registry of the court which issued the decision, by an attorney or appeal advocate, or any other public officer where the latter is entitled to do so by the provisions in force.

Article 951

Repealed.

Article 952

A judge may, by virtue of that declaration, amend or withdraw his/her decision.

In contrary cases, the clerk of the court shall forward without delay to the court registry office the case file together with the declaration and a copy of the decision.

The judge must inform the party within one month of his/her decision to examine the matter afresh or to transfer it to the court.

Article 953

The appeal shall be prepared and decided in accordance with the rules applicable to non-contentious matters before the regional court.

Chapter III
Common Provisions

Article 954

The appeal submissions must specify clearly the contentions of the parties and the grounds in fact and law upon which they are based.

They should moreover include details of the exhibits in support. For this purpose a list of documents should be attached The parties must summarize in their final submissions, the allegations and evidence which have previously been raised or referred to in their earlier submissions In default thereof they shall be deemed to be abandoned, and the court shall only rule upon the last submissions which have been filed.

Parties pleading the reversal of a judgment must explicitly state the grounds relied upon without making any reference to their pleadings before the court of first instance.

A party, who without pleading new grounds, requests the confirmation of the judgment, shall be deemed to have accepted its findings.

Article 955

Where it confirms a judgment, the court shall be deemed to have adopted the findings of that judgment which are not contrary to its own findings.

Article 955-1

Where the court assumes jurisdiction by way of an application, the parties must be advised of the date of the hearing by the registrar.

Article 955-2

Notice is given either to the appeal advocates by simple memorandum, or, in matters where the assistance of the appeal advocate shall be dispensed with, to the parties by registered mail with acknowledgment of receipt.

A copy of the application must be attached to the notice sent to the appeal advocates or to the parties.

SUB-TITLE II
THE POWERS OF THE FIRST PRESIDENT

Chapter I
Summary Orders

Article 956

In urgent matters, the first president may, in appeal cases, make through summary proceedings such orders to which no serious objections may be raised or which ought to be given owing to a dispute.

Article 957

The first president may, in appeal cases, order a stay of execution of the judgments which have been wrongly termed as being of last resort, or exercise the powers conferred upon him/her in relation to provisional enforcement.

Chapter II
Ex Parte Orders

Article 958

The first president may, during the course of the appeal proceedings, order, on an application, any urgent directions in relation to the protection of the rights of a party or of a third party when the circumstances require that such orders should not be made in the presence of all the parties.

Article 959

The application shall be presented by an appeal advocate where the proceedings require the appointment of an appeal advocate.

SUB-TITLE III
MISCELLANEOUS PROVISIONS

Chapter I
Instruction of Appeal Advocates and Pleadings

Article 960

The instruction of an appeal advocate by the respondent or by any person who becomes a party in the course of the proceedings shall be notified to the other parties by way of notification between appeal advocates.

This document must specify:

a) where the respondent is a natural person, his/her family name, first names, occupation, address, nationality, date and place of birth;

b) where the respondent is a legal person, its type, name, registered office and the organ which shall represent it legally.

Article 961

Pleadings on behalf of the parties must be signed by their appeal advocates and must be served by way of notification between appeal advocates. They will not be admissible until the particulars referred to in paragraph 2 of the preceding Article have been provided.

The service of documents produced shall be validly acknowledged by the signature of the recipient appeal advocate attached to list of documents drafted by the attorney effecting service.

Article 962

The filing at the court registry of a copy of the document of instruction and the pleadings is done either once they are notified or, if the notification pre-dates the referral of the matter to the court, contemporaneously with the filing of the copy of the declaration.

Chapter II
Judicial Administration Measures

Article 963

The appointment of judges charged with directing preparations for trial must be made in the same way as for the allocation of judges to the different chambers within the court.

The first president and the presidents of the different chambers may exercise these powers.

Article 964

More than one judge may be entrusted with the preparation of a case in one chamber; in that case, actions shall be assigned between them by the president of the particular court.

The pre-trial judges may be replaced at any stage in case of any impediment.

Article 965

The first president may delegate part or all of the functions assigned to him/her under the Sub-Titles I and II, to one or more judges of the court.

The presidents of a chamber may even delegate to the judges of their chambers part or all of the functions assigned to them under Sub-Title I.

Chapter III
The Court Registry Office

Article 966

The filing of a copy of written pleadings or of any document at the court registry office shall be entered on the record by the statement of the date of filing and the registrar's stamp on the copy as well as on the original, which shall be returned immediately.

Article 967

A copy of the declaration, of the application and of the joint application shall, as from the date of its filing at the court registry office-registry, be submitted by the registrar to the first president for the formalities of setting a date and allocation.

The decision of the first president shall be recorded by a simple note in the margin of the copy.

Article 968

To the court's file must be attached the file of the court of first instance that the registrar shall request as soon as the court assumes jurisdiction.

Article 969

Where the proceedings are on a set date, the provisions in Article 824 shall be followed.

Article 970

The registrar shall immediately advise the appeal advocates of whose appointment he/she is aware, of the case number in the general register, of the dates and time fixed by the first president to for the matter to be heard and the particular chamber to which it has been assigned.

This notice shall be given to those appeal advocates whose appointment is not yet known, as from the filing at the court registry office of their instrument of instruction.

Article 971

The appeal advocates and the attorneys of each of the parties shall be summoned or advised of their duties by the president or the judge directing preparations for the trial, according to how the matter is being prepared; they shall be convened or advised verbally, with a marginal note and a record of this on the court's file.

In case of absence, they must be notified by a simple notice, dated and signed by the registrar, and served or left by him/her at the place at the court where notifications between appeal advocates are exchanged.

Injunctive decrees must always give rise to the issue of a note.

Article 972

Where the matter has been referred back to a court of first instance or where it is resumed before that court, the file shall be sent without delay by the registrar of the court to the clerk of the lower court.

Where the decision is not the subject of any appeal, the file of the court which decided the matter at first instance is returned to the clerk of that court.

In all cases, a copy of the decision of the court shall be attached to the file.

TITLE VII
SPECIFIC PROVISIONS RELATING TO THE COURT OF CASSATION

Article 973

The parties shall, except where the contrary is indicated, be obliged to appoint an attorney at the Council of State and the Court of Cassation.

This appointment shall include the election of domicile.

Chapter I
The Procedure Where Representation by Counsel Is Mandatory

Article 974

An application to the Court of Cassation shall be made by means of a declaration to the registry office of the Court of Cassation.

Article 975

The declaration of appeal is made in a document containing:

1. a) where the appellant is a natural person: his/her family name, first names, address, nationality, place and date of birth;

   b) where the appellant is a legal person: its type, name, its registered office and the organ which will represent it legally;

2. the family name and first names of the respondent or where it concerns a legal person its name and its registered office;

3. the appointment of the of the appellant's attorney at the Council of State and at the Court of Cassation;

4. particulars of the decision being appealed;

5. the status of the enforcement procedure, unless the enforcement of the appealed decision is prohibited by law.

The declaration must specify, where appropriate, the parts of the judgment to which the appeal is limited.

It shall be signed by the attorney at the Council of State and the Court of Cassation.

Article 976

The declaration must be filed at the court registry office in as many copies as there are respondents, plus two.

The filing is entered on record by its date and with the stamp of the registrar on each of the copies of which one shall be immediately returned.

Article 977

The registrar must immediately send to the respondent by regular mail a copy of the declaration with the statement that, where he/she intends to defend the application, he/she must instruct an attorney at the Council of State and the Court of Cassation.

He/she shall request simultaneously the production of the file from the registry of the court that gave the decision in dispute.

If the copy of the declaration is returned by the postal service, the registrar of the Court of Cassation shall forward the same forthwith to the appellant's attorney who shall forward it to the respondent while reminding the latter that, where he/she contemplates defending the application, he/she shall have to retain an attorney at the Council of State and the Court of Cassation.

Article 978

At the risk of the action being time barred, the appellant to the Court of Cassation must, not later than five months from the date of the appeal, file a statement containing the grounds in law against the decision under review at the registry office of the Court of Cassation and must serve the same on the respondent.

At the risk of having it declared inadmissible by the court, a ground or part of a ground in the statement must contain only one single ground of appeal. Each ground or part of a ground must specify, subject to the same sanction:

- the ground of appeal alleged;
- the part of the decision being criticized;
- on what basis the latter is impugned.

Article 979

At the risk of the appeal being declared inadmissible by the court, the following must be filed at the court registry within the time limit for filing the statement of grounds of appeal:

- a copy of the appealed decision and its method of service;
- a copy of the judgment, upheld or reversed, by the appeal court decision;
- any other judgment given in the same dispute and to which the appealed decision has referred.

The appellant must also attach these referred documents to the application.

Article 980

Where the respondent to the appeal has not instructed any attorney, service thereof shall be on the party directly.

The document of service must inform the respondent that, where he/she intends to contest the appeal, he/she must instruct an attorney at the Council of State and the Court of Cassation and must inform him/her that where he/she does not instruct an attorney, the judgment to be given cannot be subject to any objection. This document of service must furthermore specify the time limit within which the respondent must file his/her statement in reply, or where appropriate, his/her cross-appeal.

Article 981

In the absence of the filing or service of the statement of grounds of appeal within the period prescribed in the first paragraph of Article 978, a time bar is declared by order of the first president or his/her deputy.

Article 982

The respondent to the appeal shall have a period of three months from the service of the appellant's statement of grounds of appeal to file a pleading in reply, signed by an attorney at the Council of State and Court of Cassation at the registry office of the Court of Cassation, and to serve it on the attorney acting for the appellant by way of notification between attorneys.

The period referred to in the preceding paragraph is a strict limitation period, after which a statement in defense shall automatically be declared inadmissible.

Chapter II
The Procedure Where Representation by Counsel Is Not Mandatory

Article 983

The provisions of this Chapter shall apply to appeals made in matters in which by virtue of a specific legal provision, the parties do not require the assistance of an attorney at the Council of State and the Court of Cassation.

Article 984

The appeal to the Court of Cassation is made by an oral or written declaration that the party or any representative authorized to act must deliver or send by registered mail with acknowledgment of receipt to the registry of the Court of Cassation.

Article 985

The declaration must specify the family name, first names, occupation and address of the appellant, as well as the name and address of the respondents to the application. It must specify the decision being attacked. It must indicate the status of the enforcement procedure, unless the enforcement of the decision is prohibited by law.

Article 986

The registrar shall register the appeal. He/she must state the date on which it is made and must deliver, or send by registered mail with acknowledgment of receipt, an acknowledgment of the declaration, which shall quote the provisions of Articles 989 and 994.

Article 987

The registrar shall immediately send to the respondent a copy of the declaration by registered mail with acknowledgment of receipt.

Such notification must quote the wording of Articles 991 and 994.

The registrar shall request at the same time the production of the file from the registry of the court which gave the decision being attacked.

Article 988

The registrar of the court which has delivered the appealed decision, shall send without delay the court file to the registry of the Court of Cassation, to which shall be attached:

– a copy of the appealed decision and its method of service;

– a copy of the judgment, upheld or reversed, by the appeal court decision;

– any other judgment given in the same dispute and to which the appealed decision has referred.

The appellant must also attach these referred documents to the application.

Article 989

Where the declaration of appeal does not contain the grounds of appeal, even in summarized form, against the decision being attacked, the appellant, must, at the risk of a time bar being declared by an order of the first president or his/her deputy, file at the court registry no later than three months from the filing or the receipt of the receipt of the declaration, a statement containing such grounds, and, where appropriate, the exhibits supporting the appeal.

This statement may be drafted by the representative of the party without any fresh authority to act.

Article 990

Where a statement is produced by the appellant, the registrar of the Court of Cassation must without delay notify the respondent of the same by registered letter with acknowledgment of receipt.

Article 991

The respondent to the appeal shall have at his/her disposal a period of two months to be reckoned from the notification of the statement of grounds of appeal of the appellant or from the expiration of the period of three months prescribed under Article 989 to file, on the issuance of an acknowledgment, or to address by registered letter, to the registry office of the Court of Cassation a pleading in reply and to bring, should the occasion arise, a cross-appeal.

Article 992

The registrar of the Court of Cassation shall send, without any delay, a copy of the pleading in reply to the appellant by regular mail.

In case of a cross-appeal, he/she shall send, in the same manner, a copy of the statement of grounds of appeal referred to in the first paragraph of Article 1010.

Article 993

Where an attorney at the Council of State and Court of Cassation has declared to the court registry office that he/she is acting on behalf of a party, the notification referred to in Article 990 or in Article 992 shall be substituted for a notification provided to the latter attorney.

The delivery to the attorney, in return for a receipt, of a copy of the statement of the grounds of appeal bearing the date stamp of the court registry office shall be good notification.

Article 994

In addition to the original, the appellant must provide as many copies of his/her statement of grounds of appeal as there are respondents and the respondent must provide as many copies of the statement in reply as there are appellants.

These copies are to be certified true copies by the signatory of the statement.

Article 995

Where an appeal is brought in accordance with the rules relating to mandatory representation by counsel, it shall nevertheless be admissible irrespective of the procedural track followed afterwards.

The respondent is not obliged to be represented by an attorney at the Council of State and Court of Cassation.

Chapter III
The Procedure in Electoral Matters

Section I
Disputes in Relation to Registration on Electoral Rolls in Political Elections

Article 996

The specific provisions in relation to an appeal to the Court of Cassation shall be those of the Electoral Code as follows:

"Article R. 15-1

The appeal to the Court of Cassation must be made within ten days of the notification of the decision of the district court. It is available in all cases to the prefect. It does not have a suspensive effect.

Article R. 15-2

The appeal is made by an oral or written declaration that the party or any representative authorized to act shall make, deliver or send by registered letter either to the registry office of the court which gave the decision being reviewed or to the registry office of the Court of Cassation. The declaration must specify the family name, first names, occupation and address of the appellant, as well as the name and address of the respondent or respondents to the appeal.

At the risk of it being declared inadmissible, even by the court of its own motion, the declaration must contain a statement of the grounds of appeal relied upon and must attach a copy of the impugned decision.

Article R.15-3

The court registry office which receives the appeal shall proceed to register it in its records. It shall state the date on which the appeal is made and shall deliver, or send by regular mail, an acknowledgment of receipt of the declaration.

Where there is a respondent, the court registry office which receives the appeal shall immediately send a copy of the declaration by registered mail with acknowledgment of receipt to him/her. Such notification shall reproduce the provisions of Article R.15-5.

Article R.15-4

Where the appeal is brought before the district court, the registry office of that court shall send forthwith to the registry office of the Court of Cassation the file of the case with the declaration or a copy thereof, a copy of the impugned decision as well as the documents proving the notification of the latter, and where there is a respondent, the documents in relation to the notification of the appeal to the latter. He/she shall forward to the registry office of the Court of Cassation all documents that might reach him/her subsequently.

Where the appeal is made to the Court of Cassation, the registry office of the Court of Cassation shall immediately request the case file as well as the documents relating to the notification of the impugned decision from the registry office of the district court which gave the decision.

Article R.15-5

As soon as he/she has received a copy of the declaration of the appeal, the respondent to the appeal must deliver a pleading in reply without any delay in return for an acknowledgment of receipt or shall send it by registered letter to the registry office of the Court of Cassation. He/she shall also send a copy to the appellant.

Article R.15-6

Parties shall be dispensed of the need for of an attorney at the Council of State and the Court of Cassation. If the parties or any one of them retain an attorney at the Council of State and at the Court of Cassation to represent them or him/her, the provisions of Articles 974 to 982 of the New Code of the Civil Procedure shall not apply.

When an attorney at the Council of State and the Court of Cassation has declared to the registry office of the Court of Cassation that he/she is acting on behalf of a party, the notification of the copy of the statement of grounds may be given to that attorney, and where appropriate, by way of notification between attorneys. The delivery to the attorney, in return for an acknowledgment of receipt, of a copy of the statement, bearing the stamp of the court registry office, shall be good notification.

Article R.15-7

The time limits in Articles R. 13 and 15-1 are calculated or extended in accordance with the provisions of Articles 640, 641 and 642 of the New Code of Civil Procedure."

Article 997

Repealed.

Article 998

Repealed.

Section II
Trade Elections

Article 999

The time limit to file appeal before the Court of Cassation is ten days unless the contrary is indicated.

The appeal must be made by an oral or written declaration that the party or any representative authorized to act might make, deliver, or send by registered letter to the registry of the court which gave the decision being challenged.

Article 1000

The declaration must specify the family name, first names, occupation and address of the appellant, as well as the name and address of the respondent or respondents to the appeal. It must specify the decision being challenged.

Article 1001

The clerk shall register the appeal. He/she shall state the date on which it is brought and shall deliver, or send by regular mail, an acknowledgment of the declaration, which reproduces the provisions of Articles 1004 and 1006.

Article 1002

The clerk shall immediately send to the respondent a copy of the declaration by registered letter.

Such notification shall reproduce the provisions of Article 1006.

Article 1003

The clerk shall without delay forward to the registry office of the Court of Cassation the case file with:

– a copy of the declaration;

– a copy of the impugned decision.

He/she shall immediately forward to the registry office of the Court of Cassation all documents which might subsequently be sent to him/her.

Article 1004

If the declaration of the appeal does not contain the grounds of appeal, even in summarized form, against the decision being attacked, the appellant, must, at the risk of a time bar being declared by an order of the first president or his/her deputy, file at the court registry, no later than three months from the declaration, a statement containing such grounds, and, where appropriate, the exhibits supporting the application.

This statement may be drafted by the representative of the party without any new authority to act.

Article 1005

Where a statement of grounds is produced by the appellant, the latter must, under penalty of it being automatically declared inadmissible, send, within a month of the declaration, a copy to the respondent by registered mail with acknowledgment of receipt.

Article 1006

The respondent to the application has at his/her disposal a period of fifteen days measured from the notification of the statement of grounds of appeal of the appellant or from the expiration of the period of a month prescribed under Article 1004 to file, by way of an acknowledgment of receipt, or to send by registered letter to the registry office of the Court of Cassation a pleading in reply.

Within the same time-limit, he/she shall send to the appellant, by registered letter, a copy of the pleading in reply.

Article 1007

Where an attorney at the Council of State and the Court of Cassation has declared to the court registry office that he/she is acting on behalf of a party, the notification provided in Article 1005 or under Article 1006 may be given to that attorney, and where appropriate, by way of notification between attorneys.

The delivery to the attorney, in return for an acknowledgment of receipt, of a copy of the statement bearing the date stamp of the court registry office shall constitute notification.

Article 1008

If a declaration of appeal has been made in accordance with the rules governing mandatory representation, it may nevertheless be admissible irrespective of the procedural track followed thereafter, notwithstanding the applicability of the first paragraph of Article 1004.

The respondent is not obliged to be represented by an attorney at the Council of State and the Court of Cassation.

Chapter IV
Common Provisions

Article 1009

The first president, or his/her deputy, may at the request of a party or of his/her own initiative shorten the time limit prescribed for the filing of statements and exhibits.

At the expiration of these time-limits, the president of the chamber dealing with the matter shall set the date of the hearing.

Article 1009-1

Except for those matters where the appeal obstructs the enforcement of the decision under appeal, the first president may, at the request of the respondent, and after having sought the advice of the principal State Prosecutor and of the parties, withdraw the case from the list if the appellant cannot show that he/she has enforced the decision against which a appeal lies, unless it appears to him/her that the enforcement is likely to have clearly excessive consequences.

The respondent's request must, at the risk of it being found to be automatically inadmissible, be submitted before the expiration of the time limits in Articles 982 and 981.

Article 1009-2

The time limit shall be calculated from the date of notification of the decision ordering the withdrawal from the court list. It is suspended by an act clearly showing an unequivocal intention to enforce.

Article 1009-3

The first president or his/her authorized deputy shall, unless he/she rules that the matter is time-barred, grant leave to re-enter the matter on the court list upon proof of enforcement of the decision under appeal.

The time limit granted to the respondent in Articles 982 to 991 shall run from the notification of the re-enrolment of the matter on the court list.

Article 1010

A cross-appeal, even where it is provoked, must at the risk of it being declared inadmissible automatically, be made by way of a statement of grounds of appeal and must contain the same details as the appellant's statement of grounds.

Subject to the preceding sanction, the statement of grounds of appeal must:

- be filed at the registry office of the Court of Cassation before the expiration of the time limit provided for the filing of a statement in reply;
- be sent within the same time-limit to the attorneys of the other parties to the cross-appeal. Where, in cases requiring mandatory representation by counsel, the respondent has not instructed an attorney, the statement must be served on him/her no later than the month after the expiration of this time limit.

The respondent to such an appeal shall have one month from date of notification within which to file, and where applicable, to notify his/her pleading in reply.

Article 1011

Except in cases of forfeiture as provided in Article 978, the matter shall be assigned as soon as the appellant has filed his/her statement of grounds of appeal and not later than the expiration of the time granted for that purpose.

Article 1012

The president of the bench to which the matter has been assigned shall designate a judge or auxiliary judge of that bench to act as a rapporteur.

He/she may then set the date for the hearing.

Article 1013

The reduced bench of the chamber to the which the matter is assigned shall decide after receiving a verbal report.

Article 1014

Repealed.

Article 1015

The president must inform the parties of the grounds of appeal which the court believes are available as of right and must invite them to comment on them within a time-limit which he/she shall decide.

Article 1015-1

The particular chamber hearing an appeal may seek the advice of another chamber on a point of law which is within its jurisdiction.

The parties shall be advised of the same by the president of the chamber hearing the appeal. They may submit their comments to the chamber that is asked to give its opinion.

Article 1016

In accordance with Articles 11-1 and 11-2 of Law No. 72-626 of 5 July 1972 as amended, the oral pleadings shall be in open court. The court may nevertheless reach the view that the oral pleadings shall be given or pursued in chambers if, in open court, they might invade personal privacy, or if all the parties so request, or if they might disturb order in the court.

Judgments shall be given in open court.

Article 1017

The report shall be given at the hearing.

Article 1018

The attorneys may be heard after the report if they so request. The parties may also be heard after permission has been given to that effect by the president.

Article 1019

The Court of Cassation shall issue its judgment after receiving the opinion of the State Prosecution Service.

Article 1020

The judgment shall quote the legal texts on which the decision is based.

Article 1021

The judgment must be signed by the president, the rapporteur and the registrar.

Article 1022

A copy of the judgment must be sent to the lower court which issued the decision under appeal.

Article 1022-1

In matters where the parties are dispensed with the need to instruct an attorney at the Council of State and the Court of Cassation, decisions quashing a judgment are sent by the registry office of the Court of Cassation office by registered mail with acknowledgment of receipt; decisions dismissing the appeal or decisions allowing the appeal but without recourse must be sent to parties who are not assisted or represented by an attorney at the Council of State and the Court of Cassation by regular mail.

Chapter V
Miscellaneous Provisions

Section 1
Extension of Time Limits

Article 1023

The time limits prescribed in Articles 978 and 989 may be extended:

– by one month where the appellant resides in an overseas department, in the territorial collectivity of Mayotte or in an overseas territory;

– by two months where he/she resides in a foreign country.

The time limits prescribed in Articles 982, 991 and the last paragraph of Article 1010 shall be similarly extended by a month or by two months depending on whether the respondent resides in an overseas department, in the territorial collectivity of Mayotte, in an overseas territory or in a foreign country.

Section II
Discontinuance

Article 1024

The discontinuance of the appeal shall be allowed where it contains provisos or where the respondent has already made a cross-appeal.

Article 1025

The provisions of Articles 396, 399, 400 and 403 shall apply to the discontinuance of an appeal.

Article 1026

A discontinuance is ruled upon by an order of the first president or of the president of the particular chamber to which the matter has been assigned. The first president or of the president of the bench dealing with the matter, as the case may be, shall rule on the claims made under Article 700.

However, the discontinuance may be ruled upon by way of final judgment where it occurs after the filing of the report or when the consent of the respondent, if it is necessary, is given after the said filing. The judgment shall be equivalent to an order to stop the proceedings and shall mean that Articles 628 and 630 shall apply.

Section III
Challenge

Article 1027

A request to challenge a judge of the Court of Cassation must be examined by the bench to which the matter shall be assigned.

Section IV
The Plea of Forgery

Article 1028

A plea of forgery of a document produced to the Court of Cassation must be sent to the first president.

It must be filed at the court registry office and signed by the an attorney at the Council of State and the Court of Cassation, if his/her presence is mandatory in the matter to which the application is made.

Article 1029

The first president shall decide only after having sought the opinion of the principal State Prosecutor.

He/she shall give a ruling either for a dismissal or an order allowing the application.

In cases of dismissal, the appellant may be ordered to pay a fine according to the provisions in Article 628.

Article 1030

The ruling allowing the plea of forgery must be served on the respondent within fifteen days, with a request that he/she should declare whether he/she intends to rely upon the allegedly forged document.

To this request shall be attached a copy of the application and the ruling of the first president.

Article 1031

The respondent must notify the appellant, within a period of fifteen days, whether he/she does or does not intend to rely upon the allegedly forged document.

In the first case, or where there is no answer within the period of fifteen days, the first president shall direct the parties to bring the issue before a court that he/she shall designate in order to rule upon the plea of forgery.

Chapter VI
Referral for the Opinion of the Court of Cassation

Article 1031-1

Where the judge envisages seeking the opinion of the Court of Cassation pursuant to Article L. 151-1 of the Code of Judicial Organization, he/she shall so advise the parties and the State Prosecution Service. He/she shall obtain any possible written observations from them within a time limit which he/she shall decide, unless they have already communicated their opinions on the matter.

As soon as he/she receives such observations or after the expiration of the time-limit, the judge, in a decision not subject to appeal, shall seek the opinion of the Court of Cassation by formulating the issue of law which he/she wishes to submit to the latter. He/she must stay the proceedings until the receipt of the opinion or until the expiration of the time limit referred to in Article 1031-3.

Article 1031-2

The decision seeking the opinion shall be sent, together with the pleadings and the written observations, by the clerk of the court to registry office of the Court of Cassation.

This opinion and the date the file has been transferred shall be sent to the parties by registered mail with acknowledgment of receipt.

The State Prosecution Service attached to the court shall be advised as well as the first president of the court of appeal and the principal State Prosecutor if the request for an opinion does not come from the court.

Article 1031-3

The Court of Cassation shall give its decision within three months of the receipt of the file.

Article 1031-4

In matters where representation by counsel is mandatory, the observations of the parties must be signed by an attorney at the Council of State and the Court of Cassation.

Article 1031-5

The matter is sent to the principal State Prosecutor attached to the Court of Cassation. The latter must be informed of the date of the hearing.

Article 1031-6

The opinion may state that it shall be published in the Official Journal of the French Republic.

Article 1031-7

The opinion must be sent to the court which requested it, to the State Prosecution Service attached to that court, to the first president of the court of appeal and to the principal State Prosecutor if the request does not come from a court.

It shall be sent to the parties by the registry of the Court of Cassation.

TITLE VIII
SPECIFIC PROVISIONS RELATING TO REFERRALS AFTER AN APPEAL

Article 1032

The court to which a matter is referred assumes jurisdiction by a declaration to the registry of this court.

Article 1033

The declaration must contain the particulars required for an originating process before that court; a copy of the Court of Cassation judgment must be attached to it.

Article 1034

Unless the court of referral assumed jurisdiction without any prior notification, the declaration must, at the risk of it being found to be automatically inadmissible, be made before the expiration of the period of four months from the notification of the judgment of the Court of Cassation to the party concerned. This time limit shall also run against the person who notifies.

The absence of a declaration made within the time limit or its inadmissibility shall render final the judgment of first resort if the decision which has been quashed was made on appeal against that judgment.

Article 1035

The document notifying the judgment of the Court of Cassation must, at the risk of it being invalid, indicate in clear terms the time limit set out in the first paragraph of Article 1034 as well as the procedure whereby the court of review may assume jurisdiction.

Article 1036

The clerk of the court of referral must immediately send, by regular mail, to each of the parties involved in the appeal to the Court of Cassation, a copy of the declaration with, where applicable, an indication of the need to instruct an attorney or appeal advocate.

In case of non-appearance, the defaulting parties shall be summonsed in the same manner as the respondents before the court by which the quashed decision was issued.

Article 1037

The clerk of the court of referral must without delay request the case file from the registry office of the Court of Cassation.

BOOK THREE
SPECIFIC PROVISIONS WITH RESPECT TO CERTAIN MATTERS

TITLE I
PERSONS

Chapter I
The Nationality of Natural Persons

Article 1038

The regional court shall be the only court competent to give judgment as a court of first instance in disputes over French or any foreign nationality of natural persons, subject to the provisions laid down in the Code of Nationality in relation to criminal courts with a jury.

Pleas of nationality or foreign nationality as well as pleas against jurisdiction are matters of public policy. They may be raised at any stage of the proceedings and must be raised by the judge on his/her own motion.

Article 1039

The regional court which is territorially competent is that of the judicial district where the person whose nationality is in issue resides; and if this person has not established his/her residence in France, the regional court of Paris will have jurisdiction.

Article 1040

Any action whose main cause is to seek a declaration that a natural person has or has not the status of a French National must be brought by the State Prosecution Service or against it without prejudice to the right of any interested party to intervene in the proceedings.

Article 1041

When a court of the judiciary assumes jurisdiction by way of interlocutory proceedings on a question of nationality in relation to which it lacks jurisdiction but which is necessary for the resolution of the dispute, the matter must be referred to the State Prosecution Service.

The latter shall indicate in written and reasoned pleadings, whether or not there are grounds for acknowledging the existence of a preliminary issue.

Article 1042

Where an issue of nationality is raised by a party before a court which holds that there is a preliminary issue to be decided, the court shall, within one month, refer that party to the competent regional court or to apply to the State Prosecutor.

Where the person whose nationality is contested relies upon a certificate of French nationality, or if the issue of nationality has been raised automatically, the court deciding on the merits of the case shall grant the same one month time limit to the State Prosecutor within which to inform the competent regional court.

Where the one month time-limit has not been complied with, the proceedings shall take their course. Otherwise, the court deciding on the merits of the case must defer judgment until the issue of nationality has been determined.

Article 1043

In all cases where a dispute over nationality has arisen, whether as a main or secondary issue, a copy of the writ or, where relevant, a copy of the pleadings raising the contention must be filed at the Ministry of Justice, with an acknowledgment of receipt. The filing of the documents may be substituted by way of registered mail with acknowledgment of receipt.

A civil court may not rule upon an issue of nationality before the expiration of one month calculated from the issue of the acknowledgment of filing or from the receipt of a notice of the delivery of the registered letter. However, this time-limit shall be ten days where the dispute regarding nationality has been the subject of a preliminary issue before a court hearing an electoral matter.

The writ shall lapse and the pleadings raising an issue of nationality shall be inadmissible if the procedure set out in the preceding paragraphs is not complied with.

The provisions of the present Article shall apply to rights of recourse.

Article 1044

The State Prosecutor is bound to act in accordance with the provisions of Article 1040 where so required by any public administration or by a third party who has raised the defense of nationality before a court which has deferred judgment in the manner provided in Article 1042.

The third intervening party must be joined as a third party.

Article 1045

The time limit for an appeal to the Court of Cassation shall include a stay of execution in relation to the judgment determining nationality; the appeal to the Court of Cassation brought within this period shall carry equally a stay of execution.

Chapter II
Records of Civil Status

Section I
Cancellation and Rectification of Records of Civil Status

Sub-Section 1
The Administrative Rectification

Article 1046

The State Prosecutor who is responsible in the area to deal with the administrative correction of clerical errors and omissions in a record of civil status is:

– the State Prosecutor of the area where the record was prepared or transcribed;

– the State Prosecutor of the area where the central department for civil status of the Ministry of Foreign Affairs for the records kept by this department;

– the State Prosecutor who is attached to the Regional Court of Paris for documents taking the place of records of civil status for refugees or stateless persons.

However, the application may always be made to the State Prosecutor of the area where the interested party resides, so that the matter may be referred to the State Prosecutor who is responsible for the area.

Article 1047

The President of the Regional Court has the power to order the rectification of records of civil status or equivalent documents.

The President of the Regional Court has the power to order the cancellation of records of civil status, their statements, the statements contained within them or equivalent documents as well as to rectify judgments on records of civil status that are declaratory or non-mandatory.

Article 1048

The court that has jurisdiction in an area is that within whose judicial district the party whose record of civil status is at issue resides, or if the party resides outside France, it is the Regional Court of Paris, or the President of that court. The courts of the places where the record of civil status was prepared or transcribed or where the judgment was given, also have jurisdiction.

However, only the following courts have jurisdiction:

- for records kept by the central department of civil status of the Ministry of Foreign Affairs, the court where it is situated;
- for documents taking the place of records of civil status for a refugee or stateless person, the Regional Court of Paris.

Article 1049

The action is open to any person having an interest and to the State Prosecution Service.

Article 1050

The application shall be framed, prepared and judged as a non-contentious matter.

Article 1051

The application may also be made informally to the State Prosecutor, who shall refer it to the court having jurisdiction.

However, if the State Prosecutor intends to oppose the application, it shall inform the applicant and invite him/her to refer the matter to the court him/herself.

Article 1052

The matter is notified to the State Prosecution Service for its opinion.

Where the application is made by the State Prosecutor or a third party, the person whose record of civil status is at issue or his /her heirs shall be heard or called to appear. For this purpose, the application shall state their name, first name address and date and place of birth, without prejudice to the statements contained in Article 57(1).

Article 1053

The judge may order the joinder to the proceedings of any interested party as well as the convening of the family council.

Article 1054

If he/she allows the application, the judge shall order the modification, by means of a marginal note, of any record even if it was issued, drawn up or transcribed outside of his/her judicial district. For this purpose, the terms of the decision shall be sent by the State Prosecutor to the depositary of altered records.

A cancelled record cannot be updated. It may be issued only by way of exception with the authorisation of the State Prosecutor for the judicial district where the record is kept.

Article 1055

An appeal against a decision given in non-contentious matters is framed, prepared and judged in accordance with the same procedure.

The rights of recourse are in all cases available to the State Prosecution Service.

Section II
Change of First Names

Article 1055-1

An application for a change of first name must be made to the judge within whose judicial district the birth certificate of the interested party has been prepared or within in the judicial district where he/she lives.

Where the birth certificate of the interested party is kept by the central department of civil status of the Ministry for Foreign Affairs, the application may be made to the judge within whose judicial district the department is situated.

Article 1055-2

The application for a change of first name falls within the scope of non-contentious matters.

Rights of recourse shall be open to the State Prosecution Service.

Article 1055-3

The formal order of a decision changing a first name is immediately sent by the State Prosecutor to the register of civil status who holds the birth certificate of the interested party.

Section III
Transcription and Note of Decisions in the Registers of Civil Status

Article 1056

Any decision of which the transcription or note in the registers of civil status is ordered must indicate the first names and family name of the parties as well as, where appropriate, the place where the transcription must be made or the places and dates of the documents in whose margin the note must be inserted.

Only the formal order of the decision has to be sent to the depository of the registers of civil status. The transcription and note of the order is carried out immediately.

Chapter III
The Civil Register

Article 1057

The civil register is made up of all the abstracts of applications: documents and judgments which, by virtue of special provisions referring to that register, must be filed and kept at the registry offices of the regional courts.

The abstracts shall be recorded on a register, day by day, in numerical order.

Article 1058

The filing and keeping of abstracts is carried out by the registry office of the regional court within whose judicial district the interested individual was born and by the central department of civil status for those individuals born abroad.

Article 1059

Public notice of applications, records and judgments is made by a note in the margin of the birth certificate of the party concerned. This note is inserted at the request of the registrar of the regional court or, where appropriate, at the request of the central department of civil status. The note shall have the words "civil register" followed by the reference under which the application, document or judgment is to be kept.

The date on which the note is inserted shall be stamped on the abstract which is kept at the court registry office or at the central department of civil status.

Article 1060

The note inserted in the margin of a birth certificate or a judgment dismissing an application or discharging a legal order appearing in the civil register is automatically completed by the statement that it shall include the deletion of the previous notes.

The statement of a deletion may also be inserted below the notes prescribed in Article 1292 where the party concerned has demonstrated the termination of the proceedings.

Article 1061

Copies of abstracts kept at the civil registry may be issued to any interested party.

They can only be issued on authorization from the State Prosecutor where a statement of deletion has been inserted in the margin of a birth certificate by virtue of the preceding Article.

Chapter IV
Absent Persons

Section I
The Presumption of Absence

Article 1062

An application for a presumption of absence must be brought to the guardianship judge of the district court in whose judicial district the person for whom a presumption of absence is sought resides or last resided.

In default thereof, the presiding judge shall be the one for the district court within whose judicial district the applicant resides.

Article 1063

The application must be made, prepared and decided in the manner applicable to the guardianship of minors.

Article 1064

An abstract of any decision declaring a presumption of absence or designating a person to represent somebody presumed absent and to administer his/her property or any decision varying or discharging orders previously given shall be sent to the registry office of the regional court in whose judicial district the person presumed absent was born, to be kept in the civil register and to give public notice by way of a note inserted in the margin of the birth certificate, in the manner provided in Articles 1057 to 1061. For persons born abroad, the documents must be sent to the central department of civil status.

Article 1065

Where a declaration has been given by a guardianship judge, the transmission of documents must be made by the registrar of the district court within fifteen days from the expiration of the period for appeal.

Where a decision has been given by a regional court, the transmission must be made by the registrar of the regional court within fifteen days of the judgment.

Section II
The Declaration of Absence

Article 1066

An application for a declaration of absence of a person shall be made to the regional court in whose judicial district the person resides or last resided.

Failing that, the court where the applicant resides shall have jurisdiction to deal with the matter.

Article 1067

The application is made, prepared and decided as a non-contentious matter.

Article 1068

The abstracts of a declaratory judgment of absence must be published within six months from the date of issue of that judgment; this must be stated in the abstracts which have to be published.

Article 1069

The appeal is made, prepared and decided as a non-contentious matter.

The time limit for an appeal shall run against the parties and third parties who have been notified of the judgment, one month after the expiration of the time limit fixed by the court for compliance with the formalities of public notice under Article 127 of the Civil Code.

The time limit for an appeal to the Court of Cassation suspends the enforcement of the declaratory judgment of absence. The appeal to the Court of Cassation made within this time limit shall also suspend enforcement.

Chapter IV[Bis]
Repealed.

Section I
Repealed.

Article 1069-1 - *Repealed.*

Article 1069-2 - *Repealed.*

Section II
Repealed.

Article 1069-3 - *Repealed.*

Article 1069-4 - *Repealed.*

Article 1069-5 - *Repealed.*

Article 1069-6 - *Repealed.*

Chapter V[24]
Divorce and Judicial Separation

Section I
General Provisions

Article 1070

The court which has territorial jurisdiction in divorce proceedings shall be:

- the court in whose judicial district the family resides;
- where the spouses have separate residences, the court in whose judicial district the spouse with whom the minor children reside;
- in other cases, the court in whose judicial district the spouse who did not commence the proceedings resides.

Where there is a joint application, the court that has jurisdiction shall be, according to the choice of the spouses, that of the judicial district in which one or the other of them resides.

However, where the dispute only involves maintenance, the contribution to the upkeep and education of the child, the contribution to the expenses of the marriage or the equalizing allowance, the judge who has jurisdiction may be the one of the place of residence of the creditor-spouse or the parent assuming primary responsibility for the children, even if they are adults.

---

24 Effective for divorce proceedings commenced January 1, 2005, Law No. 2004-836, August 20, 2004. For divorce proceedings commenced before January 1, 2005, see Chapter V, reproduced in The French Code of Civil Procedure in English, 2004 (Oceana Publication, Inc.).

Territorial jurisdiction is determined by the place of residence on the date of the application or, in divorce cases, when the initial petition was filed.

Article 1071

The family judge has the task of attempting to reconcile the parties.

On taking on the case, he /she may recommend mediation and, after having obtained the agreement of the parties, appoint a family mediator to proceed with it.

A decision ordering the parties to meet a family mediator pursuant to Articles 255 and 373-2-10 of the Civil Code is not subject to appeal.

Article 1072

Without prejudice to any procedural measure and subject to the provisions contained in the third paragraph of Article 373-2-12 of the Civil Code, the judge may, of his/her own initiative, order a welfare investigation where he /she considers that he/she is insufficiently informed by the facts before him/her.

The welfare investigation shall focus on the family situation as well as, where relevant, the possibilities of carrying out the arrangement of the parents or of one of them with respect to the methods of exercising parental responsibility.

It shall result in a report in which the findings made by and the solution proposed by the investigator are recorded.

The judge must provide copies of the report to the parties and set a time-limit within which they are entitled to apply for a further investigation or a counter-investigation.

Article 1073

The family judge is, where applicable, the judge directing preparations for the trial.

He/she shall perform the functions of a judge sitting in chambers.

Article 1074

Applications shall be framed, prepared and judged in the judge's chambers.

However, decisions concerning a name, first name or a divorce shall be given in public.

Article 1074-1

Measures relating to the exercise of parental authority, maintenance, the contribution to the upkeep and education of the child or the contribution to the expenses of the marriage, as well as any measures adopted pursuant to Article 255 of the Civil Code are enforceable by law on a provisional basis.

Section II
Divorce and Judicial Separation

Sub-Section 1
General Provisions

§ 1 The Applications

Article 1075

From the start of the proceedings, the spouses must, where applicable, disclose, with the details necessary to identify them, the social security fund to which they are affiliated and the department or bodies providing family benefits, pensions or any old age benefits, as well as the name of these funds, departments or bodies.

Article 1075-1

Where an equalizing allowance if applied for to a judge or contained in an agreement, each spouse must produce the sworn declaration mentioned in Article 272 of the Civil Code.

Article 1075-2

The spouses, must, at the request of the judge, justify their income and expenditures, particularly by the production of tax returns, notices of assessment and statements of taxation status.

They must also, at the judge's request, produce supporting documents relating to their assets and their living conditions in order to supplement their sworn declaration permitting the equalizing allowance to be fixed.

Article 1076

The spouse who is petitioning for divorce may, in any case, and even on appeal, substitute the application with one for judicial separation.

A reverse substitution of the above shall not be allowed.

Article 1076-1

Where one of the spouses has only requested maintenance or a contribution to the expenses of the marriage, the judge may not decree a divorce without having first invited the parties to comment upon the provision of an equalizing allowance.

Article 1077

An application can only be based on one of the grounds set out in Article 229 of the Civil Code. Any subsidiary application based on another ground shall be inadmissible.

Except for the grounds set out in Articles 247 to 247-2 of the Civil Code, it is not possible, in the course of proceedings, to substitute an application based on a ground for divorce defined in Article 229 of the Civil Code with an application based on another ground.

Article 1078 *- Repealed.*

§ 2 The Equalizing Allowance

Article 1079

An equalizing allowance cannot include any order for provisional enforcement.

However it may include such an order in whole or in part where the absence of enforcement would have clearly excessive consequences for the creditor-spouse in the event of an appeal against the equalizing allowance when the divorce is made final.

Such provisional enforcement may only take effect on the day when the divorce is made final.

Article 1080

Where assets or rights are granted by way of an equalizing allowance pursuant to Article 274(2), the approved agreement or the decision granting the divorce shall indicate their value.

Where these assets or property rights are subject to public notice for real estate transactions, the agreement or decision shall furthermore contain the statements required for such public notice in the form mandated by Decree N°55-22 of January 4, 1955 on the reform public notice for real estate transactions.

Article 1080-1 *- Repealed.*

§ 3 Public Notice of Decrees of Divorce

Article 1081

The operative parts of the decision must specify the date of the order of non-conciliation.

Article 1082

A note of the divorce shall be made in the margin of the marriage certificate, as well as in the birth certificate of each of the spouses, in light of an abstract of the decree containing only its substance together with proof of its enforceable status in accordance with Article 506.

If the marriage was celebrated abroad and in the absence of a marriage certificate kept by a French authority, a note of the terms of the decree shall be made in the margin of the birth certificate of each spouse if this document is kept in a French register. Failing that, the substance of the decree shall be kept in the register mentioned in Article 4-1 of Decree N° 65-422 of 1 June 1965 which set up the central department of civil status at the Ministry for Foreign Affairs.

Article 1082-1

As against third parties, a divorce or judicial separation shall be proven simply by the production of a copy of the decision granting it, which shall consist only of the operative provisions together with proof of its enforceability in accordance with Article 506.

§ 4 Amendments to Ancillary Orders

Article 1083

Where there is an appeal against a decree of divorce, applications for amendments to ancillary orders that are enforceable notwithstanding the appeal pursuant to Article 1074-1 may, on the emergence of a new fact, may be made only, as the case may be, to the first President of the Court of Appeal or the judge directing the preparations for trial.

Article 1084

Once the divorce has been pronounced, if it is necessary to rule upon the exercise of parental responsibility or on the modification of a maintenance order, the application must, even where a appeal to the Court of Cassation has been filed, be made to the family judge according to the procedure set out in Section III of this Chapter.

The same shall apply where the divorce is final, and there is need to review the equalizing allowance. Articles 1075-1 and 1075-2 of the present Code apply.

Article 1085

A judge may request the transfer of the file to the court that granted the divorce.

§ 5 Appeal to the Court of Cassation

Article 1086

The time limit for filing an appeal to the Court of Cassation suspends the enforcement of the decision granting the divorce. An appeal to the Court of Cassation filed within the time limit also has this effect.

Article 1087

The suspensive effect of the appeal to the Court of Cassation as well as of the time limit for bringing such an appeal shall not apply to the provisions of a decision or approved agreement that involve maintenance, the contribution to the upkeep and education of the child and the exercise of parental authority.

Sub-Section 2
Divorce on Joint Application of the Parties

Article 1088

Divorce upon a joint application is a non-contentious matter.

Article 1089

The joint application for divorce must be made in a single application.

Article 1090

The application which does not indicate the grounds for divorce must contain:

1. the family name, first names, occupation, address, nationality, date and place of birth of each spouse; the date and place of the marriage; and the same details, where applicable, for each of their children;

2. the information prescribed in Article 1075;

3. the name of the court before which the application is brought;

4. the name of the attorneys instructed by the spouses to represent them, or the one whom they have chosen for that purpose by way of common agreement;

The application will be inadmissible if it does not contain all the above.

The application must be dated and signed by each of the parties and their attorneys or it will be inadmissible.

Article 1091

At the risk of it being inadmissible, the application must have annexed to it an agreement containing a comprehensive settlement of the effects of the divorce, including in particular a division of the matrimonial property or a declaration that there is no need for such division. The division must be signed before a notary where it concerns real property that is subject to public notice.

Article 1092

The family judge shall assume jurisdiction by the filing at the court registry office of the application, which is the equivalent of pleadings.

He/she shall summon each of the spouses by regular mail sent at least fifteen days before the date of the hearing and advise the attorney or attorneys.

Article 1093 - *Repealed.*

Article 1094 - *Repealed.*

Article 1095 - *Repealed.*

Article 1096 - *Repealed.*

Article 1097 - *Repealed.*

Article 1098 - *Repealed.*

Article 1099

On the appointed day, the judge shall proceed, in accordance with Articles 250 to 250-3 of the Civil Code; he/she shall verify the admissibility of the application; he/she shall ensure that the consent of the spouses is freely given and informed and draw their attention to the importance of the commitments undertaken by them, in particular regarding the exercise of parental responsibility.

With the agreement of the parties, and in the presence of their attorney or attorneys, the judge may have deleted or amended clauses in the agreement that appear to him/her to be contrary to the interests of the children or to one of the spouses.

He/she shall give judgment immediately approving the agreement and granting the divorce.

Article 1100

If the agreement appears not to sufficiently safeguard the welfare of the children or of one of the spouses, the judge may refuse to approve it, and not pronounce the divorce. The judge shall defer, by way of an order, his/her decree until an amended agreement has been presented to him/her.

The order must specify the time limit for an appeal and the time from which it shall run.

He/she shall inform the spouses that they have to present a new agreement before the expiry of a six-month time limit. The order must specify this information and its contents.

The order shall specify the conditions or guarantee to which approval of the new agreement will be subject and, consequently, the granting of the divorce.

It shall contain, where relevant, the provisional measures approved by the judge pursuant to Article 250-2 of the Civil Code.

Article 1101

The time limit of six months to produce a new agreement is suspended where there is an appeal.

Where a new agreement is not produced within the set time limit, the judge records, of his/her own motion and by means of an order, that the petition for divorce has lapsed.

Where the spouses produce a new agreement, the parties shall be called to appear according to the procedure set out in Article 1092. If the judge refuses to approve the agreement, he/she shall issue an order by which he/she records that the petition for divorce has lapsed.

Article 1102

The decisions of the family judge shall be subject to appeal, except those approving the agreement of the spouses or those which pronounce a divorce.

The time limit for an appeal shall be fifteen days; it shall be calculated from the date of the decision.

Article 1103

The time limit to appeal to the Court of Cassation shall be fifteen days from the issue of the decision which approved the agreement between the spouses and pronounced the divorce. An appeal taken within this time limit shall also have the effect of staying the enforcement.

Article 1104

Creditors of either spouse may have the agreement which has been approved by the court declared unenforceable against them by filing a third party objection against the decision of approval within the year following the performance of the formalities referred to in Article 262 of the Civil Code.

Article 1105

The costs of the action shall be shared equally between the spouses unless their agreement provides otherwise.

Sub-Section 3
Other Divorce Proceedings

§ 1 The initial application

Article 1106

A spouse who wishes to apply for divorce must bring an application through an attorney to the judge. The application does not indicate either the legal grounds for the petition nor the facts behind it. It shall contain the requests for provisional measures and a summary of the reasons in support. He/she is obliged to appear in person when he/she requests urgent orders.

In the case of a duly recorded impediment, the judge shall go to the spouse's residence.

Article 1107

At the bottom of the application, the judge must state the date, time and place of his/her attempt to reconcile the parties.

Where necessary, the judge shall give such urgent orders as are set out in Article 257 of the Civil Code.

The order is not subject to an appeal.

§ 2 The attempt at reconciliation

Article 1108

The spouse who has not filed the application is summoned by the registrar to an attempt at reconciliation, by registered mail with acknowledgment of receipt that is confirmed on the same day by regular mail. The registered letter must be sent at least fifteen days beforehand and be accompanied by a copy of the order, or it is invalid. The registrar must inform the attorney.

The summons sent to the spouse who has not filed the application shall inform him/her that he/she must appear in person alone or assisted by an attorney. It shall specify that the assistance of an attorney is obligatory in order to accept the principle of the breakdown of the marriage at the time of the conciliation hearing. The registrar must inform the attorney of the spouse who has filed the application.

The notification by registered mail with acknowledgment of receipt should also enclose, by way of information, an explanation of the provisions of Articles 252 to 252-3 of the Civil Code.

Article 1109

In urgent cases, a family judge may, on an application, grant leave to one of the spouses to summon the other party to conciliation proceedings at an appointed date.

Article 1110

On the specified date, the judge shall first determine his/her jurisdiction, where necessary.

He/she shall inform the spouses of the provisions of Article 252-4 of the Civil Code and then proceed to attempt a reconciliation in accordance with the provisions of Articles 252-1 to 253 of the same Code.

Where one spouse is not in a position to attend at the indicated place, the judge may designate another location, within or even outside his/her judicial district, to hear the spouse who is prevented from attending or the judge shall delegate another judge to proceed with the hearing of testimony.

Article 1111

When, after having heard each of the spouses on the principle of the breakdown of the marriage, the judge notes that the petitioner is maintaining his/her application, he/she shall issue an order by which he/she may either send the parties back, in conformity with Article 252-2 of the Civil Code, to attempt anew a reconciliation or immediately allow the spouses to commence divorce proceedings.

In either case, he/she may order any or some of the interim measures mentioned in Articles 254 to 257 of the same Code.

The judge may, upon issuing a writ granting leave, refer in his/her order to the time limit in Article 1113 within which the writ must be served.

Article 1112

The order made pursuant to Articles 1110 and 1111 is subject to appeal within fifteen days of its notification, but only with respect to jurisdiction and the interim measures.

Article 1113

Within three months of the issue of the order, only the spouse who presented the initial application may commence proceedings for a divorce.

In the case of a reconciliation between the spouses or if the action is not commenced within three months of the issue of the order, all of its provisions lapse, including the authorization to commence proceedings.

§ 3 The proceedings

Article 1114

Subject to the rules set out in the first two Sections of this Chapter, the proceedings shall be framed, prepared and judged in accordance with the procedure for contentious matters that applies before the Regional Court.

Article 1115

The proposal for the settlement of the financial interests of the spouses, set out in Article 257-2 of the Civil Code, shall contain a summary of their assets and specify the intention of the applicant as regards the winding-up of the system of joint matrimonial property or joint ownership and, where relevant, the division of property.

It shall not constitute a claim within the meaning of Article 4 of this Code.

The inadmissibility provided in Article 237-2 of the Civil Code must be raised before any defence on the merits.

Article 1116 - *Repealed.*

§ 4 Interim orders

Article 1117

Where the judge has issued interim orders, he/she may take into consideration the arrangements which the spouses have agreed to between themselves.

Article 1118

In the case of the emergence of a new fact, a judge may, as long as the court still has jurisdiction over the matter, cancel, modify or supplement the provisional measures that he/she has ordered.

Before proceedings are commenced, the application shall be framed, prepared and judged according to the procedure set out in Section III of this Chapter.

Article 1119

The decision relating to interim orders shall be subject to appeal within fifteen days of its notification.

On appeal, any variation of interim orders based on the occurrence of a new fact may only be requested from the first president of the court of appeal or the judge directing the preparations for trial.

§ 5 Rights of recourse

Article 1120

An adult child who is under court protection may only agree to the judgment of divorce or refrain from appealing it with the leave of the guardianship judge.

Article 1121 - *Repealed.*

Article 1122 - *Repealed.*

§ 6 Special Provisions for Divorce by Consent

Article 1123

At any time in the proceedings, the spouses may agree to accept the principle of the breakdown of the marriage without consideration of the reason for it.

At the reconciliation hearing, this acceptance shall be set out in minutes prepared by the judge and signed by the spouses and their respective attorneys. The judge then instructs the spouses to commence proceedings so that he/she may grant the divorce and rule on its effects, the grounds for divorce being agreed. The minutes shall be annexed to the order.

Failing this, each spouse may declare in a signed written document that he/she accepts that principle of the breakdown of the marriage.

The two declarations shall be annexed to the joint application for commencement of proceedings.

During the proceedings, the application prepared pursuant to Article 247-1 of the Civil Code must be worded clearly and consistently in the submissions of the parties. Each spouse must annexe his/her declaration of acceptance to his/her submissions.

At the risk of being null and void, the minutes and the written declaration must contain the statements set out in the second paragraph of Article 233 of the Civil Code.

Article 1124

The family judge shall pronounce the decree of divorce without any reasons other than the agreement of the spouses.

Article 1125

The costs of the proceedings up to and including the petition to have the divorce granted shall be shared equally between the spouses unless the judge decides otherwise.

§ 7 Special Provisions in Divorce for Definitive Changes in Marital Relations

Article 1126

Subject to the provisions in Article 472, a judge may not of his/her own motion raise the defence of the expiry of the time limit of two years provided in the second paragraph of Article 238 of the Civil Code.

Article 1127

The costs of the proceedings shall be borne by the spouse who initiated them, unless the judge provides otherwise.

§ 8 Special Provisions for Divorce for Fault

Article 1128

An application intended to prevent the family judge, in the reasons for his/her decision, from reciting the wrongful acts and grievances of the spouses must be pleaded clearly and consistently in the submissions of the spouses.

The family judge is limited only to stating the facts which justify a divorce in accordance with the Civil Code under the Title "Divorce", Section III, Chapter I.

Sub-Section 4
Judicial Separation

Article 1129

The procedure for judicial separation follows the rules set down for the divorce procedure.

Article 1130

A declaration of the resumption of marital relations shall be recorded in the margin of the marriage certificate and the birth certificate of each of the spouses.

The same entries shall be made by the notary who drew up the document confirming the resumption of marital relations.

Sub-Section 5
Divorce upon Conversion of a Judicial Separation

Article 1131

Except in cases where the judicial separation was granted on the basis of mutual consent, the application for conversion shall be framed, prepared and judged in accordance with the procedure governing non-contentious matters.

No counter-claim shall be admissible, except in relation to ancillary matters.

Article 1132

In case of a joint application, the application for conversion must contain, or be inadmissible: the statement required in Article 1090, the particulars of the decision which pronounced the judicial separation, and a draft final agreement on ancillary matters.

Under penalty of the same sanction, the application and the draft agreement must be dated and signed by each of the spouses and their attorney.

Article 1133

In the case provided for in Article 1143, the judge can choose not to hear the spouses and to base his/her decision on an examination of the draft agreement with their attorney.

In the absence of any difficulty, the judge shall approve the agreement and pronounce the divorce.

Otherwise, the judge may, without any other formality, request that the spouses present a fresh application after having amended the agreement; where this request has not been complied with, the judge shall make an order in which he/she refuses to approve the agreement.

The judgment must state the time limit for any appeal and the time from which that period will run.

Article 1134

The order is subject to appeal within fifteen days of the decision.

The appeal must be brought, prepared and determined in accordance with the rules governing non-contentious matters.

Article 1135

The preparation of the matter and the hearing of the spouses' testimony shall be limited, whatever the circumstances, to the ancillary matters relating to the decree.

Article 1136

The costs of the proceedings for conversion shall be shared as in the case of judicial separation.

Costs relating to the appeal proceedings shall be considered as if they related to a new action.

Section III
Other Procedures Relevant to the Competence of the Family Judge

Article 1137

The judge assumes jurisdiction in the manner provided for the hearing of summary proceedings.

He/she may also assume jurisdiction by means of a petition sent or filed with the court registry jointly or by one party alone. The application shall indicate the names, first names and addresses of the parties or, where necessary, the last known address of the defendant. For legal persons, it shall indicate their type, corporate name, registered office and legal representative. It must state the purpose of the request and give a summary of the reasons in support. It must be dated and signed by the applicant or his/her attorney.

Article 1138

Within fifteen days of the petition, the registrar shall summon the defendant to a hearing by registered letter with acknowledgement of receipt. He/she shall send him/her by regular mail a copy of the request and the summons to appear.

However, where the request states that the address of the defendant is the last known address, the registrar shall invite the applicant to proceed by way of service of the summons.

The registrar shall also, by regular mail, summon the party who initiated the application. The latter may also be summoned verbally in return for his/her signature or in the manner provided for in Article 652.

At the risk of being inadmissible, the service documents and the writ of summons must mention the provisions of Articles 1139 and 1141.

Article 1139

The parties are responsible for their own defence; they have the right to be assisted or represented by an attorney.

Article 1140

The proceedings shall be oral.

Article 1141

Where the application is filed on the basis of Article L.6145-11 of the Public Health Code or Article L.132-7 of the Family and Social Action Code, any party may also, in the course of proceedings, submit his/her arguments in a letter addressed to the judge, provided that he/she can show that the opposing party had knowledge thereof prior to the hearing by registered letter with acknowledgement of receipt.

The party who makes use of this right may not appear at the hearing. The judgment of the court in such circumstances shall be deemed to be given in the presence of both parties.

Nevertheless, the judge retains the power to order the parties to appear before him/her.

Article 1142

Where the judge has assumed jurisdiction on the basis of an application, the judge may decide, either on his/her own initiative or at the request of a party, that the decision be notified by the registry by registered letter with acknowledgement of receipt.

Chapter VI
Filiation Proceedings and Allowances

Section I
General Provisions

Article 1149

Filiation proceedings and claims for allowance shall be prepared and argued in chambers.

The judgment shall be pronounced in open court, except for the cases provided for in Articles 1150 to 1153.

Article 1149-1

Where, in the case of a change of parentage, an adult child consents to a change of his/her family name, his/her consent is received by an official of civil status, a notary, a diplomatic or French consular agent or by the court which ordered the legitimization; in the latter case, this fact must be mentioned in the provisions of the order.

Section II
Legitimization

Article 1150

A request for legitimization after marriage or by leave of the court must be made by one of the parents before the regional court within the judicial district he/she has established his/her residence or by both of them jointly to the court within the judicial district one of them has established as his/her residence.

Article 1151

Legitimization shall be considered to be a non-contentious matter.

Section III
Filiation Outside of Marriage

Article 1152

Joint declarations as provided for in Articles 334-2 and 334-5 of the Civil Code shall be made to the chief registrar of the regional court of the place where the child resides.

The chief registrar immediately informs the State Prosecutor of the place of birth of the child, who must then make the necessary note in the margin of the birth certificate of the said child.

Article 1153

The change of family name of the illegitimate child by a joint declaration is a non-contentious matter.

Article 1153-1

The State Prosecution Service shall represent the State in proceedings to establish paternity made in the absence of heirs to the presumed father or where the heirs have renounced their inheritance.

Section IV
Allowances

Article 1154

Where necessary, regarding the payment of allowances pursuant to Article 342-3 of the Civil Code, the court may designate as a court guardian any person who ap pears able to look after the child.

Article 1155

The legal guardian of the child may request any relevant information from the person appointed to collect the indemnity.

If a disagreement arises between them, the court, assuming jurisdiction by the filing of a reasoned memorandum at the court registry office, resolves the disagreement without formality after having obtained explanations from the interested parties.

Article 1156

The child welfare authorities, charitable bodies or the guardian appointed by the court shall, for the purposes of the collection of allowances, be subrogated to the rights of creditors.

The amount owed to the child shall be remitted to the legal guardian as soon as possible and at the latest within one month of its receipt.

Section V
Document of Common Knowledge[25]

Article 1157

Before drawing up an official instrument relating to matters of common knowledge, a judge, if he/she deems the testimonies and documents produced to be insufficient, may, on his/her own initiative, obtain information from any person he/she chooses about the facts that are to be recorded.

Article 1157-1

The judge who issues a document of common knowledge that records the presumed status of a legitimate or an illegitimate child must immediately advise the State Prosecutor of the place where the birth certificate of the person concerned is kept.

The State Prosecutor ensures that a note of the family relationship is made in the margin of the birth certificate of the child.

Section VI
Consent to Assisted Conception

Article 1157-2

Spouses or cohabitees having recourse to assisted conception requiring the assistance of a third party donor, as referred to under Article 311-20 of the Civil Code, shall give their consent by way of joint declaration to the president or the president's deputy of the regional court of their choice, or before a notary.

The declaration is obtained in the form of an official document without the presence of third parties.

---

25 The French term "acte de notoriété" refers to an official document containing statements by a number of persons pertaining to matters of common knowledge.

A certified copy or a copy of the document may only be issued to those persons whose consent has been recorded.

Article 1157-3

Before recording the consent, the judge or notary must inform those giving it:

- that it is impossible to establish a parental link between a child artificially created and the donor, or to hold him/her liable in tort;
- of the prohibition against instituting proceedings contesting parentage or claiming status in the name of the child, unless it is alleged that the child was not born by assisted conception or that the consent was invalid;
- that there are cases where the consent is not invalid;
- of the possibility of seeking a court declaration of filiation outside of marriage of the one who, having consented to an assisted conception, does not recognize the child born as a result, and to bring an action for parental responsibility against him/her on that basis.

The document prescribed in Article 1157-2 must state that this information has been given.

Chapter VII
The Declaration of Abandonment

Article 1158

An application for a declaration of abandonment shall be brought before the regional court of the judicial district where the child lives; if it is made on behalf of the child welfare authorities, it shall be brought before the regional court of the administrative center of the department in which the child has been found.

Article 1159

The proceedings shall observe the rules relating to non-contentious matters.

Article 1160

The proceedings shall be brought by an application filed at the court registry office.

It may also be brought by the applicant by means of a simple request filed with the State Prosecutor who must remit it to the court.

The registrar must convene the parties concerned by registered mail with acknowledgment of receipt.

Article 1161

The matter shall be prepared and argued in chambers in the presence of the applicant, after the opinion of the State Prosecution Service has been obtained. The services of an attorney is not obligatory.

The parents or guardian are heard or called. In cases where these persons have disappeared, the court may order a search in the interest of the families; it shall then defer its decision for a period not exceeding six months.

The judgment shall be pronounced in open court. It shall be notified by the registrar to the applicant, the parents, and where applicable, to the guardian.

Article 1162

Where it appears necessary, the court shall in the same proceedings and in the same judgment, rule upon the delegation of parental responsibility.

Article 1163

An appeal may be brought in accordance with the procedure for non-mandatory representation by counsel. It is prepared and determined in accordance with the rules applicable to the court of first instance.

The rights of recourse are open to the persons who have been notified of the judgment as well as the State Prosecution Service.

Article 1164

An application for the return of a child shall be subject to the provisions of this Chapter.

Chapter VIII
Adoption

Section I
Consent to Adoption

Article 1165

Persons authorized to receive a consent to adoption must inform the one giving his/her consent of the possibility that the consent may be revoked and the procedures of revocation.

The document prescribed in Article 348-3 of the Civil Code must state that this information has been given.

Section II
The Procedure for Adoption

Article 1166

An application for adoption must be made to the regional court.

The court of jurisdiction shall be:

- if the applicant lives in France, the one in whose judicial district he/she resides;
- if the applicant lives abroad, the one within the judicial district of the person to be adopted;
- if the applicant and the person to be adopted live abroad, the court chosen by the applicant.

Article 1167

The proceedings for adoption fall within the scope of non-contentious matters.

Article 1168

The request for adoption is brought by way of an application.

Where the person whose adoption is requested has been living at the home of the applicant before the age of fifteen, the applicant may make the application by means of a simple request addressed to the State Prosecutor who shall remit it to the court.

Article 1169

The application must state whether the application is for a full or a simple adoption.[26]

Article 1170

The matter shall be prepared and argued in chambers, on the advice of the State Prosecution Service.

Article 1171

The court shall consider whether the legal conditions for adoption are satisfied within a time limit of six months either from the filing of the application or from its referral in the case pursuant to the second paragraph of Article 1168. Where

26 A full adoption severs all legal connection with the birth family, a simple adoption does not.

necessary, the court may appoint a medical practitioner in order to conduct such examination as it considers necessary.

The court may obtain information in relation to a ward of the State under the conditions set out in Article L. 81 of the Family and Social Assistance Code.

Article 1172

Repealed.

Article 1173

The court may, with the consent of the applicant, order a simple adoption even if a full adoption has been applied for.

Article 1174

The judgment shall be pronounced in open court. Its substance must specify whether it is a full adoption or a simple adoption and must contain the details prescribed in Article 1056. Furthermore, if the full adoption is pronounced pursuant to the second paragraph of Article 356 of the Civil Code, the judgement must state the first names and family name of the biological parent of the adopted child.

Article 1175

If it is necessary in the same proceedings, the court must rule on the changes to the first names of the adopted child, and in the event of simple adoption, to the adopted child's family name.

Article 1176

Rights of recourse shall be open to the State Prosecution Service.

Section III
The Procedure for the Revocation of a Simple Adoption

Article 1177

The proceedings must observe the rules of procedure applicable to non-contentious matters.

The matter shall be prepared and argued in chambers, after the opinion of the State Prosecution Service has been obtained.

The judgment shall be pronounced in open court.

Article 1178

An appeal may be made as in contentious matters. It shall be prepared and decided in accordance with the rules applicable to the court of first instance.

Chapter IX
Parental Authority

Section I
The Exercise of Parental Authority

Article 1179

Proceedings pursuant to the application of Article 372 to 374-2 of the Civil Code, without prejudice to the rules set forth in this Section, shall be initiated, prepared and decided in chambers, in accordance with the rules set forth in Articles 1084 to 1087.

As provided in Article 52 of Act No. 93-22 of 8th January 1993—amending the Civil Code in relation to civil status, the family and the rights of children and instituting the family judge—the parties shall be entitled to be assisted or represented in accordance with the rules applicable to the district court.

Article 1179-1

For the purpose of Articles 373-2-8 and 373-2-13 of the Civil Code, third parties may by a simple request bring a matter before the State Prosecutor who may gather any information which he/she deems necessary on the situation of the minor and his/her family.

Article 1179-2

Repealed.

Article 1180

Proceedings brought pursuant to Article 371-4 and the second paragraph of Article 373-3 of the Civil Code shall follow the rules of procedure in contentious matters; they shall be prepared and decided in chambers, once the State Prosecution Service has given its opinion.

Article 1180-1

The joint declaration referred to in Article 374 of the Civil Code shall be received by the chief registrar of the regional court of the place where the child lives. The chief registrar prepares an official report, a copy of which he/she shall send to each of the parents.

The grant of the exercise of parental authority on the basis of a joint application is dealt with as a non-contentious matter.

Article 1180-2

The order which provisionally decides on the residence of a child pursuant to Article 373-2-9 of the Civil Code shall state, in addition to the duration of the measure, the places, day and time of the hearing at which the issue of residence will again be decided.

Article 1180-3

The decision enjoining the parties to meet with a family mediator pursuant to the third paragraph of Article 373-2-10 of the Civil Code is not subject to an appeal.

Section II
Educational Measures

Article 1181

Educational measures are taken by the children's judge of the place where, as the case may be, the father, mother, guardian or the person or body to which the child was entrusted live; failing this, by the judge of the place where the child lives.

If the person mentioned in the preceding paragraph changes his/her place of residence, the judge loses jurisdiction to the judge of the place of the new residence, unless a reasoned order to the contrary is made.

As set out in Article L 228-4 of the Family and Social Assistance Code, in the case of a change of department, the president of the General Council[27] of the former residence and that of the new residence are informed of the transfer of jurisdiction.

Article 1182

The judge gives notice of the opening of the proceedings to the State Prosecutor; if they are not applicants, the judge also gives such notice to the father, mother, guardian or the person or representative of the body to whose care the child was entrusted.

The judge hears the father, mother, guardian or the person or representative of the body to which child was entrusted and the minor if he/she is capable of judgment, and informs them of the reasons for hearing the case.

The judge hears any other person whose examination appears useful to him/her.

The notice of the opening of the proceedings and the summons sent to the father and mother, guardian or the person or representative of the body to whose care the child was entrusted and to the minor setting out the right of the parties to choose an adviser or to request that one be appointed for them in accordance

27 The French term "conseil general" refers to the legislative body that runs a department.

with the provisions of Article 1186. The notice and the summons inform the parties of the possibility of consulting the case file in accordance with the provisions of Article 1187.

Article 1183

The judge may, either upon his/her own motion or on the application of the parties or the State Prosecution Service, order the provision of all information concerning the personality and the living conditions of the minor and of his/her parents, in particular by means of a child welfare investigation, medical examinations and psychiatric and psychological tests or by a measure of educational investigation and orientation.

Article 1184

Except in urgent cases that are specifically reasoned the interim measures provided for in the first paragraph of Article 375-5 of the Civil Code, as well as the informative measures provided for in Article 1183 may only be ordered if the testimony has been taken from the father, mother, guardian or representative of the body to whose care the child was entrusted.

If a placement of the child has been ordered as a matter of urgency by the judge without hearing the parties, the judge shall summon the parties to attend on a date which cannot be more than 15 days from the date of that order, failing which, at their request, the minor must be returned to his/her father, mother, guardian or the body to whose care he/she was entrusted.

If the judge assumes jurisdiction, in accordance with the provisions of the second paragraph of Article 375-5 of the Civil Code, through the State Prosecutor who has ordered as a matter of urgency a temporary placement, he/she shall summon the parties and must give a ruling within 15 days of assuming jurisdiction, failing which at their request, the minor must be returned to his/her father, mother, guardian or the body into whose care he/she was entrusted.

If the matter is urgent, the interim measures may also be taken, without prejudice to the provisions of the second paragraph of Article 375-5 of the Civil Code, by the children's judge of the place where the minor child was found, on condition that he/she should withdraw from the case within one month in favor of the judge who has territorial jurisdiction to hear the matter.

Article 1185

The substantive decision must be given within six months from the decision ordering interim measures; failing which, at their request, the child shall be returned to the father, mother, guardian or person or body to whose care he/she was entrusted.

If the preparation of the case has not been completed within the time limit prescribed in the preceding paragraph, the judge may, once the State Prosecutor has given his/her opinion, extend this time limit for a period not exceeding six months.

Article 1186

Any of: the minor who is capable of judgment, the father, mother, guardian or the person or representative of the body to whose care he/she was entrusted, may choose an adviser or request the judge to appoint one for him/herself. The appointment must be made within eight days of the request.

The parties concerned are informed of this right at the first hearing.

Article 1187

Once notice is given of the opening of the proceedings, the file may be consulted at the court registry office up to the day before the hearing by the minor's attorney and the attorney for the father, mother, guardian or the person or body to whose care the child was entrusted. The attorney may also obtain a copy of any or all documents in the court file for use exclusively in the proceedings for educational measures. He/she may not send the copies thus obtained or photocopies thereof to his/her client.

Upon the request of and on the days and times fixed by the judge, the file may also be consulted by the father, mother, guardian or person or representative of the body to whose care the child was entrusted, and by the minor child who is capable of judgment up to the day before the hearing.

The minor child who is capable of judgment may consult his/her own file in the presence of his/her father, mother or attorney. Should the parents refuse, and if the child concerned has no attorney, the judge must instruct the head of the local bar to appoint an attorney to assist the minor child or authorize the educational body in charge of the measure to accompany the child for this consultation.

In a reasoned decision, the judge may, in the absence of an attorney, exclude all or some of the documents from being consulted by one or other of the parents, guardian or person or representative of the body to whose care the child was entrusted or the minor child if this consultation might involve the risk of any serious physical or psychological danger to the minor, one of the parties or a third party.

The file may also be consulted, under the same conditions, by institutions responsible for measures under Article 1183 of this Code and Articles 375-2 and 375-4 of the Civil Code.

Once the case has been prepared, the court file is sent to the State Prosecutor who must return it within fifteen days to the judge together with his/her written opinion as to how to proceed or an indication that he/she intends to give this opinion at the hearing.

Article 1188

The hearing may be held at the children's court or the district court located in that judicial district, as indicated in the summons.

The father, mother, guardian, person or body to whose care the child was entrusted, and, where applicable, the minor child are summoned to the hearing at least eight days before the date of the hearing; the parties' advisers are also notified of the same.

Article 1189

At the hearing, the judge shall hear the minor, his/her father, mother, guardian or the person or representative of the body to whose care he/she was entrusted and any other person whose testimony seems useful to the judge. He/she may excuse the minor from having to appear or order that he/she shall not be present in court for part or all of the oral arguments.

The advisers of the parties shall be heard.

The matter shall be prepared and decided in chambers, after the State Prosecution Service has given its opinion.

Article 1190

The judge's decision shall be given within eight days to the father, mother, guardian, person or body to whose care the child was entrusted, as well to the child's adviser where one has been appointed.

The substance of the decision must be provided to a minor who is over sixteen years of age unless his/her condition does not permit it.

However, the decision to exclude certain documents from being consulted pursuant to Article 1187, must be given within eight days only to the party who requested to see them.

In any case, notice of the notification must be given to the State Prosecutor.

Article 1191

The decisions of the judge may be subject to an appeal:

- by father, mother, guardian, person or body to whose care the child was entrusted until the expiration of fifteen days from the notification;
- by the minor until the expiration of fifteen days from the notification or, failing that, from when he/she became aware of the decision;
- by the State Prosecution Service until the expiration of fifteen days following the receipt of the notice given to it.

Article 1192

The appeal shall be brought in accordance with the rules set forth in Articles 931 to 934.

The registrar must inform, by regular mail, the father, mother, guardian, person or body to whose care the child was entrusted and to a minor him/herself who is over sixteen years of age of the appeal, when they have not themselves made the appeal, and he/she must inform them that they will ultimately be summoned before the court.

Article 1193

The appeal shall be prepared and decided as a matter of priority in chambers by the chamber of the court of appeal with jurisdiction over children's matters in accordance with the procedure before a children's judge.

The court rules on appeals against decisions of temporary placement made by the children's judge pursuant to the provisions of Article 375-5 of the Civil Code within three months from the declaration of the appeal.

Article 1194

The decisions of the court of appeal shall be notified as provided in Article 1190.

Article 1195

The summons and notifications are done by the court registry office by registered mail with acknowledgment of receipt and by regular mail. The judge may, however, decide that notification be done by a court bailiff or through administrative channels.

The issue of an official copy of a judgment in return for a signed and dated acknowledgment of receipt shall constitute proper notification.

Article 1196

The appeal to the Court of Cassation is available to the State Prosecution Service.

Article 1197

Where the father and mother cannot pay all of the legal costs, the judge may fix the amount up to which they must contribute.

Article 1198

The judge may visit or have visited any minor who has been placed in care pursuant to Articles 375-3 and 375-5 of the Civil Code.

Article 1199

The judge may delegate his/her powers to the judge of the place where the minor has been placed in care, either voluntarily or by a court order, in order to arrange for one of the measures provided for in Articles 375-2 and 375-4 of the Civil Code and to follow its application.

Article 1199-1

The institution or body entrusted with implementing the measure shall send a report on the situation and the development of the minor to the children's judge who made the decision in accordance with the time frame fixed by the decision or, failing this, annually.

Article 1200

In the course of the implementation of educational measures, account must be taken of the religious or philosophical convictions of the minor and his/her family.

Article 1200-1

Educational measures which are renewed pursuant to the third paragraph of Article 375 of the Civil Code must be taken by the children's judge under the conditions set out in Articles 1181 to 1200.

Section III
Delegation and Complete or Partial Withdrawal of Parental Authority

Article 1201

Repealed.

Article 1202

Applications for the complete or partial withdrawal of parental authority must be brought before the regional court of the place where the parent against whom the action is brought resides.

Applications for the delegation of parental authority must be made to the family judge of the place where the minor resides.

Article 1203

The court or judge assumes jurisdiction on the basis of an application. The parties do not need to be represented by an attorney. The application may be sent to the State Prosecutor, who must forward it to the court or judge.

Article 1204

Where an application requests the complete or partial withdrawal of parental authority, and if the request comes from the State Prosecution Service, a member of the family or the guardian of the child, the application must be notified by the registrar to the parent against whom the action is brought.

Article 1205

The court or judge, even upon his/her own motion, must undertake or have undertaken all such inquiries as are helpful, in particular the measures to obtain information referred to in Article 1183. He/she may for this purpose appoint a children's judge.

If proceedings for educational measures have been started with regard to one or more children, the file on this must be transmitted to the court or judge.

Article 1206

The State Prosecutor shall gather such information as he/she deems necessary on the family situation of the minor and the moral conduct of his/her parents.

Article 1207

During the proceedings, the court or judge may order any interim measures with respect to the exercise of parental authority.

Article 1208

The court or judge hears the father, mother, guardian, person or representative of the body to whose care the child was entrusted and any person whose testimony shall be deemed necessary.

The matter shall be prepared and decided in chambers. Oral pleadings shall be heard in the presence of the State Prosecution Service.

Article 1209

The provisions of Article 1186, the first paragraph of Article 1187, the second paragraph of Article 1188, the first and fourth paragraphs of Article 1190, Articles 1191, the first paragraph of Article 1193 and Articles 1194 to 1197 shall apply to the procedures for delegation and the complete or partial withdrawal of parental authority, and the powers and duties of the children's judge are assumed, as the case may be, by the court or family judge.

Article 1210

Applications for the restitution of rights delegated or withdrawn must be made by way of an application to the court or judge of the place where the person to whom they have been conferred resides. It is notified to this person by the registrar. That court or judge must, furthermore, observe the rules governing applications for the delegation of parental authority.

Section IV
Provisions Relating to an Ad Hoc Guardian

Article 1210-1

Where pursuant to the provisions of Articles 388-2 and 389-3 of the Civil Code, the court proceeds with the appointment of an *ad hoc* guardian and if, in the interests of the child, it is impossible to choose this person from within the family or among the child's relatives, the court may appoint the *ad hoc* guardian from among the persons appearing on the list provided for in Article R.53 of the Code of Criminal Procedure.

Article 1210-2

The appointment of an *ad hoc* guardian may be challenged by means of an appeal by the legal representatives of the minor within fifteen days. The appeal shall not operate as a stay of execution.

The appeal must be made, prepared and decided as a non-contentious matter.

Article 1210-3

Where the *ad hoc* guardian has been selected from among the persons appearing in the list provided for in Article R. 53 of the Code of Criminal Procedure, the remuneration of that person is that which is set forth in No. 3 of Article R. 216 of the same Code.

The cost of this remuneration shall be recovered by the Treasury from the party ordered to pay costs, in accordance with the procedures and under the guarantees provided for in criminal fines. In the absence of an order for costs, the costs shall be recovered from the party specified by the judge who appointed the *ad hoc* guardian.

Chapter X
The Guardianship of Minors

Section I
Guardianship Judges

Article 1211

The guardianship judge of the place where the minor resides has jurisdiction.

Article 1212

Except where he/she assumes jurisdiction of his/her own motion, a judge acquires jurisdiction in a case on the basis of an application or a written or oral declaration made to the court registry office.

Article 1213

The sittings of the judges are not open to the public. Certified copies of their decisions may only be issued to the parties and to those persons who have been appointed guardians, unless the president of the regional court authorizes otherwise.

Article 1214

The decision of the judge is notified, on his/her initiative, within three days, to the applicant, guardian, legal representative of the minor and all those whose rights or duties are affected where they are not present.

Furthermore, in the case of Article 389-5 of the Civil Code, it is notified to the spouse who did not consent to the proceedings and, in the case of Article 468 of the same Code, to the auxiliary guardian.

Article 1215

In all cases, the decision of the judge may be appealed within fifteen days to the regional court. This remedy is available to all the persons mentioned in Article 1214 from the time of notification of the decision or, if they were present, the rendering of the decision.

Except where the decision is immediately enforceable notwithstanding an appeal, the enforcement of the decision is suspended during the time period for the appeal and during the appeal itself.

Article 1216

The appeal is brought by an application by an attorney and filed or sent by registered letter to the registry office of the district court.

Within eight days of the filing of the application or its receipt, the clerk of the court forwards the case file to the president of the regional court.

Article 1217

The registrar of the regional court gives notice of the date of the hearing to the applicant's attorney and, by registered letter with acknowledgment of receipt to those persons who could have appealed the decision.

These persons have the right to intervene before the court, which may even order that they be served with a document by a court bailiff joining them as parties to the proceedings.

Article 1218

Once the regional court has ruled upon a matter, the guardianship file, to which is added a certified true copy of the judgment, is sent back to the registrar of the district court.

Section II
The Family Council

Article 1219

The sittings of the family council are not open to the public.

Third parties may only obtain certified copies of its decisions with the authorization of the president of the regional court.

Article 1220

The decisions of the family council must be reasoned; in all cases where the decision is not unanimous, the opinion of each of its members is mentioned in the official record.

Article 1221

The decisions of the family council are self-enforceable.

However, if the judge has not made the decision immediately enforceable notwithstanding an appeal, its enforcement is suspended during the time period for the appeal set forth in Article 1222 and during the appeal itself.

Article 1222

In all cases, the decisions of the family council may be appealed to the regional court either by the guardian, the auxiliary guardian or the other members of the family council, or by the guardianship judge, irrespective of their opinion during the hearing.

The time-limit for the appeal is fifteen days; it runs from the day of the decision except in the case of Article 413 of the Civil Code where it runs, with respect to the members of the family council, from the day when they were notified of the decision.

Article 1223

The procedures set forth in Articles 1216 to 1218 apply to appeals against decisions of the family council.

When an appeal is brought by a guardianship judge, he/she adds to the case file a note explaining the reasons for his/her appeal.

The registrar of this court gives notice of the date of the hearing to the applicant's attorney and, by a registered letter with acknowledgment of receipt, to the guardian and auxiliary guardian as well as to those members of the family council who are not party to the appeal.

Section III
Common Provisions

Article 1224

Notifications that have to be given on the initiative of the guardianship judge are sent by registered letter with acknowledgment of receipt; however, a judge may decide that they shall be served by a court bailiff or delivered through administrative channels.

The issue by the court registry office of a certified true copy of a decision by a judge or a family council in return for a dated and signed receipt is equivalent to a notification.

Article 1225

Appeals against decisions of guardianship judges or family councils are entered in a register that is kept at the registry office of the district court. The name of the person bringing the appeal, that of his/her attorney, the date on which the appeal was lodged and the date of the forwarding of the case file to the regional court must be mentioned.

Article 1226

If the appeal brought against a decision of a guardianship judge or a family council is dismissed, the person who brought it, unless it is a judge, may be ordered to pay costs and even damages.

Article 1227

The appeal is conducted and heard by preference in chambers.

The court may request from the guardianship judge such information as it deems helpful.

Article 1228

The court may, even upon its own motion, substitute a new decision for that of the guardianship judge or family council.

Article 1229

The decision of the regional court is not open to appeal.

Article 1230

The amount of civil fines provided for in Articles 389-5 (*formerly*), 395, 412 and 413 of the Civil Code is at least 7.5€ and at most 75€.

The decisions are not open to the appeal specified in Article 1215.

Article 1231

When an amicable partition has been authorized in accordance with Article 466 of the Civil Code, the final scheme of division that has been approved by the parties is filed at the registry office of the district court where the members of the family council may examine it following notification by the guardianship judge.

Fifteen days after the filing or, in the case of guardianship, fifteen days after the notification to the members of the family council, the confirmation of the final scheme of division may be sought either by the legal representative of the minor or the guardian or the other parties interested in the partition.

The members of the family council who wish to object to the confirmation have to do so by way of proceedings before the regional court; a guardianship judge may object to the confirmation by a reasoned submission to this court.

The provisions of Articles 1228 and 1229 apply to the confirmation proceedings.

Section IV
Specific Provisions for Children in the Care of the State

Article 1231-1

In derogation from the provisions of Article 1223, an appeal against a decision of a family council of children in the care of the State is brought by an application signed by an attorney and submitted or sent by registered letter to the registry of the regional court.

The procedure set forth in Article 1217 applies.

Article 1231-2

An application relating to an appeal against the order of admission as a child in the care of the State that is provided for in Article 61 of the Family and Social Assistance Code is brought before the regional court in the judicial district where the order was made.

Articles 1159, 1160, 1161, (paragraph 1) and 1162 apply to the application and the proceedings.

The judgment is given in open court. It is notified by the registrar to the applicant, the guardian and the president of the Council of the department.

Chapter XI
Rules Governing the Protection of Adults

Section I
General Provisions

Article 1232

The State Prosecutor in the location where treatment takes place and the guardianship judge have the right, pursuant to Article 490-3 of the Civil Code, without prejudice to any other measures, to have protected persons examined by a doctor.

Article 1233

If the property of an adult who is a protected person within the meaning of Articles 488 and 490 of the Civil Code is possibly at risk, the judge of the district court takes all necessary measures to preserve the property on his/her own initiative or on the application of the State Prosecutor. In particular, he/she may order the affixation of seals, which is done in the manner prescribed for seals after a death.

Article 1234

Where it appears that the nature of the property does not warrant such measure, the State Prosecutor or the judge of the district court may request the chief registrar of the district court, a police captain, a commanding officer of a squad of gendarmes or the mayor to draw up a list simply describing the furniture and, if the premises are unoccupied, to ensure that they are closed and to keep the keys.

The keys are returned, in exchange for a simple receipt, to the protected person on his/her return to the premises. They may not be handed over to any other person except with the permission of the State Prosecutor or a judge of the district court.

Article 1235

The guardianship judge may, in all cases where he/she deems it helpful to hear the protected person, travel anywhere throughout the judicial district of the court of appeal, as well as in the departments that adjoin the one where he/she performs his/her duties. The judge may travel without the assistance of the registrar.

The same rules apply where the protected person is heard by a judge of the regional court.

Section II
Judicial Protection

Article 1236

The declaration for the purpose of judicial protection provided for in Article L.326-1 of the Code of Public Health is forwarded to the State Prosecutor in the location where treatment takes place, who, if appropriate, notifies the State Prosecutor of the place where the person concerned resides.

Article 1237

A judicial protection measure expires two months after the declaration; renewed measures expire six months after being declared.

Article 1238

The decision of a guardianship judge placing a person under judicial protection pursuant to the second paragraph of Article 491-1 of the Civil Code, is forwarded by him/her to the State Prosecutor of his/her judicial district, who, where appropriate, notifies the State Prosecutor of the residence or place of treatment.

Article 1239

The decision by which a guardianship judge places a person to be protected under judicial protection, pursuant to the second paragraph of Article 491-1 of the Civil Code, is not open to appeal on this ground.

Article 1240

The appointment or dismissal of the agents of persons placed under judicial protection as well as the specification of their powers are done in accordance with the procedure set down for guardianship.

Article 1241

The persons who have standing to bring an appeal against the decision that sets up the guardianship may lodge an appeal against the decision of the guardianship judge appointing, pursuant to Article 491-5 of the Civil Code, a special agent.

Article 1242

The State Prosecutor who has received the declaration for the purpose of judicial protection or the decision of the guardianship judge enters the declaration and the decision in a register kept specially for this purpose.

The declaration for the purpose of ending the protection as well as any cancellations are marked in the margin of the original entry.

Declarations for renewal are entered in the register on their date. References to the declarations are made in the margin of the initial entry.

Section III
Guardianship

Article 1243

The guardianship of adults follows the rules set down for the guardianship of minors without prejudice to the provisions that follow.

Article 1244

An application for the purpose of instituting a guardianship designates the person to be protected and states the facts that call for this protection. A certificate issued by a medical specialist, chosen from the list referred to in Article 493-1 of the Civil Code is to be enclosed with the application. The application lists the close relatives of the person to be protected to the extent that their existence is known to the applicant; it also states the name and address of the person's regular doctor.

Where the judge assumes jurisdiction on his/her own initiative for the purpose of instituting a guardianship, he/she appoints a medical specialist, chosen from the list referred to in Article 493-1 of the Civil Code, in order to assess the state of the person to be protected.

The registrar notifies the State Prosecutor of the procedure that has been commenced.

Article 1245

The list of medical specialists is drawn up each year by the State Prosecutor after consulting the prefect.

Article 1246

The guardianship judge hears the person to be protected and informs him/her of the procedure that has been commenced. The hearing may take place at the seat of the court, at the place of residence, in the institution of treatment or in any other appropriate place.

The judge may, if he/she deems it appropriate, conduct the hearing in the presence of the person's regular doctor and other people.

The State Prosecutor and the council of the person to be protected are informed of the date and place of the hearing; they may attend it.

An official report of the hearing is written.

Article 1247

Where the hearing of the person to be protected is of such a nature as to be detrimental to his/her health, a judge may, with cause and on the advice of a doctor, decide that it should not take place. He/she so notifies the State Prosecutor.

In the same decision, he/she orders that the person to be protected be informed of the procedure that has been commenced in a manner appropriate to his/her condition.

The implementation of this decision is noted in the guardianship file.

Article 1248

The judge may, either on his/her authority or on an application by the parties or the State Prosecutor's Office, order any measures to obtain information. In particular, he/she may have an investigation carried out by the social welfare authorities or findings made by any person of his/her choice.

He himself hears, as far as it is possible, the parents, close relatives and friends of the person to be protected.

Article 1249

The guardianship judge may, before reaching a decision, convene a family council constituted in the same way as set out in the Civil Code for the guardianship of minors.

The family council is called upon to give its opinion on the condition of the person for whom the institution of a guardianship is sought, as well as on the appropriateness of judicial protection.

The opinion of the family council does not bind the judge; it is not open to any appeal.

Article 1250

The case file is forwarded to the State Prosecutor a month before the date fixed for the hearing. Fifteen days before this date, the State Prosecutor returns the case file to the court registry office with his/her written opinion. These time-limits may be reduced by the judge in cases of urgency.

The judge informs the applicant and the person to be protected, if he/she seems to the judge to be in a state to benefit from such notification, or their counsel that they may consult the case file at the court registry office until the day before the hearing.

Article 1251

At the hearing, the judge hears, if he deems it appropriate, the applicant and the person to be protected.

The comments of the parties counsel are heard.

The matter is conducted and decided in chambers, after hearing the opinion of the State Prosecutor's Office.

Article 1252

An application for instituting a guardianship lapses if a decision with respect to it is not taken within a year of the application.

In cases where a judge assumes jurisdiction on his/her own motion, the proceedings are invalid and void if a decision to institute the guardianship is not taken within the year.

Article 1253

A protected person must be notified of a judgment with respect to the institution of a guardianship; the State Prosecutor is informed of it.

However, a judge may, in a reasoned decision, decide that there is no need to notify the protected person of the judgment ordering the institution of the guardianship due to his/her condition. In this case, the protected person's counsel, if he or she has one, as well as to the person among the spouses, ascending and descending relatives and brothers and sisters that the judge considers the most qualified to receive this notification, must be notified of the judgment.

If the judge deems it helpful, the persons that he/she designates from among those who the law authorizes to bring an appeal may also be notified.

Article 1254

The interested party is always notified of judgments rendered pursuant to Articles 501 and 507 of the Civil Code.

Article 1255

An appeal against a decision refusing to set up a guardianship can be brought only by the applicant.

Article 1256

An appeal against a decision to set up a guardianship or to refuse to terminate it is brought either in accordance with the provisions of Article 1216 or by a letter giving brief reasons and signed by one of the person having standing under Article 493 of the Civil Code; this letter is delivered or sent by registered mail with acknowledgment of receipt to the registry office of the district court.

Irrespective of the form of the appeal, use of counsel is not mandatory in the proceedings.

Article 1257

The recourses provided for in Articles 1255 and 1256 must be exercised within fifteen days of the judgment. With respect to persons who have been notified of the decision, the time-limit runs from the notification.

Article 1258

The State Prosecutor's Office may bring an appeal until the expiration of a period of fifteen days following receipt of the notice that has been given.

Article 1259

The registrar of the regional court informs the persons who have lodged an appeal against a decision, those persons to whom this decision has been notified as well as their attorneys, where applicable, of the hearing date.

Article 1260

An abstract of any decision ruling on the institution, modification or termination of a guardianship is forwarded to the registry office of the regional court in the judicial district the protected person was born for the purpose of being entered into the civil register and to permit a public note to be entered in the margin of the birth certificate according to the procedure set out in Chapter III of this Book.

When a decision is made by a guardianship judge, it is notified within fifteen days of the expiration of the time limits for an appeal.

When a decision has been made by a regional court, it is notified by the State Prosecutor within fifteen days of the judgment.

Article 1261

In all proceedings relating to the institution, modification or termination of a guardianship, the judge may, at any stage of the procedure and of his/her own initiative, have counsel appointed for the person to be protected or protected person if the person has not chosen one.

Section IV
Temporary Guardianship

Article 1262

Temporary guardianship is subject to the same rules as the guardianship of adults.

Article 1263

When an adult under temporary guardianship applies for a non-mandatory authorization, the judge may not rule until he/she has heard or called upon the temporary guardian.

TITLE II
PROPERTY

Chapter I
Possessory Actions

Article 1264

Subject to respecting the rules relating to public property, possessory actions may be brought, in the year in which the trespass occurred, by those persons who had been in possession or held ownership for at least a year; however, an action for re-possession against the perpetrator of a forceful ejection may be brought even though the victim of the dispossession had been in possession or held ownership for less than a year.

Article 1265

The protection of possession and the substance of the right are to be kept separate.

A judge may, however, examine titles for the purpose of establishing whether the conditions for protecting possession are met.

Procedural measures may not involve the substance of the right.

Article 1266

A person who brings an action on the substance of the right no longer has the standing to bring a possessory action.

Article 1267

A defendant in a possessory action may only bring an action on the substance of the right after having put an end to the nuisance.

Chapter II
The Rendering of Accounts and the Liquidation of Produce

Article 1268

An application for the rendering of an account is brought before the court in whose judicial district the accountant resides or, if the accountant has been appointed by a court, before the judge who appointed him/her.

Article 1269

No application for the review of an account is admissible unless it takes the form of a revision on the basis of error, omission or inaccurate presentation.

The same rules shall apply to the liquidation of produce where there is need for restitution.

Chapter III
Leases Concluded by Life Tenants by Leave of the Court

Article 1270

The leave provided for in Article 595 of the Civil Code is subject to the rules set out in Articles 1286 to 1289.

Chapter IV
The Sale of Immovables and Businesses Belonging to Minors or Adults under Guardianship

Article 1271

The sale by court order of the immovables and businesses belonging to minors or adult under guardianship may only be ordered subsequent to a decision of the family council stating the nature of the property and its estimated value.

This decision is not necessary if the property belongs at the same time to adults possessing legal capacity and if the sale is sought by them. The matter is then decided in accordance with the rules set down for partition by the court.

Article 1272

On an application by the guardian or auxiliary guardian, bids are received either by a notary appointed for this purpose by the regional court or, in a session for the sale of real property by a court, by a judge appointed by this court.

The court having jurisdiction is the one in whose judicial district the person under guardianship resides.

If the property is situated in various districts, the court may appoint a notary in each of these districts and may issue letters rogatory to each of the courts where this property is situated.

Article 1273

The court determines the reserve price of each of the items of property to be sold and the essential conditions of the sale. The court may specify that in the absence of a bid reaching this reserve price, the sale may be effected on the basis of a lower reserve price, which it sets.

The court may, if the value or nature of the property justifies it, have part or all of it valued.

Article 1274

The court shall set down the procedure for giving public notice, taking into account the value, nature and location of the property.

Article 1275

The notary who has been appointed or an attorney draws up a memorandum of the terms and conditions of sale. If the sale takes place at a court auction, this memorandum is filed with the court registry office.

The memorandum refers to the judgment ordering the sale, designates the items for sale and sets out the price and conditions of the sale. It shall indicate the judgment ordering the sale, the goods to be sold, the reserve price and the conditions of sale. If the sale involves a business, the memorandum specifies the nature and location of the business and the various assets that make it up, as well the obligations that will bind the purchaser, in particular with respect to the stock of goods of the business.

Article 1276

Pursuant to the provisions of the first paragraph of Article 459 of the Civil Code, the auxiliary guardian is summoned to the sale at least one month in advance by the person drawing up the memorandum of sale and informed that the sale will take place even in his/her absence.

Article 1277

If no bid reaches the amount of the reserve price, the judge or notary may make a record of the highest bid and award the item for the amount of this offer on a provisional basis.

Except in the case of a waiver by the seller, the court that has set the reserve price, acting on an application from the notary, the attorney or any other interested party, may either declare the award to be final and the sale concluded or order that a new sale take place; in the latter event, it fixes the time-limit for the new sale, which may not be less than fifteen days, the reserve price and the procedure for giving public notice.

Article 1278

Articles 701, 705 to 707, 733 to 741 b and 742 of the (old) Code of Civil procedure apply to this Chapter.

Nevertheless, bids are received by a notary, the auction may take place without the presence of an attorney.

In the case of a sale before a notary, if there has been a sham bid, the proceedings are continued before a court. The certificate recording that the highest bidder has not fulfilled the conditions is issued by the notary. The official report of the auction is filed at the court registry office.

Article 1279

Within ten days following the definitive sale by auction, any person may make an overbid higher by one tenth as long as they comply with the formalities and time limits set out in Articles 708 to 710 of the (old) Code of Civil procedure.

In cases where the auction took place before a notary, the court, in its judgment upholding the overbid, refers the new auction to the same notary, who proceeds in accordance with the memorandum of the terms and conditions of sale that was drawn up previously.

Where a second auction takes place after an overbid, no further overbid is permitted for the same items.

Article 1280

The overbid provided for in the second paragraph of Article 459 of the Civil Code is made, within ten days following the auction, by way of declaration to the registry office of the court in whose judicial district the notary who carried out the sale resides.

Notice of this declaration is given to the person or residence of the highest bidder within the time period provided for in Article 709 of the (old) Code of Civil Procedure.

Furthermore, the rules of Article 1279 apply.

Article 1281

Nothing derogates from the respective powers of the various public officers with respect to the sale of businesses.

Chapter V
The Distribution of Funds Outside Execution Procedures

Article 1281-1

If it is necessary, outside of any execution procedure, to distribute a sum of money between creditors, the first party to act may apply for a summary order to the president of the regional court in the judicial district in which the debtor resides, which judge appoints a person to make the distribution.

The person appointed for the distribution is the receiver of the funds unless the deposit has not been ordered.

Article 1281-2

The receiver appointed for the distribution must offer guarantees for the sums that have been distributed.

Article 1281-3

The registrar serves a copy of the order by ordinary mail on the person charged with the distribution and, if the deposit has been ordered, the Bank for Official Deposits.

The person charged with the distribution advises the creditors, by registered letter with acknowledgment of receipt, that they must, within a period of one month, send him a declaration comprising a breakdown of the sums claimed with respect to principal, interest and ancillary costs. Where applicable, this declaration mentions the preferential rights and securities attached to the claim. The supporting documents are attached to the declaration.

If a creditor is in default of a declaration within the time period referred to in the preceding paragraph, the creditor loses the right to participate in the distribution.

Article 1281-4

The person charged with the distribution prepares a plan for distribution within two months following the last notice referred to in the second paragraph of Article 1281-3.

Such notice is served on the debtor and each creditor by registered letter with acknowledgment of receipt.

If it is not to be invalid, the notification indicates to the recipients:

1. That he/she raises, within a period of fifteen days from receipt of the letter, and sends by registered letter with acknowledgment of receipt, an objection, giving reasons and accompanied by the necessary supporting documents, with the person charged with the distribution.

2. That, failing a reply within the time allowed, he/she is deemed to have accepted the plan and that the plan will become final if no objection is raised.

In case of difficulty, the time period referred to in the first paragraph of the Article may be extended by the president of the regional court acting on an *ex parte* application by the person charged with the distribution.

Article 1281-5

In the absence of any objection with the fifteen days following the last notification referred to in the second paragraph of Article 1281-4, the plan for distribution becomes final.

When the person charged with the distribution holds the sum to be distributed, he/she then pays the creditors within fifteen days.

Where the funds have been deposited, the person charged with the distribution serves the finalized plan for distribution on the Bank for Official Deposits, which proceeds to pay within fifteen days.

Article 1281-6

In the case of objection, the person charged with the distribution summons the parties by registered letter with acknowledgment of receipt with a view to attempting to achieve a friendly settlement, which must happen within the month following the first objection.

The summons reproduces the wording of the second paragraph of Article 1281-7.

Article 1281-7

If an agreement is reached, a formal document recording it is drawn up and a copy of it delivered or sent by regular mail to all the parties. Payment is then made under the conditions set out in the second and third paragraphs of Article 1281-5.

A person who is duly summoned and who does not appear is deemed to have accepted the agreement.

Article 1281-8

In the absence of a friendly settlement, the person charged with the distribution draws up a document setting out the points of disagreement.

The sums available for distribution are immediately deposited if they have not already been deposited by virtue of the decision appointing the person charged with the distribution.

The first party to act may bring the matter before the regional court, which makes the distribution.

Article 1281-9

In the absence of a plan for distribution within the periods allowed, the matter proceeds as is provided for in the second and third paragraphs of Article 1281-8.

Article 1281-10

The payments must be made fifteen days at the latest after the Bank for Official Deposits has been notified that the judgment of distribution has become final.

Article 1281-11

The remuneration of the person charged with the distribution is deducted from the funds to be distributed and borne by the creditors proportionately to the sum that is due to them.

In case of any dispute, the remuneration is fixed by the president of the regional court.

Article 1281-12

In commercial matters, the powers conferred upon the regional court and its president are exercised by the Commercial Court and by its president.

TITLE III
MATRIMONIAL REGIMES, SUCCESSION AND DONATIONS

Chapter I
The Rights of Spouses and Matrimonial Regimes

Section I
Leave and Authorizations

Article 1286

Applications for leaves and authorizations provided for by law, in particular by Articles 217, 219, the second paragraph of Article 1426 and Articles 2139, 2140 and 2163 of the Civil Code are brought before the regional court.

Article 1287

The application is conducted and judged as a non-contentious matter except in those cases where it aims at circumventing the spouse's refusal.

Article 1288

When the application for leave aims at circumventing the spouse's refusal, the applying spouse makes an application to the president with a view to summoning his/her spouse to appear on a certain day. The court hears the other spouse before giving a ruling unless this spouse, after being duly served, does not appear. The matter is conducted and decided in chambers.

Article 1289

An appeal is brought, conducted and decided as a non-contentious or contentious matter, as the case may be; in the latter event, the matter is conducted and decided in chambers.

Section II
Urgent Measures

Article 1290

The urgent measures provided for in Article 220-1 of the Civil Code are prescribed by a family judge in a summary proceeding or, where necessary, by an order given on an *ex parte* application.

Section III
Transfers by Court Order of Administration and the Early Liquidation of Equity Claims

Article 1291

The actions provided for in the first and third paragraphs of Article 1426 and in Articles 1429 and 1580 of the Civil Code are governed by the rules applicable to applications for the separation of property.

Section IV
Court-Ordered Separation of Property

Article 1292

An application for the separation of property is brought before the regional court where the family resides.

A copy of the application is forwarded by the attorney of the applicant to the registry offices of the regional courts in whose judicial districts the spouses were born, with a view to keeping it in the civil register and publishing it by a note in the margin of the birth certificate in accordance to the procedure set out in Chapter III of Title I of the present Book.

A copy of the application may, in addition, be published in a newspaper distributed in the judicial district of the court dealing with the matter.

Article 1293

The judgment may only be rendered one month after the note referred to in the preceding Article has been inserted in the margin of the birth certificate of each of the spouses or, if this document is not kept in a French register, after a copy of the application has been filed in the civil register referred in Article 4 of Decree No. 65-411 of 1 June 1965 on the creation of a central department for civil status at the Ministry for Foreign Affairs.

Article 1294

The judgment ordering the separation is published in the newspaper distributed in the judicial district of the court that rendered it.

The registrar at the place where the marriage was celebrated is notified of the formal order of the judgment, so that a note of it may made in the margin of the marriage certificate. If the marriage was celebrated in a foreign country and a marriage certificate has been drawn up or transcribed into a French register, the authority responsible for this register, is notified of the formal order of the judgment.

Where a marriage contract was entered into by the spouses, the formal order of the decision is sent by registered letter with acknowledgment of receipt to the notary holding the original of the contract. The notary is obliged to make a note of the decision on the document and must no longer issue a copy of it, enforceable or not, without reproducing this note, otherwise, he/she is liable in damages.

In the cases referred to in the two preceding paragraphs, the notification is accompanied by proof of the enforceable character of the decision in accordance with Article 506.

Article 1295

The formalities set out in Article 1294 are performed by the applicant.

Article 1296

A judgment dismissing the application for the separation of property is published in accordance with the second paragraph of Article 1292.

Article 1297

The implementation of the decision may not be raised against creditors of the spouses if it has been started before the formalities set out in Article 1294 have been performed.

Article 1298

Within the year following compliance with these formalities, the creditors of either spouse may bring a third party objection against the judgment of separation of property.

Article 1299

The admission of the respondent spouse does not constitute proof, even if there is no creditor.

Section V
Approval by the Court of a Change of the System of Matrimonial Property

Article 1300

An application for the approval of a change of the system of matrimonial property is brought before the regional court where the family resides.

Article 1301

The approval of a change of the system of matrimonial property is considered a non-contentious matter.

Article 1302

A certified copy of the notarized document that modifies or changes entirely the system of matrimonial property is enclosed with the application.

Article 1303

Paragraphs 2 and 3 of Article 1292, Articles 1293 to 1296 and Article 1298 apply to the approval of a change of the system of matrimonial property.

Section VI
Public Notices in International Matters

§ 1 The designation of the law applicable to the system of matrimonial property done during the course of the marriage

Article 1303-1

Where the marriage certificate is kept by a French authority, this authority notes in the margin of that document, at the request of one or both of the spouses, the document containing the designation of the law applicable to the system of matrimonial property, public notice of which is required by Article 1397-3 of the Civil Code.

In the absence of a marriage certificate kept by a French authority and if the document containing the designation of the law applicable to the system of matrimonial property has been drawn up in its official form in France, or if one of the spouses is French, the said document or certificate issued by the person with the authority to draw it up is, at the request of one or both of the spouses, entered for safekeeping in the supplementary civil register referred to in Article 4-1 of Decree No. 65-422 of 1 June 1965 on the creation of a central department for civil status at the Ministry for Foreign Affairs.

Article 1303-2

Where a marriage contract has been concluded in France, one or both of the spouses send to the notary holding the original of the contract, by registered letter with acknowledgment of receipt, a copy of the document containing the designation of the law applicable to the system of matrimonial property. If the marriage contract was executed in the presence of a French diplomatic or consular official, one or both of the spouses inform the Minister for Foreign Affairs.

The notary, the French diplomatic or consular official, or the Minister for Foreign Affairs makes a note of the applicable law that is so designated on the original of the marriage contract and must not issue any copy or abstract of it that does not contain this note.

§ 2 Change of the system of matrimonial property by virtue of a foreign law

Article 1303-3

Where the marriage certificate is kept by a French authority, the change of a system of matrimonial property that is obtained pursuant to a foreign law governing the marriage property is noted in the margin of this certificate.

In the absence of a marriage certificate kept by a French authority, this change of the system of matrimonial property, if it has given rise to a decision of a French court or to a document drawn up in France in its official form, or if one of the spouses is French, is entered for safekeeping in the supplementary civil register referred to in Article 4-1 of Decree No. 65-422 of 1 June 1965 on the creation of a central department for civil status at the Ministry for Foreign Affairs.

Article 1303-4

If this change has given rise to a decision of a French court, the note in the margin of the marriage certificate or its entry in the supplementary civil register is done in accordance with the second, third and fourth paragraphs of Article 1294. In other cases, the State Prosecutor of the place where the marriage certificate or the supplementary civil register is kept has this note or entry made at the request of one or both of the spouses.

Article 1303-5

Where a marriage contract has been concluded in France, one or both of the spouses send to the notary holding the original of the contract, by registered letter with acknowledgment of receipt, a copy or an abstract of the marriage certificate updated in accordance with Articles 1303-3 and 1303-4 or a certificate of registration in the supplementary civil register referred to in Article 4-1 of the aforecited Decree no. 65-422 of June 1st, 1965. If the contract of marriage ha been received by French consular or diplomatic official, one or both of the spouses notifies the Minister for Foreign Affairs.

The notary, the French diplomatic or consular official or the Minister for Foreign Affairs make a note of the change of the system of matrimonial property on the original of the marriage contract and must not issue any copy or abstract of it that does not contain this note.

§ 3 Change of the system of matrimonial property taking place abroad by virtue of French law

Article 1303-6

By virtue of French law, the public notice requirements set out in the second paragraph also apply to cases of a change of the system of matrimonial property taking place abroad.

Chapter II
Succession and Donations

Section I
Protective Measures Taken after the Commencement of Succession Proceedings

Sub-Section 1
Seals

§ 1 The affixation of seals

Article 1304

The affixation of seals may be applied for:

1. by a spouse;

2. by any person claiming a right in the succession;

3. by the executor of the will;

4. by the State Prosecution Service;

5. by the owner of the premises;

6. by any creditor in possession of a writ of execution or permission from a judge;

7. in the absence of the spouse or heirs or, if there are among the heirs minors who do not have a legal representative, by persons who were living with the deceased, the mayor, a police captain, or the commanding officer of a gendarmerie brigade.

Article 1305

The decision is made by the chief registrar of the district court in whose judicial district is located the property that is the subject-matter of the requested measure.

Article 1306

The chief registrar affixes the seals by way of a special seal that stays in his/her possession and the mould of which is kept at the registry.

Article 1307

The affixation may only be carried out after the completion of the inventory, unless this inventory is challenged and it is not so ordered by the judge of the district court.

Article 1308

The chief registrar may take such steps as are necessary to affix the seals.

Where the premises are closed, he/she may gain access to them by any means or affix the seals to the door if the applicant does not request the premises to be opened.

Article 1309

The chief registrar appoints a custodian of the seals if the composition and apparent value of the property justifies this.

Where persons remain in the premises to which the seals are affixed, the custodian is chosen from among them.

The custodian cannot be chosen from among the members of the staff of the registry.

Article 1310

If papers or closed packages are found, they are placed in a piece of furniture to which seals are affixed.

Article 1311

If a will is discovered, the chief registrar initials it in the presence of other persons. He then deposits it in the hands of a notary.

Article 1312

The chief registrar deposits any documents, sums of money, securities, jewels or other precious objects for which the affixation of seals does not appear to be a sufficient precaution either in the registry or with a notary or banking institution.

Article 1313

If papers or closed packages appear, by their address or any other proof in writing, to belong to a third party, the chief registrar deposits them in the registry.

The judge of the district court summons these third parties before him/her within a time period that he/she sets down so that they may take part in the proceedings.

If, during the proceedings, it is shown that the papers or packages are extraneous to the succession, the judge returns them to the parties concerned. If these parties do not appear or if the papers or packages are germane to the succession, the judge orders them to be deposited either in the registry or with a notary.

Article 1314

The official record of the affixation is signed and dated by the chief registrar. It contains:

1. the grounds for the affixation;

2. the name and address of the applicant or applicants and the capacity in which they have sought the affixation;

3. a brief account of the declarations of the persons present and the tracing rights that may have been accorded to them;

4. the designation of the premises and the furniture to which the seals have been affixed;

5. a brief description of the objects which were not put under seal;

6. an indication of the steps taken to ensure the preservation of the premises and goods and the safekeeping of the domestic animals;

7. a note on the formalities carried out pursuant to Articles 1310 to 1313;

8. where applicable, information on the person appointed guardian.

Article 1315

If there are no movables, the chief registrar draws up an official report *invalida bona*.

If there are items that are necessary for use by the persons remaining on the premises or to which seals cannot be affixed, the registrar draw up a description of them.

§ 2 The removal of seals

Article 1316

The removal of the seals may be requested by the persons having the right to apply for their affixation and by the state property department if it has been charged with managing the succession.

Article 1317

The applicant submits to the chief registrar a list of the persons who should be summoned to the removal of the seals, which includes those persons who had requested the affixation, those entitled to succeed, or the state property department that has been appointed to manage the succession and, where applicable, the executor of the will.

The chief registrar fixes the date and time when the seals will be removed.

Unless the persons who should be present at the removal of the seals have not explicitly exempted him/her from doing so, the applicant summons them, by registered letter with acknowledgment of receipt or by a document served by a court bailiff, to be present at the removal of the seals. In the latter case, the removal may not take place unless it is proved that the summons were received eight days before the date set for the removal of the seals.

Article 1318

The chief registrar gives notice of the removal of the seals to persons who, by means of a written declaration with reasons, have requested to be present.

Article 1319

The seals may be removed without an inventory when all parties that have been summoned are present or represented and do not object.

Otherwise, an inventory is drawn up even if some parties do not appear, as long as they have been duly summoned. The spouse where there is community of property in the marriage, the heirs, the executor of the will and the persons to whom the testator leaves all or a share of his/her estate may agree on the choice of one or two notaries, auctioneers or experts. If they do not agree or are not present or represented, the matter is dealt with by one or two notaries, auctioneers, or experts appointed by a judge of the district court.

Article 1320

The official report of the removal of the seals is dated and signed by the chief registrar. It includes:

1. a note of the request for removal and the decision of the chief registrar setting down the date and time of the removal;

2. the name and address of the applicant or applicants;

3. the name and address of the parties who were present, represented or summoned;

4. the acknowledgment that the seals are safe and intact or, if they are not, the state of the alterations;

5. the comments of the applicants and the parties that appeared and the tracing rights that may have been accorded to them;

6. information about the notary who did the inventory.

Article 1321

The seals are removed in succession and in line with the preparation of the inventory; they are re-affixed at the end of each session.

Article 1322

If the need arises, the chief registrar may proceed with a provisional removal of the seals, which will have to be re-affixed immediately after the operation that made their removal necessary has been performed.

The registrar draws up an official record of the steps that he/she has taken.

A provisional removal followed by an immediate re-affixation is not subject to the provisions of Articles 1316 to 1321.

Sub Section 2
Other Protective Measures

Article 1323

Where it appears that the composition of the goods does not justify the affixation of seals, the chief registrar in charge of the matter draws up a description of the movables; in the absence of an heir present, he/she ensures that the premises are closed if they are unoccupied and delivers the keys to the registry.

After having acknowledged their composition in the presence of the chief registrar, any heir may obtain the keys by giving a discharge for the furniture in the description. Under the same conditions, the keys may be given, with the permission of the district court, to a universal legatee that has the right to take possession of the deceased's property without formalities.

The public property department may also request the keys where it has been designated to administer the succession.

Article 1324

One month after the death, where there is no known person entitled to inherit and if the rental contract has come to an end, the judge of the district court may authorize the owner of the premises to which the seals have been affixed or in which a description of the movables has been drawn up, to have the movables removed and to have them either deposited in another place or put aside in a part of the premises that was occupied by the deceased person. The costs of removal and safe-keeping of the movables are advanced by the landlord.

The chief registrar is present at the moving of the movables and draws up an official report of the operation.

If seals had been affixed, he/she removes them and then re-affixes them in the place where the judge has authorized the depositing or putting aside of the movables.

Where a description has been drawn up, the chief registrar ensures that the premises where the movables have been deposited or put aside are closed and keeps the keys at the registry.

Article 1325

The provisions of Articles 1307, 1308 and 1311 to 1313 apply to the protective measures provided for in the Sub-section.

Sub-Section 3
Common Provisions

Article 1326

In the event that he/she is unable to act, the chief registrar may delegate his authority to carry out any of the measures provided for in the present Section to a registrar of his/her court.

Article 1327

If difficulties arise in the execution of the provisions of this Section, the parties or the chief registrar may bring the matter before the judge for the district court by way of an *ex parte* application.

If there is a dispute between the parties themselves, the judge of the district court deals with it by way of summary proceedings.

Articles 1328 to 1404

Reserved.

TITLE IV
OBLIGATIONS AND CONTRACTS

Chapter I
Administrative Enforcement Procedures

Section I
Order to Pay

Article 1405

An application for the recovery of a debt using an order to pay may be made where:

1. the debt arises from a contract or arises from an obligation defined by statute and amounts to a fixed amount; in matters of contract, the decision is made on the basis of the terms of the contract including, where applicable, the penalty clause;

2. the commitment arises from the acceptance or drawing of a bill of exchange, the subscription of a promissory note, the endorsement or guarantee of one or the other of these instruments or the acceptance of an assignment of debts in accordance with the Act No. 81-1 of 2 January 1981 facilitating loans to enterprises.

Article 1406

The claim is brought before the district court, local court or the president of the regional court in accordance with the jurisdiction of these courts.

The judge has territorial jurisdiction where the debtor or one of the debtors who is being sued resides.

The rules set down in the preceding paragraphs are in the public interest. Any clause to the contrary is null and void. A judge must establish, on his/her own initiative, his/her lack of jurisdiction, in which case Article 847-5 applies.

Article 1407

The claim is made by an application that is delivered or sent, as the case may be, to the court registry office or court registry by the creditor or by any agent.

The application contains:

- the family names, first names, occupations and places of residence of the creditors and debtors or, for legal persons, their form, name and registered office;
- a precise indication of the amount of the sum claimed with a breakdown of the various items of the debt as well as the legal basis for the claim.

It is accompanied by the supporting documents.

Article 1408

The creditor may, in the application for an order to pay, request that, in the case of an objection, the matter be immediately referred to a court that he/she considers has jurisdiction.

Article 1409

If, in light of the documents submitted, the claim appears to be well-founded in part or in full, the judge makes an order to pay for the sum that he/she decides.

If the judge dismisses the application, the judge's decision cannot be appealed by the creditor unless the creditor pursues the matter through ordinary legal procedures.

If the judge only grants the application in part, the judge's decision cannot be appealed by the creditor unless the creditor decides not to serve the order and to pursue the matter through ordinary legal procedures.

Article 1410

The decision bearing the order to pay and the application are kept as official records in the court registry office or court registry. The documents submitted in support of the application are kept provisionally at the court registry office or court registry.

Where the application is dismissed, the application and the documents submitted are returned to the applicant.

Article 1411

A certified true copy of the application and of the decision are on each of the debtors on the initiative of the creditor.

Article 1412

The debtor may object to the decision bearing the order to pay.

Article 1413

In order to be valid, the instrument by which the decision bearing the order to pay is served must contain, in addition to the information required for documents of the court bailiff, a formal summons:

- either to pay to the creditor the amount of the sum set out in the decision as well as interest and registry costs, the amount of which must be specified;

- or, if the debtor is to raise a defense, to make an objection, which has the effect of bringing the initial claim of the creditor and the whole suit before the court.

Subject to the same sanction, the document of service:

- sets out the time-limit within which an objection must be made, the court before which it must be brought and the manner in which it must be done;
- advises the debtor that he/she may inspect the documents submitted by the creditor at the court registry office or court registry and that, in the absence of an objection within the stated time limit, he/she will have no remedy and may be compelled by any appropriate legal means to pay the sums claimed.

Article 1414

Where service is made to the debtor personally, the court bailiff must inform the debtor of the matters set out in Article 1413; the performance of this formality is noted in the record of service.

Article 1415

An objection shall be brought, according to the case, before the district court which pronounced the injunctive decree to pay or before the Commercial Court whose president gave the order.

It shall be brought to the registry, either by declaration, on the issuance of an acknowledgment, or by registered letter.

Article 1416

An objection must be made within the month following service of the decision.

However, if no-one has been personally served, an objection may be made up to the expiration of a period of one month following the first instrument personally served, or, failing this, following the first measure of execution that has the effect of rendering all or part of the debtor's property incapable of free disposal.

Article 1417

The court rules upon the claim for recovery.

It deals, within the limits of its powers, with the initial claim and all the additional claims and the defenses on the merits of the case.

Where the court declines jurisdiction or in the case referred to in Article 1408, the matter is referred to the court having jurisdiction in accordance with the rules laid down under Article 97.

Article 1418

Registrar calls the parties to a hearing by a registered letter with acknowledgment of receipt.

The convocation is sent to all the parties, even to those who have not raised an objection.

Article 1419

If none of the parties are present, the court records the termination of the proceedings, which renders null and void the decision bearing the order to pay.

Article 1420

The judgment of the court is substituted for the decision bearing the order to pay.

Article 1421

The court rules subject to appeal where the amount of the claim exceeds the sum up to which it has jurisdiction as a court of last instance.

Article 1422

In the absence of an objection within the month following service of the decision bearing the order to pay, whatever form the service takes, or where the debtor withdraws his/her objection, the creditor may request that an authority to execute be affixed to the decision. The withdrawal by the debtor is subject to the rules set out in Articles 400 to 405.

The decision has all the effect of a judgment rendered after hearing both parties. It is not open to appeal even if it grants a period for payment.

Article 1423

The application for affixing the writ of execution is made to the court registry, either by means of a deposition or by regular mail.

The decision is null and void if the creditor's application has not been submitted within a month following the expiration of the time limit for an objection or the withdrawal by the debtor.

Article 1424

The documents produced by the creditor and kept provisionally at the court registry office or registry are returned to him/her on his/her request once an objection is raised or when the order is accompanied by writ of execution.

Article 1425

Before a Commercial Court, the costs of the order to pay are advanced by the creditor and deposited at the court registry no later than fifteen days from the application referred to in Article 1405, failing which the application lapses.

The objection is received free of charge by the registrar, who immediately invites the creditor by registered letter with acknowledgment of receipt to deposit the fees for the objection at the registry within fifteen days, failing which the application referred to in Article 1405 lapses.

Section II
Order to Act

Article 1425-1

Specific performance of an obligation resulting from a contract concluded between individuals, not all of whom have the status of a commercial person, may be requested from the district court if the value of the obligation whose performance is requested does not exceed the amount within the court's jurisdiction.

The local judge has jurisdiction within the limits set out in the Code of Judicial Organization and under the conditions of Article 847-4 of the present Code.

Article 1425-2

The application is made, at the plaintiff's choice, either to the court of the place where the defendant resides or the district court of the place of performance of the obligation.

Article 1425-3

The request is made by means of an application deposited or sent to the court registry by the beneficiary of the obligation or by the persons referred to in Article 828.

The application contains:

1. in the case of natural persons, the family name, first names, occupation and address of the parties or, in the case of legal persons, the name and registered office;

2. a precise statement of the nature of the obligation whose performance is sought as well as the basis for it;

3. possibly, the damages which will be claimed in case of failure to carry out the order to act.

It is accompanied by supporting documents.

The limitation period and the time limits for taking action are interrupted by the registration of the application at the court registry.

Article 1425-4

If, in light of the documents submitted, the claim appears to be well-founded, the judge makes a decision bearing the order to act that is not open to appeal.

The judge fixes the subject matter of the obligation as well as the time-limit and the conditions for its performance.

The decision states, in addition, the place, date and time for the hearing at which the matter will be examined unless the plaintiff has made known that the order has been carried out.

Article 1425-5

The registry notifies the parties of the decision by registered letter with acknowledgment of receipt. The registry sends a copy of this notification by regular mail on the same day. The letter of notification mentions the provisions of Articles 1425-7 and 1425-8.

Article 1425-6

The decision bearing the order to act and the application are kept as official records in the registry where the documents submitted in support of the application are provisionally kept.

Article 1425-7

The plaintiff informs the registrar if the order to act has been carried out in the stated time limit. The matter is then taken off the list of cases.

Failing such communication or if the plaintiff does not appear at the hearing without a legitimate reasons, the court strikes the proceedings for an order to act off the list.

The striking off the list may be revoked if the plaintiff informs the court registry within a period of fifteen days the legitimate reason that he/she was not able to appear at the proper time. In this event, the parties are called to a subsequent hearing.

Article 1425-8

The court, in cases of failure to comply fully or partially with the order to act that it has issued, rules on the application after having attempted to reconcile the parties.

It deals, within the limits of its powers, with the initial application and all the additional claims and the defenses on the merits of the case.

Where the court declines jurisdiction, the matter is referred to the court having jurisdiction in accordance with the rules contained in Article 97.

Article 1425-9

If the judge dismisses the application, the decision cannot be appealed by the applicant unless he/she proceeds by way of regular legal procedures. The application and the documents submitted are returned to the applicant.

Chapter II
Offers for Payment and Deposits of Funds

Article 1426

The official record of formal tenders of performance or payment specifies what is offered; if it concerns a sum of money, it specifies the amount thereof and the method of payment.

It states in all cases the place where the funds will be deposited if the offers are not accepted.

Article 1427

The official report makes mention of the reply, refusal or acceptance by the creditor and indicates if the creditor has signed, refused to sign or stated that he/she is not able to sign.

Article 1428

If the creditor rejects the offers, the debtor may so as to escape liability, divest of the sum or thing offered by depositing it with interest, where applicable, up to the date of deposit.

A garnishee who is prevented from paying by an objection may avoid liability by making a deposit without having to make a formal tender.

A public official prepares an official report of the deposit and serves it on the creditor.

Article 1429

Incidental disputes about the validity of the offers or the deposit are dealt with by the judge in charge of the principal matter.

Chapter III
The Reconstruction of Destroyed Instruments

Article 1430

An application for the reconstruction of the original of an official or private instrument that has been destroyed, in any place, as a result of war or disaster is brought before the regional court.

Article 1431

The court having jurisdiction is that of the place where the instrument was drawn up or, if the instrument was drawn up in a foreign country, that of the place where the applicant resides; if the applicant resides in a foreign country, it is the regional court of Paris.

Article 1432

The reconstruction of a court decision is done by the court that gave it.

Article 1433

The application is brought, conducted and judged as a non-contentious matter.

Article 1434

A court may proceed to a partial reconstruction of an instrument in cases where proof is brought of certain clauses alone as long as they are self-standing.

Chapter IV
The Issue of Copies of Instruments and Registers

Article 1435

Public officers or officials or all other depositories of instruments are obliged to issue, on payment of their fees, duplicates or copies of instruments to the parties themselves, their heirs and legal successors.

Article 1436

In the case of refusal or failure to reply on the part of a depository, the president of the regional court, assuming jurisdiction on the basis of an application, makes a decision after having heard or summoned the applicant and the depository.

Article 1437

The decision is enforceable on a provisional basis.

An appeal is brought, conducted and judged as a non-contentious matter.

Article 1438

A party may obtain a copy of an instrument that has not been registered or which is defective; he/she must request it from the president of the regional court. The request is presented in the form of an *ex parte* application.

In the case of refusal or failure to reply on the part of the depository of the instrument, the matter is referred to the president of the regional court.

Article 1439

A party seeking the issue of a second enforceable copy of an official instrument must request it from the president of the regional court. The request is presented in the form of an application.

In the case of refusal or failure to reply on the part of the depository of the instrument, the matter is referred to the president of the regional court.

Article 1440

Registrars and depositaries of registers and public record books are obliged to issue a copy or abstract to anyone who so requests, on payment of their fees.

Article 1441

Any person capable of seeking a remedy under the conditions set out in the first paragraph of Article 11-1 of Act No. 91-3 of 3 January 1991 on the transparency and proper conduct of market procedures and subjecting the conclusion of certain contracts to rules of public notice and competitive bidding, must, if he/she intends to commence such proceedings, first give formal notice, by registered mail with acknowledgment of receipt, to the legal person that is bound by the obligations of public notice and competitive bidding to which the conclusion of the contract is subject, to comply with them.

An appeal is brought, conducted and judged as a non-contentious matter.

Chapter V
Litigation in Relation to the Conclusion of Works Contracts

Article 1441-1

Any person having the capacity to enter an appeal under the conditions set out in the first paragraph of Article 11-1 of Act No. 91-3 of 3 January 1991 on the transparency and proper conduct of market procedures and subjecting the conclusion of certain contracts to rules of public notice and competitive bidding, must, if he/she intends to commence such an action, first give formal notice, by registered letter with acknowledgment of receipt, to the legal person bound by the obligations of public notice and competitive bidding to which the conclusion of the contract is subject, to comply with them.

In the case of a refusal or failure to reply within a period of ten days, the person giving formal notice may bring the matter before the president of the court having jurisdiction or his/her delegate, who rules within a period of twenty days.

Article 1441-2

Article 1441-1 applies to the State Prosecution Service in the case provided for in the second paragraph of Article 11-1 of Act No. 91-3 of 3 January 1991.

Article 1441-3

The decision of the president of the court dealing with the matter or his/her delegate is subject to an appeal on a point of law within fifteen days of its notification.

Chapter VI
Settlement Agreement

Article 1441-4

The president of the regional court, who has taken jurisdiction upon an application by a party to a settlement, confers enforceability on the instrument that is presented to him/her.

BOOK FOUR
ARBITRATION

TITLE I
ARBITRATION AGREEMENTS

Chapter I
Arbitration Clause

Article 1442

An arbitration clause shall provide that the parties to a contract undertake to refer any disputes which might arise under the contract to arbitration.

Article 1443

An arbitration clause must, at the risk of it otherwise being invalid, be in writing in the principal agreement or in a document which the agreement shall incorporate.

Subject to the same sanction, the arbitration clause must either appoint the arbitrator or arbitrators, or provide for the method of their appointment.

Article 1444

Where, once a dispute has arisen, the constitution of the arbitration tribunal is presented with an obstacle by reason of the acts of one of the parties or because of the implementation of the method of appointment, the president of the regional court shall appoint the arbitrator or arbitrators.

However, such an appointment shall be made by the president of the Commercial Court where the agreement has expressly provided for this eventuality.

Where the arbitration clause is either on the face of it, invalid or insufficient to allow for the constitution of an arbitration tribunal, the president shall record this fact and declare that the tribunal has not been appointed.

Article 1445

The dispute shall be referred to an arbitration tribunal either jointly by the parties or by the party who takes the initiative.

Article 1446

Where it is invalid, the arbitration clause shall be deemed to be unwritten.

Chapter II
The Arbitration Agreement

Article 1447

The arbitration agreement is the agreement by which the parties to a dispute that has already arisen refer it to arbitration before one or more persons.

Article 1448

The arbitration agreement must specify the subject matter of the dispute if it is not to be invalid.

Subject to the same sanction, the arbitration agreement must name the arbitrator or arbitrators, or provide for the manner of their appointment.

The arbitration agreement lapses if an arbitrator that it names declines the appointment conferred upon him/her.

Article 1449

The arbitration agreement must be in writing. It may be incorporated in an official document signed by the arbitrator and the parties.

Article 1450

The parties shall have the right to submit a matter to arbitration even where they are in the midst of proceedings commenced before another court.

Chapter III
Common Rules

Article 1451

The task of arbitrator may only be granted to a natural person; the latter must enjoy the full exercise of his/her civil rights.

Where the arbitration agreement appoints a corporate entity, the latter only has the power to organize the arbitration.

Article 1452

The constitution of the arbitration tribunal shall only be completed when the arbitrator or arbitrators accept the task given to them.

The arbitrator who considers him/herself open to being challenged must inform the parties. In that case, he/she may only agree to his/her appointment with the approval of the parties.

Article 1453

The arbitration tribunal must consist of one arbitrator or an odd number of several arbitrators.

Article 1454

Where the parties have appointed an even number of arbitrators, the arbitration tribunal shall be completed by an additional arbitrator chosen either in accordance with the intentions of the parties or, in the absence of any such intentions, by the appointed arbitrators or, failing an agreement between the arbitrators, by the president of the regional court.

Article 1455

Where a natural person or corporate entity is designated to organize the arbitration, the task of arbitration shall be conferred upon one or more arbitrators who are accepted by all the parties.

Failing such acceptance, the person or entity charged with organizing the arbitration shall invite each party to appoint an arbitrator and shall proceed, where applicable, with the appointment of the arbitrator necessary to complete the arbitration tribunal. Where the parties fail to appoint an arbitrator, the latter shall be appointed by the person or entity charged with organizing the arbitration.

The arbitration tribunal may also be constituted from the start in accordance with the procedure set out in the preceding paragraph.

The person or entity charged with organizing the arbitration may provide that the arbitration tribunal will only issue a draft award and that, if this draft is challenged by one of the parties, the matter shall be submitted to a second arbitration tribunal. In this case, the members of the second tribunal shall be appointed by the person or entity charged with organizing the arbitration, each party having the right to replace one of the arbitrators so appointed.

Article 1456

Where the arbitration agreement does not specify a time limit, the task of the arbitrators shall last for only six months calculated from the day on which the last of them accepted the said task.

The legal or contractual time limit may be extended either with the agreement of the parties or, on the request of one of them or of the arbitration tribunal, by the president of the regional court or, in the case referred to in the second paragraph of Article 1444, by the president of the Commercial Court.

Article 1457

In the cases referred to in Articles 1444, 1454, 1456 and 1463, the president of the court, assuming jurisdiction by way of a summary proceeding on behalf of one of the parties or the arbitration tribunal, shall make an order which is not subject to appeal.

However, this order may be subject to appeal if the president rules against the appointment of arbitrators on the basis of the grounds referred to in the third paragraph of Article 1444. The appeal shall be filed, prepared and decided as in the procedure for a plea objecting to the jurisdiction.

The president who has jurisdiction shall be the one of the court which has been designated in the arbitration agreement or, failing that, the one in whose judicial district the agreement has located the arbitration proceedings. Where the agreement is silent on this, the president who has jurisdiction shall be the one of the court of the place where one or more of the defendants in the proceedings lives or, if the defendant does not reside in France, the court of the place where the plaintiff lives.

Article 1458

Where a dispute over which the arbitration tribunal has jurisdiction by virtue of an arbitration agreement is brought before a court of law of the State, the latter must decline jurisdiction.

If the arbitration tribunal has not yet taken jurisdiction, the court must also decline jurisdiction unless the arbitration agreement is obviously invalid.

In both cases, the court may not of its own motion raise its lack of jurisdiction.

Article 1459

Any provision or agreement which is contrary to the contained in the present Chapter shall be deemed invalid and void.

TITLE II
THE ARBITRATION PROCEEDINGS

Article 1460

The arbitrators establish the rules for the arbitration proceedings without being bound by the rules governing the courts of law, unless the parties have decided otherwise in the arbitration agreement.

However, the governing principles for proceedings set out in Articles 4 to 10, the first paragraph of Article 11 and Articles 13 to 21 shall always be applicable to arbitration proceedings.

Where a party has in his/her possession an item of evidence, the arbitrator may compel production.

Article 1461

The preparatory steps and the official records are done by all of the arbitrators if the arbitration agreement does not authorize them to assign these tasks to one among them.

Third parties shall be heard without an oath being administered.

Article 1462

An arbitrator must see his/her commission through until its completion.

An arbitrator cannot be removed without the unanimous consent of the parties.

Article 1463

An arbitrator may not withdraw him/herself or be challenged unless it is on a ground for a challenge which has become apparent or which has arisen subsequent to his/her appointment.

Difficulties arising in relation to the application of the present Article shall be brought before the president of the court that has jurisdiction.

Article 1464

Arbitration proceedings shall terminate, subject to any specific agreements between the parties:

1. by the dismissal, death or impediment of an arbitrator as well as the loss of the full exercise of his/her civil rights;
2. by the withdrawal of or challenge to an arbitrator;
3. by the expiration of the time limit for the arbitration.

Article 1465

The interruption of arbitration proceedings shall be governed by the provisions of Articles 369 to 376.

Article 1466

If, before an arbitrator, one of the parties challenges either the principle or the scope of the arbitrator's powers, it shall be for the latter to rule upon the validity or limits of his/her appointment.

Article 1467

Unless there is agreement to the contrary, an arbitrator has the power to determine the preliminary issue of verifying handwriting or forgeries in accordance with the provisions of Articles 287 to 294 and of Article 299.

Where there is an allegation of forgery, Article 313 shall be applicable before the arbitrator. The time limit for the arbitration proceedings shall continue to run from the date on which the preliminary issue has been resolved.

Article 1468

The arbitrator shall fix the date on which the matter shall be considered.

After this date, no claim may be brought or new issue raised. No comments may be submitted nor any document be produced unless it is at the request of the arbitrator.

TITLE III
THE ARBITRAL AWARD

Article 1469

The deliberations of the arbitrators shall be in camera.

Article 1470

The arbitral award shall be given by way of a majority of votes.

Article 1471

The arbitral award must set out succinctly the respective claims of the parties and grounds in support.

The award must be reasoned.

Article 1472

The arbitral award must contain the following particulars:

– the name of arbitrators who made it;

– the date;

– the place where it was given;

– the family name, first names or business name of the parties, as well as their address or registered office;

– where applicable, the name of the attorneys or any person who represented or assisted the parties.

Article 1473

The arbitral award must be signed by all the arbitrators.

However, if a minority of them refuses to sign, the others shall recite this in the award and it shall have the same effect as if it had been signed by all the arbitrators.

Article 1474

An arbitrator must determine a dispute in accordance with the rules of law unless, in the arbitration agreement, the parties assigned him/her the task of deciding in the capacity of a mediator.

Article 1475

The award shall terminate the arbitrator's jurisdiction over the dispute.

The arbitrator nevertheless still retains the power to interpret the award, to correct any material errors and omissions affecting it and to complete it where he/she has omitted to rule upon one of the heads of claim. Articles 461 to 463 shall apply. Where an arbitration tribunal cannot be re-constituted, such powers shall vest in the court which would have had jurisdiction in the absence of the arbitration.

Article 1476

The arbitral award, from the moment that it has been made, shall be final as regards the dispute which it has determined.

Article 1477

The arbitral award shall only be enforced by virtue of an order made by the regional court in the jurisdiction of which the award was made.

For this purpose, the original award together with a copy of the arbitration agreement must be filed by one of the arbitrators or by the first party to act at the court registry.

Article 1478

Any order refusing enforcement must be reasoned.

Article 1479

The rules governing the provisional enforcement of judgments shall be applicable to arbitral awards.

In case of an appeal or an application for annulment, the first president or the judge charged with the preparation for trial, once he/she assumes jurisdiction, may make an order for enforcement of the arbitral award including provisional enforcement. He/she may also order provisional enforcement in the manner provided for in Articles 525 and 526; his/her decision is the equivalent of an order for enforcement.

Article 1480

The provisions of the second paragraph of Article 1471 and Article 1472 in relation to the names of arbitrators and the date of the award, and Article 1473 are mandatory at the risk of the award otherwise being invalid.

TITLE IV
RIGHTS OF RECOURSE

Article 1481

The arbitral award is not subject to an objection or an appeal to the Court of Cassation.

It may be subject to a third party objection made to the court which would otherwise have had jurisdiction in the absence of the arbitration, subject to the provisions of the first paragraph of Article 588.

Article 1482

The arbitral award shall be subject to an appeal unless the parties have waived such a right in the arbitration agreement. However, it is not subject to appeal where the arbitrator was given the task of deciding as a mediator unless the parties have expressly retained this right in the arbitration agreement.

Article 1483

Where, following the provisions of Article 1482, the parties have not waived the right to appeal or have expressly retained this right in the arbitration agreement, an appeal only shall be available if it is intended to reverse the arbitral award or seek its annulment. The appeal judge shall decide the matter as a mediator where the arbitrator was accorded this task.

Article 1484

Where, following the provisions of Article 1482, the parties have waived the right of appeal or have not expressly retained this right in the arbitration agreement, an application to annul an instrument named as an arbitral award may nevertheless be made notwithstanding any contrary provisions.

It is only available in the following cases:

1. where the arbitrator has ruled upon the matter without any arbitration agreement or where this agreement is invalid or has expired;

2. where the arbitration tribunal has been invalidly constituted or the sole arbitrator invalidly appointed;

3. where the arbitrator has made a ruling that is not in accordance with the task conferred upon him/her;

4. where the principle of involving all the parties has not been complied with;

5. in all the cases of invalidity referred to in Article 1480;

6. where the arbitrator has acted in breach of a rule of public policy.

Article 1485

Where a court which is requested to annul the award does so, it shall decide upon the merits of the case within the limits of the arbitrator's terms of reference, unless there is a contrary intention by all the parties concerned.

Article 1486

The appeal and the application to annul must be made to the court of appeal in whose judicial district the arbitral award was given.

These recourses are admissible from the time when the award is made; they shall cease to be so if they have not been exercised within one month from the service of the award endorsed with the order for enforcement.

The time limit for exercising these rights of recourse shall operate to stay the enforcement of the arbitral award. A recourse exercised within the time limit shall also stay the enforcement.

Article 1487

The appeal and application to annul are made, prepared and decided in accordance with the rules governing the procedure for contentious matters before the court of appeal.

The legal classification given by the parties to the right of recourse at the time when the declaration is made may be amended or refined up to the time when the court of appeal assumes jurisdiction.

Article 1488

The order granting enforcement shall not be subject to any appeal.

However, an appeal or application to annul an award shall include, within the limits of the court's jurisdiction, a recourse against the order of the enforcement judge or the removal of the case from this judge.

Article 1489

The order refusing enforcement is subject to appeal up to one month from its service. In this case, the court of appeal will consider, at the request of the parties, the grounds which they would have been able to raise against the arbitral award by way of an appeal or an application to annul the award, as the case may be.

Article 1490

The dismissal of the appeal or the application to annul the award shall render the arbitral award or such of its provisions which are not objected to by the court enforceable.

Article 1491

An application for reconsideration shall be available against the arbitral award in the cases and under the same conditions as for judgments.

It must be made to the court of appeal which would have otherwise had jurisdiction to have heard the other rights of recourse against the award.

TITLE V
INTERNATIONAL ARBITRATION

Article 1492

An international arbitration is one where international commercial interests are involved.

Article 1493

Directly or by reference to a set of arbitration rules, the arbitration agreement may appoint the arbitrator or arbitrators or provide for the method of their appointment.

If, in arbitrations to be conducted in France or for those in relation to which the parties have provided that French civil procedure should apply, the constitution of the arbitration tribunal is faced with difficulties, the first party to act, unless there is a clause to the contrary, may inform the president of the regional court of Paris in accordance with the manner set out in Article 1457.

Article 1494

The arbitration agreement may, directly or by way of reference to a set of arbitration rules, lay down the procedure to be applied for the arbitration proceedings; it may also submit the proceedings to a procedural law which it shall decide.

Where the agreement is silent, the arbitrator shall lay down the procedure to the extent that it is necessary, either directly or by reference to a law or a set of arbitration rules.

Article 1495

Where an international arbitration is governed by French law, the provisions of Titles I, II and III of the present Book shall only apply in the absence of any specific agreement and subject to Articles 1493 and 1494.

Article 1496

The arbitrator shall rule on the dispute in accordance with the rules of law which the parties have chosen; in the absence of such a choice, he/she shall rule in accordance with those which he/she shall deem to be appropriate.

He/she must in all cases consider trade customs and usages.

Article 1497

The arbitrator shall rule as a mediator if the agreement between the parties confers such a function upon him/her.

TITLE VI
RECOGNITION, ENFORCEMENT AND RECOURSES WITH RESPECT TO ARBITRAL AWARDS GIVEN ABROAD OR IN MATTERS OF INTERNATIONAL ARBITRATION

Chapter I
Recognition and Enforcement of Arbitral Awards Given Abroad or in Matters of International Arbitration

Article 1498

Arbitral awards are recognized in France if their existence is proved by the party claiming entitlement under it and where its recognition would not obviously be contrary to international public policy.

Under the same conditions, the awards shall be declared enforceable in France by the judge in charge of enforcement.

Article 1499

The existence of an arbitral award shall be proven by the production of the original decision together with the arbitration agreement or copies of the same satisfying the conditions required for their authenticity.

Where these documents are not written in the French language, a party must produce a certified translation from a translator registered on the list of experts.

Article 1500

The provisions of Articles 1476 to 1479 shall apply.

Chapter II
Rights of Recourse Against Arbitral Awards Given Abroad or in Matters of International Arbitration

Article 1501

A decision refusing the recognition or enforcement of an award shall be subject to appeal.

Article 1502

An appeal against the decision which grants the recognition or enforcement of an award shall only be available in the following cases:

1. where the arbitrator has ruled upon the matter without any arbitration agreement or where this agreement is invalid or has expired;

2. where the arbitration tribunal has been invalidly constituted or the sole arbitrator invalidly appointed;

3. where the arbitrator has made a ruling that is not in accordance with the task conferred upon him/her;

4. where the principle of involving all the parties has not been complied with;

5. if the recognition or enforcement are contrary international public policy.

Article 1503

The appeal referred to in Articles 1501 and 1502 must be made to the court of appeal to which the judge who ruled upon the matter is subject. It may be made up until the expiration of one month from the service of the decision of the judge.

Article 1504

An arbitral award made in France in matters of international arbitration may be subject to an application for annulment in the cases mentioned in Article 1502.

The order allowing the enforcement of this award is not be subject to any appeal. However, an application to annul an award shall include automatically, within the limits of the court's jurisdiction, a recourse against the order of the enforcement judge or the removal of the case from this judge.

Article 1505

The application to annul an award referred to in Article 1504 must be made to the court of appeal within whose judicial district the award was given. This application shall be admissible immediately the award is given; it shall cease to be admissible where this right has not been exercised within one month of the service of the award which has been rendered enforceable.

Article 1506

The time limit for making the application referred to in Articles 1501, 1502 and 1504 shall operate as a stay of enforcement of the arbitral award. An application made within this time limit shall also operate as a stay of enforcement.

Article 1507

The provisions of Title IV of this Book, except those in the first paragraph of Article 1487 and in Article 1490, do not apply to rights of recourse.

SELECTED FRENCH LEGAL TERMS

A

à concurrence de	up to the limit (amount) of
à dire d'expert	according to expert opinion
à due concurrence	pro tanto
à échoir	accruing, due in the future/at a future date
à la diligence de	on the initiative of, by
à l'amiable	amicably, out of court, privately
à l'audience	in court
à l'issue de	at the end of
à ordre	to order
à peine de forclusion	if it is not to be out of time, on pain of loss of rights
à peine de nullité	in order to be valid
à quelque titre que ce soit	in any capacity whatsoever
à terme	future
à titre conservatoire	as a preventive measure
à titre de	by way of
à titre gratuit	free of charge, gratuitously
à titre onéreux	for value, for consideration
à un (certain) délai de vue	after sight
à vue	on sight
abaisser	to reduce
abandon	withdrawal, waiver
abus de confiance	breach of trust, fraudulent conversion
abusivement	unfairly, unreasonably, wrongfully
acceptance par intervention	acceptance for honor
accessoire	ancillary
accomplir	to perform
accord d'entreprise	company agreement
accueillir	to uphold
acompte	down-payment, advance payment
acompte sur dividende	interim dividend
acquit	release, receipt, discharge
action en nullité	action for rescission
activité salariée	paid employment
acte	document, act, instrument
acte authentique	notarized document
acte de commerce	commercial transaction
acte de disposition	conveyance
acte de saisie	seizure, attachment
acte de société	corporate statutes
acte extrajudiciaire	extrajudicial act, formal notice
action	share

action à dividende prioritaire	preferred dividend share
action à titre irréductible	whole share
action à titre réductible	fractional share
action d'apport	share issued in return for a contribution in kind
action de jouissance	dividend share
action de numéraire	cash share
action de priorité	preference share
action de travail	employee share
action en garantie	action to enforce a guarantee
action en justice	legal proceedings
action en répétition	proceedings for repayment
action en restitution	action to recover a possession
action en revendication	action to establish ownership/title
action en responsabilité	action for damages
action individuelle	personal action
action indivise	undivided share
action publique	criminal proceedings
action résolutoire	action for rescission
actionner	to sue, to bring an action/legal proceedings against
actions de capital	capital stock
adjoindre	to associate, to add, to appoint
adjudicataire	purchaser (at an auction), highest bidder
adjudication (publique)	sale by public auction
adjuger	to sell (by auction)
admettre	to authorize, to allow
admettre aux négociations sur un marché réglementé	to list for trading on a regulated stock market
administrateur	director
administrateur judiciaire	court-appointed administrator/receiver
administration	public authorities
adresser	to send
affaires en cours	current business
affectation	utilization, type of use, classification
affecter	to assign, to allocate, to set aside for, to appropriate
afférant à	pertaining to
affichage	posting
affirmer sous serment	to swear
agence	office
agglomération	built-up area, urban center
agir	to take action
agir en désignation de	to apply for the appointment of
agir en justice	to bring legal proceedings
agissements	dealings
agréé	authorized, recognized, approved
agrément	approval, consent

aliéner	to transfer
allié	relative by marriage
allocation	allowance
allonge	rider
altérer	to damage
aménagement	development
aménagement du territoire	town and country planning, regional planning
amiable	private
amortissement	redemption (of capital), depreciation
amortir	to redeem, to write off
année civile	calendar year
année culturale	growing season
annonce	notice, advertisement
annuler	to annul, to set aside, to rescind, to declare void
antérieur	previous, earlier
antériorité	priority
anticipé	early, premature, before the due date
antidater	to antedate, to backdate
appareil	structure
appel	appeal (to a court of appeal)
appel de fonds	call on shareholders
appel publique à l'épargne	public offering (of shares)
appeler	to require, to call upon
application	application, implementation
appliquer	to observe
appointement	stipend, fee
apport en industrie	contribution in the form of services
apport en nature	contribution in kind
apport en numéraire	cash contribution
apport en société d'un fonds de commerce	contribution to a company or partnership in the form of a business
apposer	to insert
appréciation	finding, assessment
apprécier	to value, to assess
apurement	clearing, settlement
apurer	to pay off, to discharge, to settle
archive	record
arrérage	instalment (of an annuity or pension)
arrêté	order
arrêter	to draw up, to prepare, to make an order for, to adopt
arrondissement	district, borough
artisanal	artisanal
aspect	implication
assiette	basis (of taxation)
assignation	summons, writ, petition

associé	partner, shareholder, member
associé commandité	active partner
associé unique	sole member
assorti	accompanied by, together with
assurance	insurance policy, insurance company
assurer	to effect
attester	to certify
attribuer	to allocate, to grant, to allot, to accord, to confer
attribution	allotment, grant, allocation
au gré de	with the agreement of, at the will of
au jour le jour	on a day-to-day basis
au marc le franc	in proportion to, proportionally, pro rata
au nom de	on behalf of
au préalable	beforehand
au préjudice de	to the detriment of
au profit de	for the benefit of
au regard de	in the eyes of, upon examining, according to
au sens de	within the meaning of
au titre de	in respect of, pursuant to
au vu de	based on, in light of
auprès de	attached to
auteur	perpetrator
autorisation d'exploitation commerciale	business operating permit
Autorité des marches financiers	Financial Markets Authority
autorités administratives	public authorities
autorités judiciaires	court authorities, legal authorities
aux termes de	under, according to
aval	signature guaranteeing a bill, endorsement
avaliseur	guarantor, endorser
avantage	privilege
avis	notice, opinion, recommendation, advice
aviser	to give notice, notify
avoir communication de	to be informed of
avoir droit à	to be entitled to
avoir pour objet	to be intended
avoir qualité de	to be empowered to
ayant cause	successor
ayants droits	legal successors, successors in title, beneficiaries

B

bail emphytéotique	long-term lease
bail rural	agricultural lease/tenancy
bailleur de gage	pledgor
banqueroute	criminal bankruptcy
base d'imposition	taxable value, basis for taxation

barême	list, schedule
bénéfice	benefit, profit
bénéfice de discussion	right to require prior execution against the principal debtor
bénéficier de	to take advantage of, to benefit from
biens	property, goods, assets, chattels
biens immobiliers	immovable property, real property
biens mobiliers	movable property, personal property
biffer	to strike off, to cross off/out, to delete
bilan	balance sheet, assessment
billet à ordre	promissory note
blâme	reprimand
blanc	gap
bloqué	frozen
boni de liquidation	surplus upon winding-up
bon de souscription	subscription voucher
branche	sector
bulletin	slip, gazette
bulletin de gage	security/pledge instrument
Bulletin official de la concurrence, de la consommation et de la repression des frauds	Official Gazette on Competition, Consumer Affairs and the Prevention of Fraud
Bulletin official des annonces civiles and commerciales	Official Gazette of Civil and Commercial Notices
bureau de jugement	trial body

C

cadre	manager
cahier des charges	terms and conditions, rules
caisse	fund
Caisse de dépôts et consignation	Bank for Official Deposits
capitaine au long cours	master mariner
capital (social)	(share) capital
capitaux propres	equity capital
carence	deficiency
cas	case, event, circumstances
catégorie	class (shares)
caution	guarantor, security, surety, guarantee
caution bancaire	banker's guarantee
caution solidaire	guarantor jointly and severally liable with the principal debtor
cautionnement	bond, contract of guarantee
cédant	assignor
céder	to assign
cessation de commerce	discontinuance of business
certificat de droit de vote	certificate of voting right
cessation de paiements	suspension of payments, insolvency

certificat d'investissement	investment certificate
cessionnaire	assignee
chambre de compensation	clearing house
chambre de discipline	disciplinary board
chambre des comptes	board of accounts
chambre des métiers	trades chamber
chambre du conseil	judge's chambers
charge	encumbrance
charger	to entrust, to charge, to make someone responsible for, to instruct
chef d'entreprise	entrepreneur, head of a business
chef-lieu	chief town
circuit de distribution	distribution channel
citer	to summon, to convoke
classement	classification
clause à ordre	order clause
clause de retour sans frais	clause in a bill excluding the requirement of a protest
coalition	combination
code de déontologie	code of professional ethics
collaborateur	colleague, assistant
collectivité locale	local government authority
collectivité publique	public authority
collectivité territoriale	territorial authority
Comité de la réglementation comptable	Committee on Accounting Rules
comité d'entreprise	works council
commandement	summons to pay
commanditaire	limited partner
commandité	active partner
commerçant	commercial person
commerce	outlet, business, trade
commercial	commercial, business, trade (adj.)
commercialisation	marketing, commercialization
commettre	to assign, to appoint
commissaire à exécution du plan	commissioner responsible for the implementation of the plan
commissaire aux apports	valuer of contributions in kind
commissaire du gouvernement	government commissioner
commissaire priseur	valuer and auctioneer
commission	committee, commission, board
Commission des opération de Bourse	Securities and Exchange Commission
commissionnaire	commission agent
communauté	joint ownership
commune	municipality
communication	handing-over

communiquer	to communicate, to make known, to transmit, to submit, to inform, to report, to forward
commutatif	for mutual consideration
Compagnie nationale des commissaires aux comptes	National Company of Auditors
compensation	set-off
compenser	to set off, to compensate, to offset, to clear (as in clearing house)
compétent	appropriate, relevant, having jurisdiction
complémentaire	supplementary
complété de	supplemented by
complice	accomplice, accessory
comporter	to include, to entail, to involve
comprendre	to include
compromettre	to submit for arbitration
compromis	arbitration agreement, settlement, sales agreement
compte de résultat	profit and loss account
compte d'exploitation	operating account
compte rendu	record, report
compte tenu	taking into account
comptes	accounts, financial statements
concéder	to grant, to accord
concessionnaire	licensee, franchisee
concourir	to be a party to, to participate in, to contribute to
condamner	to convict
condition résolutoire	condition subsequent
conditionnement	packaging
confection	making, preparation
conforme	consistent
conformément à	in accordance with
congé	period of notice
conjointement	jointly
connaissement	bill of lading
connaître	to hear (court)
connexe	related
consecutive à	resulting from
Conseil de la concurrence	Council on Competition
conseil de prud'hommes	industrial relations tribunal
Conseil des marchés financiers	Financial Markets Supervisory Board
Conseil des ventes volontaires de meubles aux enchères	Commission for Voluntary Sales of Chattels by Public Auction
Conseil d'Etat	Council of State
Conseil général des ponts et chaussées	General Highways Council
conseil municipal	local council
Conseil national de comptabilité	National Accounting Board

Conseil national de la consommation	National Consumer Council
conseiller	counselor
consentir	to grant
conservation	safe-keeping
conservatoire	precautionary, interim
Conservatoire des arts et métiers	Paris School of Engineering
conserver	to maintain
consigner	to record, to indicate, deposit
consistance	composition
constater	to record, to evidence, to note, to conclude, to find
constituer	to give, to grant (security)
constitution	setting-up, formation
consulaire	trade (adj), commercial
contester	to dispute, challenge, object
continuation	recovery, continued existence
contradictoire	in the presence of both (all) parties
contravenant	offender
contre	in exchange for
contre récépissé	in return/exchange for a receipt
contrepartie	consideration
contrôle	audit, supervision
conventionnel	contractual, agreed
conversion	redeployment, transformation, conversion
convoquer	to convene, to call, to call together
co-obligé	co-promisor, person jointly liable
corrélatif	corresponding
cotiser	to contribute
coupure d'action	subshare
Cour de Cassation	Court of Cassation
Cour des comptes	Court of Auditors
courtier de commerce	trade broker
courtier de marchandises	commodities broker
courtier interprète et conducteur de navires	shipping broker
courtier maritime	ship broker
créance à terme	claim subject to a stipulation as to time of payment
créance mobilière	chose in action
créancier chirographaire	unsecured creditor
créancier gagiste	pledgee, secured creditor
créancier hypothécaire	mortgagee
créancier saisissant	execution creditor
crédit-bail	leasing
credits	funds
créer	to set up, to draw (bill)

D

d'office	on their own authority, ex officio, by virtue of their office,
dans la limite de	up to a limit of
de ce fait	by virtue of this fact
de façon habituelle	on a regular basis
de gré à gré	by private agreement, privately
de plein droit	automatically, by operation of law
de premier degré	of first instance
débours	disbursement
décharge	discharge
déchéance	forfeiture (of rights)
déchéance du terme	forfeiture of the term
déchet	deterioration
décider	to rule, to decide
décision de justice	court order
décision en force de chose jugée	final/definitive decision
décision judiciaire	court order
déclaration d'utitilité publique	expropriation for public purposes
décompte	detailed account, breakdown, final balance
décret-loi	legislative order
dédit	repudiation
défaillance	default
défaut	default
défaut de paiement	default in payment
définitif	final
définir	to define, to describe, to set out
délai	period of time, time limit
délai congé	termination notice
délai de vue	period after sight
délais de paiement	payment by instalments, deferred payment
déliberation	resolution, decision, deliberation
délibérer	to deliberate, to decide, to consider
délivrer	to issue
demande	application, request
demander	to request, to apply for, to call upon
demander devant le tribunal	to apply to the court
demander en justice	to apply to the court
demander en référé	to apply to the court for a summary order
dénégation	denial
dénommé	known as
dénomination	designation
dénomination sociale	business name
dénoncer	to indicate, to disclose, to report, to make a complaint, to give notice of
dénonciation	report. complaint, notice

déontologie	professional (code of) ethics
déplacement	transfer, relocation
déposant	depositor
déposer	to file, to lodge
déposer des conclusions	to file pleadings
dépôt	filing, deposit
dépôt d'usine	factory warehouse
député	deputy
déroulement	conduct, progress
déséquilibre	imbalance
désigner	to appoint, to designate
désintéresser	to pay off, to satisfy, to buy out
désorganiser	to disrupt
déspécialisation	extension of activities
desserte	service, access
destitution	dismissal
déterminé	specific
déterminer	to determine, to lay down, to set, to assess
détourner	to misappropriate, to embezzle
dévolu	passed on, handed down, bestowed, assigned
diffuser	to circulate
diligences	steps (taken)
diminué de	minus, less
directeur-général	general manager
directeur-général délégué	associate general manager
directeur-général unique	sole general manager
directoire	managing board
dirigeant	executive
diriger	to direct, to manage
discretion	duty of confidentiality
dispensation	exemption
dispenser	to exempt
dispositions législatives et réglémentaires	legislative and regulatory provisions
dissiper	to waste
distinct	separate
divertir	to misappropriate
divulgation	disclosure
domicile	address, place of residence, domicile
données chiffrées	financial data
donner acte de	to confirm, to take formal/judicial notice of
donner avis à	to notify
donner lieu à	to require, to give rise to
donneur d'ordre	principal
dresser	to prepare, to draw up
droit au bail	tenant's/lessee's right to a lease

droit de communication	right to have documents made available for inspection
droit de créance	right of claim
droit de mutation	transfer duty
droit de recours	right of recourse
droit de retention	lien. right to remain in possession, right of retention
droit de suite	right to follow into the hands of a purchaser
du (seul) fait de	(merely) by virtue of
durable	lasting, long-term
durablement	for the long term
durée	term (*e.g.* of a lease)

E

échéance	due date, date for payment, maturity
échu	matured, outstanding
école professionnelle	vocational school
écrit	document
effet	bill, effect, impact
effet de commerce	negotiable instrument
effectif	actual
effectuer	to conduct, to carry out, to effect
éléments d'appréciation	relevant factors
éléments incorporels	fixed assets
émargement	initials, signature
émarger	to initial, to sign
emphytéote	long-term lessee
emplacement	location, space
emporter	to imply, to entail
en application de	pursuant to, under
en blanc	in blank
en connaissance de cause	with full knowledge of the facts
en cours	current
en dernier ressort	at last instance, final judgment
en double exemplaire	in duplicate
en exécution de	pursuant to
en faveur de	for the benefit of
en fonction de	according to
en fonctions	serving (adj)
en l'état	as is, as the case stands, in an unaltered state
en matière de	as regards, in terms of
en méconnaissance de	in disregard of
en rapport avec	in proportion to
en recouvrement	for collection
en temps utile	in due time
en vertu de	pursuant to, under the terms of, by virtue of
enchère	bid

encourir	to be liable to
enfreindre	to infringe, to violate, to be in breach of
engagement	obligation, commitment, undertaking
engager	to initiate, to institute
enjoindre	to enjoin, to call upon, to charge
énoncer	to state, to refer to
énonciations	terms, statements
enregister	to register, to record
enseigne	sign
ensemble	series, body, unit, complex
entente	understanding
entraîner	to cause, to entail, to lead to
entreprise individuelle	independent business
enterprise unipersonelle à responsabilité limitée	sole proprietorship with unlimited liability
énumérer	to list
envisager	to propose
envoi	dispatch
équipement	facilities
escompte	discount
établir	to prepare, to draw up, to show, to provide proof of, to create, to prove
établissement d'utilité publique	public service institution
établissements publics français	French public institutions
état	statement, list,
état nominatif	list of names
étendue	scope, extent, area
être libératoire	to constitute a discharge
être substitué pour	to replace
éventuellement	possibly, potentially
évolution	trend
exception	exception, defense, objection
exécuter	to enforce, to implement
exécuter un contrat	to perform a contract
exécution	performance, enforcement,
exécution provisoire	order annulling the suspensive effect of an appeal, enforcement order
exécutoire	enforceable
exerciser	to exercise, to perform
exigible	payable, due, owing
exonérer	to exempt
expédition	office copy
expertise	expert assessment
exploit	writ
exploitation	business
exploitation agricultural	agricultural holding

exploiter	to operate, to carry on
exposé de motifs	explanatory memorandum, statement of reasons
exposer	to set out, to explain
exprimer son suffrage par correspondance	to vote by mail
extrait	summary, abstract
	F
facteurs locaux de commercialité	local market factors
faculté	right, option, authority
faillite personnelle	culpable bankruptcy
faire acte de	to carry out
faire apparaître	to show, to uncover
faire appel à	to call on
faire connaître	to communicate, to inform, to give notice of, to make known
faire droit à	to allow
faire échec à	to frustrate, to put a stop to
faire état de	to specify, to state, to refer to
faire foi	to be authentic
faire l'objet de	to be the subject (matter) of
faire mention de	to enter (in a register)
faire prélèvement sur	to deduct from
faire publiquement appel à l'épargne	to offer shares to the public
faire valoir	to put forward, to exercise (rights)
fait	matter, act, fact
fait incriminé	alleged act/fact
faits reprochés	alleged facts/acts
fausser le jeu de	to distort
faute	fault, misconduct, error, misfeasance, negligence
faute lourde	gross negligence
faux	forged (adj), forgery
favoriser	to promote, encourage
fictif	false, sham, fictitious
figurer	to appear (on a list)
finalités	purposes
fixer	to fix, to lay down, to set down, to specify
folle enchère	sham/frivolous bid
fonctions	office, position, duties, functions
fondateur	founder
fonds commun de créances	debt investment trust
fonds commun de placement	mutual fund
fonds commun de placement d'entreprise	company mutual fund
force de chose jugée	res judicata
forclusion	loss of rights, forfeiture
formalités de publicité	publication formalities

formes	procedure
formule	wording
fraction	percentage, portion, share
frais	fees, costs
frais de justice	court fees
	G
gage	pledge, pawn, security
gage commercial	commercial security
garantie	guarantee, security, cover (insurance), warranty
garantir	to guarantee, to warrant, to secure
garde	custody
Garde des Sceaux	Minister of Justice
gestionnaire	administrator
global	overall
Grand-livre de la dette publique	Public Debts Ledge
greffe	court registry
greffier	clerk of the court
grever	to encumber
groupement d'intérêt économique (européen)	(European) economic interest grouping
	H
habilité	authorized, empowered, competent
habiliter	to authorize, to empower
habituel	regular, usual
hall	(covered) market
Haut conseil du commissariat aux comptes	High Council of the Auditorship
homologuer	to approve, to confirm
honoriat	honorary title
huissier	bailiff
hypothèque légale	statutory mortgage
	I
illicite	unlawful
immatriculation	registration
immeuble	building
immeuble par destination	fixture
immeubles	immovable property, real property
impératif	mandatory
impérativement	necessarily
implantation	site plan, siting, location
implanter	to establish
imposer	to impose, to require
impuissance	inability
imputer sur	to charge to, to set off against, to deduct from

inacessibilité	unassignability, freezing
inaliénable	non-transferable, non-negotiable
incidence	effects
inconvénients	problems
indéfiniment responsable	with unlimited liability
indemnité	compensation
indemnisation	compensation
indépendamment	regardless
indication	statement, detail
indications	information
indiquer	to show, to indicate, to state, to name
indispensable	essential
indivisibilité	joint liability
infirmation	setting-aside
infliger	to impose
information	inquiry
informer	to inform, to notify
infraction	breach, infringement
insaisissable	non-attachable
inscription	entry in the register, enrolment, registration
inscription nominative	registration by name
Inspection générale des finances	Public Auditor's office
instance	body, proceedings
instances en cours	current proceedings
instituer	to lay down
instruction	preparatory stages, examination
interdiction	deprivation
intéressé	concerned (adj), relevant, affected
intéressement	employee profit-sharing scheme
interêts de retard	late interest charges
interjeter appel	to lodge an appeal
intermédiaire	interim (adj), intermediary
intervenir	to occur, to take place
intervenir à	to be a party to
intervention	involvement
introduire une action	to bring an action
irrégulier	improper

J

joindre	to append, to enclose, to attach
jouissance	use, enjoyment
jour franc	clear day
journal d'annonces légales	a newspaper authorized to publish legal notices
judiciaire	court-ordered
judiciairement	by court order
juge-commissaire	bankruptcy judge

juges des référés	judge in charge of summary orders/proceedings
juge d'instance	trial judge
jugement de condamnation	conviction and sentence
juridiction administrative	administrative courts
juridiction commerciale	commercial courts
juridiction compétente	court having jurisdiction, court hearing the case
juridiction d'instruction	investigating court
juridiction de jugement	trial court. court hearing the case
juridiction judiciaire	ordinary courts
juridiction répressive	criminal courts
juridiction saisie	the court to which the matter has been referred, the court hearing the case
juridique	legal
jusqu'à due concurrence	up to the full amount
justification	supporting documents, evidence, proof
justifier de	to prove you have something, to be able to produce something

L

laisser prévenir	to indicate, to suggest
lettre de change	bill of exchange
lettre de voiture	consignment note, waybill
lettre recommandée avec accusé de réception	registered letter with acknowledgement of receipt
licenciement	dismissal, redundacy
lié	affiliated
lieu	place, district
liquidation judiciaire	court-ordered liquidation
limitrophe	adjacent
litigieux	disputed
local	premises
local d'habitation	residential premises, dwelling place
location	lease
location-gérance	management lease
locataire-gérant	lessee-manager
locaux	premises
loueur	lessor

M

magasin général	bonded warehouse
magistrat	law officer, judge
magistrat du siège	judge
mainlevée	lifting, discharge
maître d'ouvrage	contracting authority
majoration	penalty, surcharge
majoration de retard	penalty for late payment
majoré de	plus

mandat	agency, power of attorney, authority, duties, position
mandat d'administrateur	directorship
mandat de virement	transfer order
mandataire	agent, representative, proxy
mandataire judiciaire	court-appointed administrator
mandataire judiciare au redressement et à la liquidation des entreprises	court-appointed administrator for the restructuring and liquidation of undertakings
mandataire social	company official, company agent
mandater	to appoint as an agent/representative
manifestement	clearly
manquement	breach
marché public	public procurement contracts
marge commerciale	trading margin
masquer	to conceal
masse	group, body
matériel	equipment
matériellement	physically
méconnaître	to ignore
membre de profession libérale	member of the professions
mémoire	memorandum, statement
mention	note, annotation, statement, words
mentionner	to annotate, to state, to mention, to set out, to note, to define, to list, to refer to
mentions	details, information
menue mercerie	small dry goods
méprise	mistake
mettre à la disposition de	to make available to, to put at the disposal of
mettre en cause	to implicate, to join to an action, to adversely affect, to summon to appear, to involve
mettre en oeuvre	to implement, to make use of, to exercise, to carry on
mettre en recouvrement	to place on collection
meubles	movable property, personal property
mieux-disant	highest bidder
ministère public	State Prosecution Service
mise à pied	laying off
mise à prix	upset price
mise en demeure	formal notice
mise sous scellés	placing under seal
mission	instructions, duties, position, task
mobilier	chattels
mobilisation de fonds	raising of funds
modalités	terms and conditions, procedure, method, ways and means
modalités d'application	implementing provisions
modes d'application	implementing provisions

motif	ground, reason, cause
motif de fond	substantial grounds
mutuelle	friendly society
	N
nanti	secured by a charge
nantissement	pledge, charge, security
négliger de	to fail to
négociant	merchant
nom commercial	trade name
nom supposé	fictitious name
nombre entier	round number
nominatif	registered
nommer	to appoint
non-conformité	discrepancy, non-conformity
non-lieu	discharge
notable	significant
notablement	significantly
notamment	notably, in particular, inter alia
notification	notification, notice, service
notifier	to report, to serve, to notify, to forward
notoire	acknowledged, well-known
nul	void
nullité	invalidity, nullity, annulment, cancellation
numéraire	cash
	O
objet	subject matter
obligataire	debenture holder, bondholder
obligation	liability, obligation, bond
obligation à lot	premium bond
obligation de garanti	statutory warranty, seller's warranty
obligatoire	compulsory, obligatory, mandatory
obligé	promisor, debtor, obligor
observation	observation, remark, comment
observatoire	monitoring center
observer	to comply with
obtenir communication de	to inspect
officier de police judiciaire	senior police officer
officier public/ministériel	public officer
omettre de	to fail to
opération	transaction, operation
opération d'animation commercial	sales promotion campaign
opération de rachat	buy-out
opposable à	binding on
opposer une signature	to place a signature
opposition	objection

organe collective	corporate body, collegial body
organe de contrôle	audit body
organe de direction	executive body
organisme	agency, body
organisme de placement collectif en valeurs mobilières	undertaking for collective investment in transferable securities (UCITS)
orientations	guidelines

P

par décision de	by order of
par le ministère de	by the use of
par l'intermédiaire de	through
par procuration	for collection
par rapport à	in comparison with, in relation to
par son fait	personally
par voie de référé	by a summary order
parquet	State Prosecutor's office
part	portion, share, proportion
part bénéficiaire	founder's share
part de fondateur	founder's share
part d'intérêt	partnership share
participation	(share) holding
participation ouvrière	employee participation
particulier	specific
partie civile	person claiming damages (in criminal proceedings)
partie en cause	party to the proceedings
partie la plus diligente	first party to act
partie poursuivante	plaintiff, applicant
partie principale	party to the proceedings (State)
passer outre	to disregard, to carry on regardless
passible de	liable to, subject to
passif exigible	current liabilities
patrimoine	assets, possessions, estate
patrimonial	economic, financial
peine	penalty
percevoir	to collect, to levy
période	term (of a lease)
periodicité	frequency
permission de voirie	permission to occupy part of the public highway or another public place
perquisition	search
personalité civile	legal personality
personne interposée	third person, intermediary
personne morale de droit privé	legal person under private law
personne physique	natural person
personnel	employees, workforce
perspectives d'activité	business prospects

pièces justificatives	supporting documents
plan d'épargne d'entreprise	company savings plan
plan d'occupation du sol	land-use plan
poursuivre	to prosecute, to sue
port d'attache	home port
portable	payable at the creditor's place of residence of business
porter atteinte à	to interfere with, to adversely affect, to cause loss to, to harm
porter sur	to involve, to be concerned with, to relate to
porteur d'obligation	bondholder
poser des questions par écrit	to submit written questions
posséder	to hold
poste	item (on balance sheet)
pour encaissement	for collection
pour l'application de	for the purposes of
pour mémoire	for the record, as a token entry
poursuite	progress
poursuite judiciaire	court proceedings
pourvoi en cassation	appeal to the Court of Cassation
pouvoirs publics	public authorities
préalablement	beforehand
préciser	to state, to set out, to specify
préjudice	damage, loss, injury
prélèvement	deduction
prélever sur	to pay out of, to deduct from
prendre connaissance de	to acquaint oneself with, to examine, to study
prendre en gage	to take as security
préposé	servant, employee
préposer	to appoint, to put in charge of
préretraite	early retirement
préscription	instruction
présenter	to put forward/before, to submit, to present
president	president, presiding judge
président-directeur-général	chief executive officer
présider	to chair, to preside over
prestation	thing, service, benefit
prêt sur nantissement	loan secured by a pledge/charge
prétendre	to claim
prévenir	to inform, to forewarn
prévisible	foreseeable
prévision	estimate, forecast
prévisionnel	preliminary, provisional
prévoyance	(social) welfare
prévoir	to provide for, to specify, to set out, to lay down
prévu par la loi	statutory

prime	bonus, premium
primitif	original
prisée	valuation
privatif	exclusive
privilège	preference, (right of) priority, preferential right
procéder à	to perform, to carry out
procédure d'exécution	execution procedure
procédure judiciaire	court proceedings
procès-verbal	minutes, official record
procès-verbal de carence	official record of failure
procuration	power of attorney
procureur de la République	State Prosecutor
productions en cours	work in progress
produits	income
profession	profession, occupation, business
profession libérale	(independent) profession
professionel	professional, business, trade, trader
projet de....	proposed..., draft......
prolonger	to extend
promoteur	promoter
prononcé du jugement	verdict
prononcé	passing, giving, imposition (judgment)
prononcer	to order
proportionnel	proportionate
provenir de	to arise from
provisions	funds
provisoire	interim, interlocutory
provisionnel	provisional, interim
provoquer	to call for
publication	publication, public notice
publicité	publicity, public notice(s)
pur et simple	unconditional
purge	discharge, clearing

Q

qualité	status, position
quittance	receipt, discharge
quitter	to vacate
quote-part	proportion, proportionate share
quotité	portion, proportion, quota, amount, share

R

rabais	rebate, discount
radiation	cancellation, striking off
rang de privilège	rank in priority, priority ranking
rapport de gestion	annual report
rapporter	to indicate, to cancel, to revoke

rapporteur	rapporteur
rapports	dealings, relations
réalisation	creation
réaliser	to fulfill, to achieve, to realize, to carry out, to implement, to attain, to set up
réalisation forcée	forced sale
réalisible	liquid (asset)
réalité	existence
receler	to handle (stolen goods)
recettes	income
recevable	admissible (a legal action)
récépissé-warrant	warehouse warrant
reclassement	relocation, re-grading
reconnaître	to acknowledge
reconnaître à	to accord to
recours	remedy, right of action, appeal, application
recours en annulation	application to set aside
recours en cassation	appeal on a point of law to the Court of Cassation
recouvrement	collection
recouvrer	to collect, to recover (debts)
recto	reverse side, back
recueil	collection, compendium
recueillir	to gather, to collect, to obtain, to record
récusation	challenge
rediger	to draw up
redevable	liable
redevances	fees
redressement judiciaire	court-ordered restructuring
référé	summary order, summary proceeding
en régie	state run
régime	scheme, rules governing
registre à souches	counterfoil book/register
registre de procès-verbaux	minute book
registre du commerce et des sociétés	corporate and commercial register
règlement	settlement
règlement entre banquiers	inter-bank settlement
règlement judiciaire	simple bankruptcy
régler	to govern, to regulate, to deal with, to sort out, to settle, to govern
régler en valeur	to pay with a instrument
regroupement	consolidation (of shares)
regrouper	to gather, to group together
régularisation	compliance
régulariser	to rectify
régularité	validity, proper form

régulier	in due form, valid
réintégrer	to reinstate, to restore
relater	to confirm, to record, to state
relaxe	acquittal
relever	to note, to uncover, to identify, to come across, to release
relever de	to come under, to be a matter for
remboursement des parts	redemption of the shares
remettre	to send, to deliver
remettre en garantie	to give as security
remise	discount, remission
remplir les devoirs	to discharge or carry out the duties
rendre	to deliver
rendre compte de	to report on, to account for
renonciation	waiver
renseignements	information
réparation civile	civil damages
répartition	allocation, apportionment, distribution
répertoire	record book, register
répertoire des métiers	trades register
répertoirier	to record, to note
répétition	repayment, recovery
répondre à	to comply with
répondre indéfiniment	to have unlimited liability
report	postponement
reprendre	to resume
reputé avoir qualité de	deemed to be authorized to
reputé non écrit	deemed null and void
requérant	applicant
requérir	to apply for, to ask for
requête	*ex parte* application
réserver	to preserve, to reserve
réserves légales	statutory reserves
résiliation	cancellation
résilier	to terminate, to repudiate, to cancel
résoudre	to rescind
responsabilité	responsibility, liability
ressort	judicial district
résultat	result, outcome, profits, final account(s)
résultant de	resulting from, under
retenir	to use, to deduct
retour sans frais	free return
retraite	redraft
revendication	claim of ownership/title
reverser	to repay
revêtir	to mark (a document), to take the form of

revocation	removal
ristourne	refund, rebate
rompu	fractional share
rupture	breach (of a contract), termination

S

s'acquitter de	to discharge, to perform
s'adresser à	to apply to, to speak to
s'entendre de	to be defined as, to mean
s'obliger à	to commit oneself, to undertake, to agree to
s'opposer à	to object to
saisie	attachment, seizure
saisine	referral
saisir	to attach, to seize, to put in possession, to arrest (ship)
saisir la jurisdiction compétente	to refer the matter to the competent court
sanction pécuniaire	financial penalty
sans motif légitime	except for a good/legitimate reason
sans protêt	without protest
satisfaire à	comply with
sauf stipulation contraire	unless specified otherwise
schéma directeur	master plan, basic development scheme
scindé	divided (of a company)
scission	division (of a company)
scrutin uninominal	single candidate ballot
se constituer partie civile	to bring a civil suit for damages (in criminal proceedings
se dérouler	to be conducted
se libérer	to escape liability
se porter	to act as
se pourvoir en référé	to apply to the court for a summary order
se prévaloir de	to avail oneself of, to take advantage of, to make use of
se prononcer	to make an order, to rule, to decide, to vote
se regrouper en	to form (e.g. an association)
se réunir	to be held
séance de bourse	trading day
séquestre	trustee
services déconcentrés	local services of the State
siège	registered office
signaler	to point out, to indicate
signification	service of notice
signifier à	to serve on
situation	situation, affairs, position, statement
social	corporate, company
société	corporation, partnership, company
société anonyme (SA)	public limited company

société à responsabilité limitée (SARL)	private limited company
société civile	non-commercial company or partnership
société commerciale	commercial company or partnership
société commerciale cooperative de main d'oeuvre	workers' cooperative commercial company
société coopérative de credit	friendly society
société coopérative de main d'oeuvre	workers' cooperative society
société coopérative ouvrière de production	workers' production cooperative society
société de capitalisation	investment company
société de capital-risque	capital risk company
société d'économie mixte	partly state-owned company
société de droit privé	company under private law
société en commandite par actions	limited partnership with shares
société en commandite simple	limited partnership
société en nom collectif	general partnership
société en participation	joint venture, undisclosed partnership
société financière d'innovation	venture capital company
société immobilière pour le commerce et l'industrie	leasing company for commercial and industrial premises
société d'investissement à capital variable	open-end investment company
société par actions	stock company
soin	task
solde	balance, clearance sale
solidairement	jointly and severally
sommation	formal demand
sommes	proceeds
soulte	balancing adjustment
sous réserve de	subject to, without prejudice to
sous seing privé	private document
souscrire	to subscribe to, to sign
souscrire à titre réductible	to subscribe for fractions of shares
souscrire à titre irréductible	to subscribe for whole shares
soustraire	to misappropriate, to remove, to shield
spécial	special, specific
stage	training course
statuant en référé	by way of a summary order
statuer	to rule, to give judgment
statuer en dernier ressort	to give a final ruling
statuer en référé	to make a summary order
statuer sur le fond	to give judgment on the merits of the case
statut	corporate statutes, rules governing
stipulation	requirement, stipulation
stipuler	to require, to stipulate, to specify

subside	grant, subsidy
subsidiaire	secondary
subsister	to survive, to continue to exist
succession bénéficiaire	encumbered succession
successivement	in succession
succursale	branch
suppléance	substitution
suppléant	alternate
suppléer	to make up for, to be substituted for
supplémentaire	additional
support	media
supposer	to imply
sur décision de	at the discretion of
sur dernière convocation	at the final time of asking
sur option	voluntarily, at the option of
surenchère	overbid
sûreté	security, surety, guarantee
suroffre	over-supply
surplus	balance

T

talon	counterfoil
tarif	scale of fees/charges
taux de compétence	sum up to which a court has jurisdiction, financial limit of the jurisdiction of a court
taxe professionnelle	business tax
texte	provisions, legislation, wording
texte reglémentaire	regulation
tierce opposition	third-party objection
tiré	drawee
tirer	to draw
tirer pour compte	to draw on account
tireur	drawer
titrage	titration
titre	instrument, security, title, certificate, qualification
titre de capital	equity security
titre de créance	debt security
titre exécutoire	writ of execution
titre nominatif	registered security
titulaire	holder, owner
totalité	full amount
tradition	delivery
traite	draft, payment
transfert	relocation
transformer	to convert, to process
transiger	to settle, to compromise
transmettre	to forward

transmission	transfer
transmission à titre universel	transmission of entire estate
tribunal consulaire	commercial court
tribunal de commerce	commercial court
tribunal de grande instance	district court
tribunal d'instance	local court
troubler	to disturb
tutelle	supervision
type (adj)	standard

U

urbanisme	town/city planning
usages	custom and practice
usages normaux du commerce	normal usages of the trade
usufruitier	holder of a life interest, life tenant
utile	useful, helpful

V

valeur	amount, value, security
valeur d'exploitation	working asset
valeur en gage	pledged security
valeur en garantie	pledged security
valeur mobilière	transferable security
valider	to uphold
valoir	to be deemed to be the equivalent of
veiller à	to ensure
vendre à la folle enchère	to sell by auction without reserve prices
venir en concurrence	to rank equally
vente à cri public	public auction
vente au déballage	special-offer sale
vente en magasin d'usine	factory shop sale
vente publique	public sale
ventilation du prix	breakdown of the price
verbalement	by word of mouth, verbally
vérification	check, audit, examination
verser	to pay out, to lay out
vice de forme	formal defect
violation	breach, infringement, contravention
visa	sighting (instrument), mark of approval
visant	concerning, involving
viser	to initial, to specify, refer to, to countersign
voie de recours	appeal
voies d'exécution	execution procedure
volant	leaf
volontairement	deliberately
vote	vote, ballot
vote prépondérante	casting vote

W

warrant hotêlier	hotel warrant
warrant pétrolier	oil warrant
warranter	to cover by a warrant

Z

zone	area
zone de chalandaise	catchment area

TOPICAL INDEX

A

B

C

D

F

G

I

W